Early praise for *Python Testing with pytest, Second Edition*

The knowledge and experience Brian brings to these pages has made this the definitive pytest resource for me. New or experienced, this book will be your one-stop shop for all of your real-world pytest needs.

➤ **Julian Sequeira**
   Cofounder of PyBites

If you are into coding books and Python, this is a great and fun way to learn and acquire testing skills like a pro, much faster than figuring it out on your own.

➤ **Sebastián Ramírez**
   Creator of FastAPI and Typer

This is my pytest go-to book—thorough coverage, great code examples, and accessible. If you want to write great test code and become proficient in what I think is the best Python testing framework out there, study this book.

➤ **Bob Belderbos**
   Python coach and Cofounder of PyBites

This book truly is an excellent resource on pytest. I've been recommending the first edition when people ask me for a book during my pytest trainings. While reading through the second edition, I sometimes thought, "I wish the pytest documentation would explain this topic just as well."

➤ **Florian Bruhin**
   Founder, Bruhin Software

Python Testing with pytest, Second Edition

Simple, Rapid, Effective, and Scalable

Brian Okken

The Pragmatic Bookshelf

Raleigh, North Carolina

Many of the designations used by manufacturers and sellers to distinguish their products are claimed as trademarks. Where those designations appear in this book, and The Pragmatic Programmers, LLC was aware of a trademark claim, the designations have been printed in initial capital letters or in all capitals. The Pragmatic Starter Kit, The Pragmatic Programmer, Pragmatic Programming, Pragmatic Bookshelf, PragProg and the linking *g* device are trademarks of The Pragmatic Programmers, LLC.

Every precaution was taken in the preparation of this book. However, the publisher assumes no responsibility for errors or omissions, or for damages that may result from the use of information (including program listings) contained herein.

For our complete catalog of hands-on, practical, and Pragmatic content for software developers, please visit *https://pragprog.com*.

The team that produced this book includes:

CEO: Dave Rankin
COO: Janet Furlow
Managing Editor: Tammy Coron
Development Editor: Katharine Dvorak
Copy Editor: Karen Galle
Indexing: Potomac Indexing, LLC
Layout: Gilson Graphics
Founders: Andy Hunt and Dave Thomas

For sales, volume licensing, and support, please contact *support@pragprog.com*.

For international rights, please contact *rights@pragprog.com*.

ISBN-13: 978-1-68050-860-4
Book version: P1.0—February 2022

Contents

Part III — Booster Rockets

Acknowledgments

I first need to thank Michelle, my wife and best friend. I wish you could see the room I get to write in. Monitor, keyboard, and recording equipment arranged neatly-ish atop a vintage oak desk. Next to the desk, an antique secretary to hide away papers, spare cables, and a growing microphone collection. Behind me, tech and sci-fi books, retro space toys, and juggle balls arranged in a glass-front bookcase. In front, a fabric-covered wall to dampen sound echos (and it looks great with vintage frames, quirky posters, and old medical illustrations). I love writing here not just because it's wonderful and reflects my personality, but because it's a space that Michelle and I created together. She and I have always been a team, and she has been incredibly supportive of my crazy ideas to write a blog, start a podcast or two, and write a pytest book, and now, rewrite the same book. She helps me find time for writing, researching, and recording. I really, really couldn't do this without her.

I also have two amazingly awesome, curious, and brilliant daughters, Gabriella and Sophia, who are two of my biggest fans. They tell anyone talking about programming that they should listen to my podcasts, and anyone interested in Python that they should learn how to test their code better by reading my book.

There are so many more people to thank.

My editor, Katharine Dvorak. She has helped tremendously through both editions. I'm a better writer and a better teacher because of her involvement in this project. She was incredibly helpful for the first edition. During the second edition, I wanted the book to be a smooth progression of complexity. We re-arranged the order several times to get here, and it wasn't easy. With her help, I think we've got a great story to tell with this book.

Thank you to Dave Rankin, Tammy Coron, and the rest of The Pragmatic Bookshelf for maintaining such an amazing publishing company.

The technical reviewers have been instrumental in suggesting fixes and updates to the second edition. Thank you to Bob Belderbos, Oliver Bestwalter, Florian Bruhin, Floris Bruynooghe, Paul Everitt, Matt Harrison, Michael Kennedy, Matt Layman, Kelly Paredes, Raphael Pierzina, Sebastián Ramírez, Julian Sequeira, Anthony Sottile, and Sean Tibor. Many on that list are also pytest core developers and/or maintainers of incredible pytest plugins. The suggestions, direction, and tips from reviewers have really helped make this edition great.

Special thanks to Florian Bruhin. In the midst of the pytest 7 release and the 2021 holiday season, he also found time to review this second edition with a fine-toothed comb. If there are mistakes left in the book, it's probably because I didn't listen to Florian in all the places I should have.

Special thanks to Matt Harrison, not only for reviewing this edition, but for arranging my first in-person pytest training. It got me hooked. Teaching people in person is an amazing experience. The second edition was heavily influenced by my new-found little voice in my head saying, "Would you really teach someone this if they were sitting there with you in person?" If not, I took it out. If not then, I moved it to later in the book.

Thank you to the entire pytest-dev team for creating such a cool testing tool, and for answering my pytest questions over the years. Even during the writing of this edition, I sent many quick emails to many on the team to clarify my understanding. They've been supportive of the book. For that, I'm deeply grateful. Special thanks to Holger Krekel for creating pytest in the first place, and Florian Bruhin, Ran Benita, Bruno Oliveira, Ronny Pfannschmidt, Anthony Sottile, and so many others for keeping it going and keeping the pytest contributor environment healthy.

Python and pytest are amazing communities that I'm proud to be part of. I am humbled and profoundly grateful for all of the encouragement and help I have received in my goal to get software developers to learn to love testing.

Paul Everitt told me that the first edition changed his attitude toward testing from something he should do to something he enjoys doing. He even calls it "the joy of testing." I hope the second edition lives up to the first. I hope you find joy in testing.

Brian Okken
February 2022

Preface

The use of Python is increasing not only in software development, but also in fields such as data science, machine learning, data analysis, research science, finance, and just about all other industries. The growth of Python in many critical fields also comes with the desire to properly, effectively, and efficiently put software tests in place to make sure the programs run correctly and produce the correct results. In addition, more and more software projects are embracing continuous integration and including an automated testing phase. There is still a place for exploratory manual testing—but thorough manual testing of increasingly complex projects is infeasible. Teams need to be able to trust the tests being run by the continuous integration servers to tell them if they can trust their software enough to release it.

Enter pytest. pytest is a robust Python testing tool that can be used for all types and levels of software testing. pytest can be used by development teams, quality assurance teams, independent testing groups, and individuals practicing test-driven development, for both commercial and open-source projects. In fact, projects all over the Internet have switched from unittest or nose to pytest, including Mozilla and Dropbox. Why? Because pytest offers powerful features such as assert rewriting, a third-party plugin model, and a powerful yet simple fixture model that is unmatched in any other testing framework.

Why pytest?

pytest is a software testing framework, which means pytest is a command-line tool that automatically finds tests you've written, runs the tests, and reports the results. It has a library of goodies that you can use in your tests to help you test more effectively. It can be extended by writing plugins or installing third-party plugins. And it integrates easily with other tools like continuous integration and web automation.

Here are a few of the reasons pytest stands out above many other testing frameworks:

- Simple tests are simple to write in pytest.

- Complex tests are still simple to write.

- Tests are easy to read.

- Tests are easy to read. (So important it's listed twice.)

- You can get started in seconds.

- You use assert in tests for verifications, not things like self.assertEqual() or self.assertLessThan(). Just assert.

- You can use pytest to run tests written for unittest or nose.

pytest is being actively developed and maintained by a passionate and growing community. It's so extensible and flexible that it will easily fit into your work flow. And because it's installed separately from your Python version, you can use the same version of pytest on multiple versions of Python.

Learn pytest While Testing a Sample Application

In this book, you're going to learn pytest by writing tests against an example project that I hope has many of the same traits of applications you'll be testing after you read this book.

The sample application is called Cards. Cards is a minimal task-tracking application with a command-line user interface. It has enough in common with many other types of applications that I hope you can easily see how the testing concepts you learn while developing tests against Cards are applicable to your projects now and in the future.

Cards has a command-line interface (CLI). The CLI interacts with the rest of the code through an application programming interface (API). The API is the interface where you'll direct most of your testing. The API interacts with a database control layer, which interacts with a document database, TinyDB.

This isn't the most sophisticated task-management application, but it's complicated enough to use it to explore testing.

How This Book Is Organized

The book is organized into three parts. In Part I, Primary Power, on page 1, you'll install pytest and start to explore its primary features using the Cards project along the way. You'll learn how to run simple test functions on the command line. You'll then use pytest fixtures to push setup and teardown code out of the test functions. You'll learn how to use many of pytest's builtin fixtures to help with common testing problems like temporary directories. You'll also learn how to turn one test into many test cases with parametrization. And finally, you'll learn how to use markers to run a subset of tests.

In Part II, Working with Projects, on page 97, you'll look at some real-world issues around testing projects, as well as explore more of the power of pytest. You'll start by exploring a simple testing strategy process and applying it to the Cards project. You'll take a look at configuration files and all of the other non-test files involved in testing projects. You'll use coverage analysis to look at where our testing holes are with respect to Cards, and use mocking to help test the user interface and fill in some coverage gaps. Really all testing involves some debugging of both code and tests, so you'll take a look at some of the great features pytest has to help us debug test failures. Many projects utilize continuous integration (CI). Tox is a popular framework to simulate a local CI system. You'll look at using pytest with tox and with hosted CI systems. Part II also includes a look at the Python search path. The Cards project is an installable Python package; however, not all testing projects involve installed packages. This chapter in Part II looks at how you can tell pytest to find your source code.

In Part III, Booster Rockets, on page 195, you'll take your tests to the next level. You'll learn how to use third-party plugins to extend the capabilities of pytest and learn how to build your own plugins. You'll also learn advanced parametrization techniques that build on what you learned in Part I.

What You Need to Know

Python
> This book assumes that you are fairly comfortable with Python. You don't need to know a lot of Python—the examples don't do anything super weird or fancy—but Python isn't explained in detail.

pip
> You should use pip to install pytest and pytest plugins. If you want a refresher on pip, check out Appendix 2, pip, on page 237.

A command line
> I wrote this book and captured the example output using zsh on a Mac laptop. However, the only commands I use in zsh are cd to go to a specific directory, and pytest, of course. Because cd exists in Windows cmd.exe and all Unix shells that I know of, all examples should be runnable on whatever terminal-like application you choose to use.

That's it, really. You don't need to be a programming expert to start writing automated software tests with pytest.

Why a Second Edition?

Both Python and pytest have changed since the first edition of this book was published in 2017. There have been updates to pytest that are now reflected in the book:

- New builtin fixtures
- New flags
- The addition of package scope fixtures

There have also been updates to Python that are reflected in the book:

- The adoption of f-strings and pathlib
- The addition of dataclasses

Also, since publication of the first edition, I have taught many, many people about pytest, and I think I've learned how to be a better teacher. The second edition not only expands on what is covered in the first edition—it grew from 7 to 16 chapters!—but also it presents the material in what I think is a more gradual, digestible manner.

So what's in all of these new chapters?

- *More on parametrization, markers, coverage, mocking, tox and continuous integration, and third-party plugins.* All of these topics were covered in the first edition, but in this edition I expand that coverage. I pulled the discussion of parametrization into its own chapter and added a discussion of advanced parametrization techniques. I delve more deeply into markers and include an example of how to pass data from markers to fixtures (which is super cool). I also take you on a deeper dive into test coverage, mocking, and CI, and using and building your own plugins to extend pytest's capabilities.

- *A discussion of test strategy.* Feedback from the first edition was that the book was great for the mechanics of how to use pytest, but the "What test do I write?" information was a bit lacking. The new Chapter 7, Strategy, on page 99 is a push in the right direction of what tests to write. A complete treatment of test strategy would be a book in itself; however, this chapter will get you started.

- *Information about the Python search path.* A lot of readers reached out to me asking about how to get their tests to see their test code, and the first edition didn't cover it. The project in this book, Cards, doesn't have that problem because it's an installed Python package. However, lots of user projects are applications or scripts or lots of other things that are not installed packages. This chapter offers a focused look at the problem and provides some solutions.

I consolidated the information about debugging test failures into a chapter of its own. In the last edition, this information was spread all throughout the book. It is my hope that when you are faced with a deadline and a failing test suite, bringing this information together into one chapter will help you figure out an answer quickly and ease some stress.

Finally, the example project changed. The first edition used a project called Tasks to illustrate how to use pytest. Now it's called Cards. Here's why:

- It's easier to say out loud. (Try it. Say "tasks" three times, then "cards" three times. Right?)

- The new project itself is different because it uses Typer instead of Click for command-line functionality. Typer code is easier to read.

- The project also uses Rich for formatting the output. Rich didn't exist (neither did Typer) when the first edition was written.

The code examples have also been simplified. The directory structure of the first edition code examples followed a progression of a possible test directory within a project, with most of the project removed. Seriously, I think it made sense to me at the time. In this edition, there is a project in its own directory, cards_proj, with no tests. Then, each of the chapters have test code (if appropriate) that either work on the one project or on some local code. Trust me, I think you'll agree that it's way easier to follow along now.

Example Code and Online Resources

The examples in this book were written and tested using Python 3.7+ (including 3.10) and pytest 6.2 and 7.0. If you're reading this with later versions of pytest and wondering if this book still applies, the odds are that it does. There are places where this book depends on pytest 7 features. However, because pytest 7 is very new, I've noted differences with pytest 6.2 when necessary. I have worked with many core pytest contributors to make sure the content of this book will apply to future versions of pytest as well. There is also an errata page set up at both pythontest.com[1] and at pragprog.com[2]

---

1. https://pythontest.com/pytest-book
2. https://pragprog.com/titles/bopytest2

that notes any updates you need to be aware of for future versions of pytest and this book.

The source code for the Cards project, as well as for all of the tests shown in this book, is available through a link on the book's web page.[3] You don't need to download the source code to understand the test code; the test code is presented in usable form in the examples. But to follow along with the Cards project, or to adapt the testing examples to test your own project (more power to you!), you must go to the book's web page to download the project.

To learn more about software testing in Python, you can also check out pythontest.com[4] and testandcode.com,[5] a blog and podcast I run that discuss the topic.

I've been programming for decades, and nothing has made me love writing test code as much as pytest. I hope you learn a lot from this book, and I hope you'll end up loving test code as much as I do.

---

3. https://pragprog.com/titles/bopytest2/source_code
4. https://pythontest.com
5. https://testandcode.com

Part I

Primary Power

## CHAPTER 1

Getting Started with pytest

This is a test:

```
ch1/test_one.py
def test_passing():
    assert (1, 2, 3) == (1, 2, 3)
```

This looks very simple. It is. But there's still a lot going on. The function test_passing() will be discovered by pytest as a test function because it starts with test_ and is in a file that starts with test_. And when the test is run, the assert statement will determine if the test passes or fails. assert is a keyword built into Python and has the behavior of raising a AssertionError exception if the expression after assert is false. Any uncaught exception raised within a test will cause the test to fail. Although any type of uncaught exception can cause a test to fail, traditionally we stick with AssertionError from assert to determine pass/fail for tests.

We'll get into the nitty-gritty of all of that later. First, I'd like to show you what it looks like to run a test on the command line. And in order to run this test, we'll need to install pytest. So let's do that now.

Installing pytest

The headquarters for pytest is https://pytest.org. That's the official documentation. But it's distributed through PyPI (the Python Package Index) at https://pypi.org/project/pytest.

Like other Python packages distributed through PyPI, use pip to install pytest into the virtual environment you're using for testing:

```
$ python3 -m venv venv
$ source venv/bin/activate
(venv) $ pip install pytest
```

The (venv) added before the command prompt lets you know that you are using a virtual environment. For the examples in the rest of the book, we'll always use a virtual environment. However, in order to save a little clutter on the page, (venv) has been removed. We'll also always be using python3, but will shorten it to python.

If you are not familiar with venv or pip, I've got you covered. Check out Appendix 1, Virtual Environments, on page 235 and Appendix 2, pip, on page 237.

What About Windows?

The example for venv and pip should work on many POSIX systems, such as Linux and macOS, and many versions of Python, including Python 3.7 and later.

Note that the source venv/bin/activate line won't work for Windows. For cmd.exe, use venv\Scripts\activate.bat instead:

```
C:\> python -m venv venv
C:\> venv\Scripts\activate.bat
C:\> pip install pytest
```

For PowerShell, use venv\Scripts\Activate.ps1 instead:

```
PS C:\> python -m venv venv
PS C:\> venv\Scripts\Activate.ps1
PS C:\> pip install pytest
```

What About virtualenv?

With some distributions of Linux, you will need to use virtualenv. Some people also just prefer virtualenv for various reasons:

```
$ python3 -m pip install virtualenv
$ python3 -m virtualenv venv
$ source venv/bin/activate
(venv) $ pip install pytest
```

Running pytest

With pytest installed, we can run test_passing(). This is what it looks like when it's run:

```
$ cd /path/to/code/ch1
$ pytest test_one.py
========================= test session starts =========================
collected 1 item

test_one.py .                                                    [100%]

========================= 1 passed in 0.01s =========================
```

The dot after test_one.py means that one test was run and it passed. The [100%] is a percentage indicator showing how much of the test suite is done so far. Because there is just one test in the test session, one test equals 100% of the tests. If you need more information, you can use -v or --verbose:

```
$ pytest -v test_one.py
====================== test session starts ======================
collected 1 item

test_one.py::test_passing PASSED                        [100%]

==================== 1 passed in 0.00 seconds ====================
```

If you have a color terminal, PASSED and the bottom line appear green. It's nice.

This is a failing test:

ch1/test_two.py
```
def test_failing():
    assert (1, 2, 3) == (3, 2, 1)
```

The way pytest shows you test failures is one of the many reasons developers love pytest. Let's watch this fail:

```
$ pytest test_two.py
====================== test session starts ======================
collected 1 item

test_two.py F                                           [100%]

============================ FAILURES ============================
_____ test_failing _____

    def test_failing():
>       assert (1, 2, 3) == (3, 2, 1)
E       assert (1, 2, 3) == (3, 2, 1)
E         At index 0 diff: 1 != 3
E         Use -v to get the full diff

test_two.py:2: AssertionError
==================== short test summary info ====================
FAILED test_two.py::test_failing - assert (1, 2, 3) == (3, 2, 1)
===================== 1 failed in 0.03s =====================
```

Cool. The failing test, test_failing, gets its own section to show us why it failed. And pytest tells us exactly what the first failure is: index 0 is a mismatch. If you have a color terminal, much of this appears in red to make it really stand out. This extra section showing exactly where the test failed and some the surrounding code is called a *traceback*.

That's already a lot of information, but there's a line that says Use -v to get the full diff. Let's do that:

```
$ pytest -v test_two.py
====================== test session starts ======================
collected 1 item

test_two.py::test_failing FAILED                          [100%]

=========================== FAILURES ============================
_____ test_failing _____
    def test_failing():
>       assert (1, 2, 3) == (3, 2, 1)
E       assert (1, 2, 3) == (3, 2, 1)
E         At index 0 diff: 1 != 3
E         Full diff:
E         - (3, 2, 1)
E         ?    ^     ^
E         + (1, 2, 3)
E         ?    ^     ^

test_two.py:2: AssertionError
==================== short test summary info ====================
FAILED test_two.py::test_failing - assert (1, 2, 3) == (3, 2, 1)
====================== 1 failed in 0.03s ========================
```

Wow. pytest adds little carets (^) to show us exactly what's different.

So far we've run pytest with the commands pytest test_one.py and pytest test_two.py, so we know we can give pytest a filename and it will run the tests in the file. Let's run it a few more ways.

To run pytest, you have the option to specify files and directories. If you don't specify any files or directories, pytest will look for tests in the current working directory and subdirectories. It looks for .py files starting with test_ or ending with _test. From the ch1 directory, if you run pytest with no commands, you'll run two files' worth of tests:

```
$ pytest --tb=no
====================== test session starts ======================
collected 2 items

test_one.py .                                             [ 50%]
test_two.py F                                             [100%]

==================== short test summary info ====================
FAILED test_two.py::test_failing - assert (1, 2, 3) == (3, 2, 1)
================== 1 failed, 1 passed in 0.03s ==================
```

I also used the --tb=no flag to turn off tracebacks, since we don't really need the full output right now. We'll be using various flags throughout the book.

We can also get the same set of tests to run by specifying them or by listing the directory name:

```
$ pytest --tb=no test_one.py test_two.py
===================== test session starts =====================
collected 2 items

test_one.py .                                         [ 50%]
test_two.py F                                         [100%]

==================== short test summary info ====================
FAILED test_two.py::test_failing - assert (1, 2, 3) == (3, 2, 1)
================= 1 failed, 1 passed in 0.03s =================
$ cd ..
$ pytest --tb=no ch1
===================== test session starts =====================
collected 2 items

ch1/test_one.py .                                     [ 50%]
ch1/test_two.py F                                     [100%]

==================== short test summary info ====================
FAILED ch1/test_two.py::test_failing - assert (1, 2, 3) == (3...
================= 1 failed, 1 passed in 0.04s =================
```

We can also specify a test function within a test file to run by adding ::test_name to the file name:

```
$ pytest -v ch1/test_one.py::test_passing
===================== test session starts =====================
collected 1 item

ch1/test_one.py::test_passing PASSED                   [100%]

===================== 1 passed in 0.00s =====================
```

Test Discovery

The part of pytest execution where pytest goes off and finds which tests to run is called *test discovery*. pytest was able to find all the tests we wanted it to run because we named them according to the pytest naming conventions.

Given no arguments, pytest looks at your current directory and all subdirectories for test files and runs the test code it finds. If you give pytest a filename, a directory name, or a list of those, it looks there instead of the current directory. Each directory listed on the command line is examined for test code, as well as any subdirectories.

Here's a brief overview of the naming conventions to keep your test code discoverable by pytest:

- Test files should be named test_<something>.py or <something>_test.py.
- Test methods and functions should be named test_<something>.
- Test classes should be named Test<Something>.

Because our test files and functions start with test_, we're good. There are ways to alter these discovery rules if you have a bunch of tests named differently. I'll cover how to do that in Chapter 8, Configuration Files, on page 113.

Test Outcomes

So far we've seen one passing test and one failing test. However, pass and fail are not the only outcomes possible.

Here are the possible outcomes of a test:

- PASSED (.)—The test ran successfully.

- FAILED (F)—The test did not run successfully.

- SKIPPED (s)—The test was skipped. You can tell pytest to skip a test by using either the @pytest.mark.skip() or @pytest.mark.skipif() decorators, which are discussed in Skipping Tests with pytest.mark.skip, on page 74.

- XFAIL (x)—The test was not supposed to pass, and it ran and failed. You can tell pytest that a test is expected to fail by using the @pytest.mark.xfail() decorator, which is discussed in Expecting Tests to Fail with pytest.mark.xfail, on page 77.

- XPASS (X)—The test was marked with xfail, but it ran and passed.

- ERROR (E)—An exception happened either during the execution of a fixture or hook function, and not during the execution of a test function. Fixtures are discussed in Chapter 3, pytest Fixtures, on page 31, and hook functions are discussed in Chapter 15, Building Plugins, on page 205.

Review

Congratulations! You've done quite a bit so far in this chapter and are on a good pace to master pytest quickly. Here's a quick review of what was covered in the chapter:

- pytest is installed into a virtual environment with the following steps:

    - python -m venv venv

    - source venv/bin/activate (or venv\Scripts\activate.bat / venv\Scripts\Activate.ps1 on Windows)

    - pip install pytest

- pytest can be run in several different ways:

  - pytest: With no arguments, pytest searches the local directory and subdirectories for tests.

  - pytest <filename>: Runs the tests in one file

  - pytest <filename> <filename> ...: Runs the tests in multiple named files

  - pytest <dirname>: Starts in a particular directory (or more than one) and recursively searches for tests

- Test discovery refers to how pytest finds your test code and depends on naming:

  - Test files should be named test_<something>.py or <something>_test.py.
  - Test methods and functions should be named test_<something>.
  - Test classes should be named Test<Something>.

- The possible outcomes of a test function include: PASSED (.), FAILED (F), SKIPPED (s), XFAIL (x), XPASS (X), and ERROR (E).

- The -v or --verbose command-line flag is used to reveal more verbose output.

- The --tb=no command-line flag is used to to turn off tracebacks.

Exercises

This chapter, and the rest of the book, is designed so that you can follow along on your own. Doing the exercises at the end can help cement your learning. They should only take a few minutes.

The following exercises are intended to

- get you comfortable with virtual environments,
- make sure you can install pytest, and
- get you writing a few test files and using different types of assert statements.

pytest allows you to write new small tests quickly. Seeing for yourself just how quickly by writing some tests on your own should be fun. Actually, testing should be fun. Starting now to learn how to play with test code will help you avoid fear of writing tests in the future.

Also, you really need to know about any trouble you have installing or running pytest now, or the rest of the book is going to be decidedly not fun.

1. Create a new virtual environment using python -m virtualenv or python -m venv. Even if you know you don't need virtual environments for the project you're working on, humor me and learn enough about them to create one for trying out things in this book. I resisted using them for a very long time, and now I always use them. Read Appendix 1, Virtual Environments, on page 235 if you're having any difficulty.

2. Practice activating and deactivating your virtual environment a few times.
   - $ source venv/bin/activate
   - $ deactivate

   On Windows:
   - C:>venv\scripts\activate.bat (or C:>venv\scripts\Activate.ps1 for PowerShell)
   - C:>deactivate

3. Install pytest in your new virtual environment. See Appendix 2, pip, on page 237 if you have any trouble. Even if you thought you already had pytest installed, you'll need to install it into the virtual environment you just created.

4. Create a few test files. You can use the ones we used in this chapter or make up your own. Practice running pytest against these files.

5. Change the assert statements. Don't just use assert something == something_else; try things like:
   - assert 1 in [2, 3, 4]
   - assert a < b
   - assert 'fizz' not in 'fizzbuzz'

What's Next

In this chapter, we looked at where to get pytest, how to install it, and the various ways to run it. However, we didn't discuss what goes into test functions. In the next chapter, we'll look at writing test functions, and grouping tests into classes, modules, and directories.

## CHAPTER 2

Writing Test Functions

In the last chapter, you got pytest up and running and saw how to run it against files and directories. In this chapter, you'll learn how to write test functions in the context of testing a Python package. If you're using pytest to test something other than a Python package, most of this chapter still applies.

We're going to write tests for a simple task-tracking command-line application called Cards. We'll look at how to use assert in tests, how tests handle unexpected exceptions, and how to test for expected exceptions.

Eventually, we'll have a lot of tests. Therefore, we'll look at how to organize tests into classes, modules, and directories.

Installing the Sample Application

The test code we write needs to be able to run the application code. The "application code" is the code we are validating, and it has many names. You may hear it referred to as production code, the application, code under test (CUT), system under test (SUT), device under test (DUT), and so on. For this book, we'll use the term "application code" if it's necessary to distinguish the code from the test code.

The "test code" is the code we are writing in order to test the application code. Ironically, "test code" is fairly unambiguous and doesn't have many names other than "test code."

In our case, the Cards project is the application code. It is an installable Python package, and we need to install it in order to test it. Installing it will also allow us to play with the Cards project on the command line. If the code you are testing is not a Python package that can be installed, you'll have to use other ways to get your test to see your code. (Some alternatives are discussed in Chapter 12, Testing Scripts and Applications, on page 165.)

If you haven't already done so, you can download a copy of the source code for this project from the book's web page.[1] Download and unzip the code to a location on your computer you are comfortable working with and can find easily later. For the rest of the book, I'll be referring to this location as /path/to/code. The Cards project is at /path/to/code/cards_project, and the tests for this chapter are at /path/to/code/ch2.

You can use the same virtual environment you used in the previous chapter, create new environments for each chapter, or create one for the whole book. Let's create one at the /path/to/code/ level and use that until we need to use something different:

```
$ cd /path/to/code
$ python -m venv venv
$ source venv/bin/activate
```

And now, with the virtual environment activated, install the local cards_proj application. The ./ in front of ./cards_proj/ tells pip to look in the local directory, instead of trying to install from PyPI.

```
(venv) $ pip install ./cards_proj/
Processing ./cards_proj
...
Successfully built cards
Installing collected packages: cards
Successfully installed cards
```

While we're at it, let's make sure pytest is installed, too:

```
(venv) $ pip install pytest
```

For each new virtual environment, we have to install everything we need, including pytest.

For the rest of the book, even though I will be working within a virtual environment, I'll only show $ as a command prompt instead of (venv) $ merely to save horizontal space and visual noise.

Let's run cards and play with it a bit:

```
$ cards add do something --owner Brian
$ cards add do something else
$ cards
  ID   state   owner   summary
 ─────────────────────────────────────────
  1    todo    Brian   do something
  2    todo            do something else
```

---

1. https://pragprog.com/titles/bopytest2/source_code

```
$ cards update 2 --owner Brian
$ cards
  ID   state   owner   summary
  ─────────────────────────────────────────
  1    todo    Brian   do something
  2    todo    Brian   do something else
$ cards start 1
$ cards finish 1
$ cards start 2
$ cards
  ID   state     owner   summary
  ─────────────────────────────────────────
  1    done      Brian   do something
  2    in prog   Brian   do something else
$ cards delete 1
$ cards
  ID   state   owner   summary
  ─────────────────────────────────────────
  2    in prog   Brian   do something else
```

These examples show that a todo item, or "card," can be manipulated with the actions add, update, start, finish, and delete, and that running cards with no action will list the cards.

Nice. Now we're ready to write some tests.

Writing Knowledge-Building Tests

The Cards source code is split into three layers: CLI, API, and DB. The CLI handles the interaction with the user. The CLI calls the API, which handles most of the logic of the application. The API calls into the DB layer (the database), for saving and retrieving application data. We'll look at the structure of Cards more in Considering Software Architecture, on page 101.

There's a data structure used to pass information between the CII and the API, a data class called Card:

cards_proj/src/cards/api.py
```
@dataclass
class Card:
    summary: str = None
    owner: str = None
    state: str = "todo"
    id: int = field(default=None, compare=False)

    @classmethod
    def from_dict(cls, d):
        return Card(**d)
```

```
def to_dict(self):
    return asdict(self)
```

Data classes were added to Python in version 3.7,[2] but they may still be new to some. The Card structure has three string fields: summary, owner, and state, and one integer field: id. The summary, owner, and id fields default to None. The state field defaults to "todo". The id field is also using the field method to utilize compare=False, which is supposed to tell the code that when comparing two Card objects for equality, to not use the id field. We will definitely test that, as well as the other aspects. A couple of other methods were added for convenience and clarity: from_dict and to_dict, since Card(**d) or dataclasses.asdict() aren't very easy to read.

When faced with a new data structure, it's often helpful to write some quick tests so that you can understand how the data structure works. So, let's start with some tests that verify our understanding of how this thing is supposed to work:

ch2/test_card.py

```
from cards import Card


def test_field_access():
    c = Card("something", "brian", "todo", 123)
    assert c.summary == "something"
    assert c.owner == "brian"
    assert c.state == "todo"
    assert c.id == 123


def test_defaults():
    c = Card()
    assert c.summary is None
    assert c.owner is None
    assert c.state == "todo"
    assert c.id is None


def test_equality():
    c1 = Card("something", "brian", "todo", 123)
    c2 = Card("something", "brian", "todo", 123)
    assert c1 == c2


def test_equality_with_diff_ids():
    c1 = Card("something", "brian", "todo", 123)
    c2 = Card("something", "brian", "todo", 4567)
    assert c1 == c2
```

---

2. https://docs.python.org/3/library/dataclasses.html

```python
def test_inequality():
    c1 = Card("something", "brian", "todo", 123)
    c2 = Card("completely different", "okken", "done", 123)
    assert c1 != c2


def test_from_dict():
    c1 = Card("something", "brian", "todo", 123)
    c2_dict = {
        "summary": "something",
        "owner": "brian",
        "state": "todo",
        "id": 123,
    }
    c2 = Card.from_dict(c2_dict)
    assert c1 == c2


def test_to_dict():
    c1 = Card("something", "brian", "todo", 123)
    c2 = c1.to_dict()
    c2_expected = {
        "summary": "something",
        "owner": "brian",
        "state": "todo",
        "id": 123,
    }
    assert c2 == c2_expected
```

Do a quick test run:

```
$ cd /path/to/code/ch2
$ pytest test_card.py
===================== test session starts =====================
collected 7 items

test_card.py .......                                    [100%]

===================== 7 passed in 0.04s =====================
```

We could have started with one test. However, I want to demonstrate just how quickly and concisely we can write a bunch of tests. These tests are intended to demonstrate how to use a data structure. They aren't exhaustive tests; they are not looking for corner cases, or failure cases, or looking for ways to make the data structure blow up. I haven't tried passing in gibberish or negative numbers as IDs or huge strings. That's not the point of this set of tests.

The point of these tests is to check my understanding of how the structure works, and possibly to document that knowledge for someone else or even for a future me. This use of checking my own understanding, and really of using tests as little playgrounds to play with the application code, is super powerful, and I think more people would enjoy testing more if they start with this mindset.

Note also that all of these tests use plain old assert statements. Let's take a look at them next.

Using assert Statements

When you write test functions, the normal Python assert statement is your primary tool to communicate test failure. The simplicity of this within pytest is brilliant. It's what drives a lot of developers to use pytest over other frameworks.

If you've used any other testing framework, you've probably seen various assert helper functions. For example, following is a list of a few of the assert forms and assert helper functions from unittest:

pytest	unittest
assert something	assertTrue(something)
assert not something	assertFalse(something)
assert a == b	assertEqual(a, b)
assert a != b	assertNotEqual(a, b)
assert a is None	assertIsNone(a)
assert a is not None	assertIsNotNone(a)
assert a <= b	assertLessEqual(a, b)
...	...

With pytest, you can use assert <expression> with any expression. If the expression would evaluate to False if converted to a bool, the test would fail.

pytest includes a feature called "assert rewriting" that intercepts assert calls and replaces them with something that can tell you more about why your assertions failed. Let's see how helpful this rewriting is by looking at an assertion failure:

```
ch2/test_card_fail.py
def test_equality_fail():
    c1 = Card("sit there", "brian")
    c2 = Card("do something", "okken")
    assert c1 == c2
```

This test will fail, but what's interesting is the traceback information:

```
$ pytest test_card_fail.py
===================== test session starts =====================
collected 1 item

test_card_fail.py F                                     [100%]

=========================== FAILURES ==========================
_____ test_equality_fail _____

    def test_equality_fail():
        c1 = Card("sit there", "brian")
        c2 = Card("do something", "okken")
>       assert c1 == c2
E       AssertionError: assert Card(summary=...odo', id=None) ==
E                              Card(summary=...odo', id=None)
E
E         Omitting 1 identical items, use -vv to show
E         Differing attributes:
E         ['summary', 'owner']
E
E         Drill down into differing attribute summary:
E           summary: 'sit there' != 'do something'...
E
E         ...Full output truncated (8 lines hidden),
E         use '-vv' to show

test_card_fail.py:7: AssertionError
=================== short test summary info ===================
FAILED test_card_fail.py::test_equality_fail - AssertionError...
===================== 1 failed in 0.07s =======================
```

That's a lot of information. For each failing test, the exact line of failure is shown with a > pointing to the failure. The E lines show you extra information about the assert failure to help you figure out what went wrong.

I intentionally put two mismatches in test_equality_fail(), but only the first was shown in the previous code. Let's try it again with the -vv flag, as suggested in the error message:

```
$ pytest -vv test_card_fail.py
===================== test session starts =====================
collected 1 item

test_card_fail.py::test_equality_fail FAILED            [100%]

=========================== FAILURES ==========================
_____ test_equality_fail _____

    def test_equality_fail():
        c1 = Card("sit there", "brian")
        c2 = Card("do something", "okken")
>       assert c1 == c2
E       AssertionError: assert Card(summary='sit there',
E         owner='brian', state='todo', id=None) ==
```

```
E           Card(summary='do something',
E             owner='okken', state='todo', id=None)
E
E           Matching attributes:
E           ['state']
E           Differing attributes:
E           ['summary', 'owner']
E
E           Drill down into differing attribute summary:
E             summary: 'sit there' != 'do something'
E             - do something
E             + sit there
E
E           Drill down into differing attribute owner:
E             owner: 'brian' != 'okken'
E             - okken
E             + brian

test_card_fail.py:7: AssertionError
==================== short test summary info ====================
FAILED test_card_fail.py::test_equality_fail - AssertionError...
===================== 1 failed in 0.07s =====================
```

Well, I think that's pretty darned cool. pytest listed specifically which attributes matched and which did not, and highlighted the exact mismatches.

The previous example only used equality assert; many more varieties of assert statements with awesome trace debug information are found on the pytest.org website.[3]

Just for reference, we can see what Python gives us by default for assert failures. We can run the test, not from pytest, but directly from Python by adding a if _name_ == '_main_' block at the end of the file and calling test_equality_fail(), like this:

ch2/test_card_fail.py
```python
if __name__ == "__main__":
    test_equality_fail()
```

Using if _name_ == '_main_' is a quick way to run some code from a file but not allow the code to be run if it is imported. When a module is imported, Python will fill in _name_ with the name of the module, which is the name of the file without the .py. However, if you run the file with python file.py, _name_ will be filled in by Python with the string "_main_".

Running the test with straight Python, we get this:

---

3. https://doc.pytest.org/en/latest/example/reportingdemo.html

```
$ python test_card_fail.py
Traceback (most recent call last):
  File "/path/to/code/ch2/test_card_fail.py", line 12, in <module>
    test_equality_fail()
  File "/path/to/code/ch2/test_card_fail.py", line 7, in test_equality_fail
    assert c1 == c2
AssertionError
```

That doesn't tell us much. The pytest version gives us way more information about why our assertions failed.

Assertion failures are the primary way test code results in a failed test. However, it's not the only way.

Failing with pytest.fail() and Exceptions

A test will fail if there is any uncaught exception. This can happen if

- an assert statement fails, which will raise an AssertionError exception,
- the test code calls pytest.fail(), which will raise an exception, or
- any other exception is raised.

While any exception can fail a test, I prefer to use assert. In rare cases where assert is not suitable, use pytest.fail().

Here's an example of using pytest's fail() function to explicitly fail a test:

```
ch2/test_alt_fail.py
import pytest
from cards import Card


def test_with_fail():
    c1 = Card("sit there", "brian")
    c2 = Card("do something", "okken")
    if c1 != c2:
        pytest.fail("they don't match")
```

Here's what the output looks like:

```
$ pytest test_alt_fail.py
========================= test session starts =========================
collected 1 item

test_alt_fail.py F                                              [100%]

============================== FAILURES ===============================
_____ test_with_fail _____

    def test_with_fail():
        c1 = Card("sit there", "brian")
        c2 = Card("do something", "okken")
        if c1 != c2:
```

```
>               pytest.fail("they don't match")
E               Failed: they don't match

test_alt_fail.py:9: Failed
======================= short test summary info ========================
FAILED test_alt_fail.py::test_with_fail - Failed: they don't match
========================= 1 failed in 0.16s ===========================
```

When calling pytest.fail() or raising an exception directly, we don't get the wonderful assert rewriting provided by pytest. However, there are reasonable times to use pytest.fail(), such as in an assertion helper.

Writing Assertion Helper Functions

An *assertion helper* is a function that is used to wrap up a complicated assertion check. As an example, the Cards data class is set up such that two cards with different IDs will still report equality. If we wanted to have a stricter check, we could write a helper function called assert_identical like this:

ch2/test_helper.py
```python
from cards import Card
import pytest

def assert_identical(c1: Card, c2: Card):
    __tracebackhide__ = True
    assert c1 == c2
    if c1.id != c2.id:
        pytest.fail(f"id's don't match. {c1.id} != {c2.id}")

def test_identical():
    c1 = Card("foo", id=123)
    c2 = Card("foo", id=123)
    assert_identical(c1, c2)

def test_identical_fail():
    c1 = Card("foo", id=123)
    c2 = Card("foo", id=456)
    assert_identical(c1, c2)
```

The assert_identical function sets __tracebackhide__ = True. This is optional. The effect will be that failing tests will not include this function in the traceback. The normal assert c1 == c2 is then used to check everything except the ID for equality.

Finally, the IDs are checked, and if they are not equal, pytest.fail() is used to fail the test with a hopefully helpful message.

Let's see what that looks like when run:

```
$ pytest test_helper.py
=========================== test session starts ===========================
collected 2 items

test_helper.py .F                                                  [100%]

============================== FAILURES ===============================
_____ test_identical_fail _____

    def test_identical_fail():
        c1 = Card("foo", id=123)
        c2 = Card("foo", id=456)
>       assert_identical(c1, c2)
E       Failed: id's don't match. 123 != 456

test_helper.py:18: Failed
======================= short test summary info =======================
FAILED test_helper.py::test_identical_fail - Failed: id's don't match...
===================== 1 failed, 1 passed in 0.15s =====================
```

If we had not put in the _tracebackhide_ = True, the assert_identical code would have been included in the traceback, which in this case, wouldn't have added any clarity. I could have also used assert c1.id == c2.id, "id's don't match." to much the same effect, but I wanted to show an example of using pytest.fail().

Note that assert rewriting is only applied to conftest.py files and test files. See the pytest documentation[4] for more details.

Testing for Expected Exceptions

We've looked at how any exception can cause a test to fail. But what if a bit of code you are testing is supposed to raise an exception? How do you test for that?

You use pytest.raises() to test for expected exceptions.

As an example, the cards API has a CardsDB class that requires a path argument. What happens if we don't pass in a path? Let's try it:

```
ch2/test_experiment.py
import cards


def test_no_path_fail():
    cards.CardsDB()
```

```
$ pytest --tb=short test_experiment.py
===================== test session starts =====================
collected 1 item

test_experiment.py F                                        [100%]
```

---

4.   https://docs.pytest.org/en/latest/how-to/assert.html#assertion-introspection-details

```
=========================== FAILURES ===========================
_____ test_no_path_fail _____
test_experiment.py:4: in test_no_path_fail
    c = cards.CardsDB()
E   TypeError: __init__() missing 1 required positional argument: 'db_path'
==================== short test summary info ====================
FAILED test_experiment.py::test_no_path_fail - TypeError: __i...
===================== 1 failed in 0.06s =====================
```

Here I used the --tb=short shorter traceback format because we don't need to see the full traceback to find out which exception is raised.

The TypeError exception seems reasonable, since the error occurs when trying to initialize the custom CardsDB type. We can write a test to make sure this exception is thrown, like this:

ch2/test_exceptions.py
```python
import pytest
import cards


def test_no_path_raises():
    with pytest.raises(TypeError):
        cards.CardsDB()
```

The with pytest.raises(TypeError): statement says that whatever is in the next block of code should raise a TypeError exception. If no exception is raised, the test fails. If the test raises a different exception, it fails.

We just checked for the type of exception in test_no_path_raises(). We can also check to make sure the message is correct, or any other aspect of the exception, like additional parameters:

ch2/test_exceptions.py
```python
def test_raises_with_info():
    match_regex = "missing 1 .* positional argument"
    with pytest.raises(TypeError, match=match_regex):
        cards.CardsDB()


def test_raises_with_info_alt():
    with pytest.raises(TypeError) as exc_info:
        cards.CardsDB()
    expected = "missing 1 required positional argument"
    assert expected in str(exc_info.value)
```

The match parameter takes a regular expression and matches it with the exception message. You can also use as exc_info or any other variable name to interrogate extra parameters to the exception if it's a custom exception. The exc_info object will be of type ExceptionInfo. See the pytest documentation[5] for full ExceptionInfo reference.

Structuring Test Functions

I recommend making sure you keep assertions at the end of test functions. This is such a common recommendation that it has at least two names: Arrange-Act-Assert and Given-When-Then.

Bill Wake originally named the Arrange-Act-Assert pattern in 2001.[6] Kent Beck later popularized the practice as part of test-driven development (TDD).[7] Behavior-driven development (BDD) uses the terms Given-When-Then, a pattern from Ivan Moore, popularized by Dan North.[8] Regardless of the names of the steps, the goal is the same: separate a test into stages.

There are many benefits of separating into stages. The separation clearly separates the "getting ready to do something," the "doing something," and the "checking to see if it worked" parts of the test. That allows the test developer to focus attention on each part, and be clear about what is really being tested.

A common anti-pattern is to have more a "Arrange-Assert-Act-Assert-Act-Assert…" pattern where lots of actions, followed by state or behavior checks, validate a workflow. This seems reasonable until the test fails. Any of the actions could have caused the failure, so the test is not focusing on testing one behavior. Or it might have been the setup in "Arrange" that caused the failure. This interleaved assert pattern creates tests that are hard to debug and maintain because later developers have no idea what the original intent of the test was. Sticking to Given-When-Then or Arrange-Act-Assert keeps the test focused and makes the test more maintainable.

The three-stage structure is the structure I try to stick to with my own test functions and the tests in this book.

Let's apply this structure to one of our first tests as an example:

```
ch2/test_structure.py
def test_to_dict():
    # GIVEN a Card object with known contents
    c1 = Card("something", "brian", "todo", 123)
```

---

5. https://docs.pytest.org/en/latest/reference/reference.html#exceptioninfo
6. https://xp123.com/articles/3a-arrange-act-assert
7. https://en.wikipedia.org/wiki/Test-driven_development
8. https://dannorth.net/introducing-bdd

```
# WHEN we call to_dict() on the object
c2 = c1.to_dict()

# THEN the result will be a dictionary with known content
c2_expected = {
    "summary": "something",
    "owner": "brian",
    "state": "todo",
    "id": 123,
}
assert c2 == c2_expected
```

- *Given/Arrange*—A starting state. This is where you set up data or the environment to get ready for the action.

- *When/Act*—Some action is performed. This is the focus of the test—the behavior we are trying to make sure is working right.

- *Then/Assert*—Some expected result or end state should happen. At the end of the test, we make sure the action resulted in the expected behavior.

I tend to think about tests more naturally using the Given-When-Then terms. Some people find it more natural to use Arrange-Act-Assert. Both ideas work fine. The structure helps to keep test functions organized and focused on testing one behavior. The structure also helps you to think of other test cases. Focusing on one starting state helps you think of other states that might be relevant to test with the same action. Likewise, focusing on one ideal outcome helps you think of other possible outcomes, like failure states or error conditions, that should also be tested with other test cases.

Grouping Tests with Classes

So far we've written test functions within test modules within a file system directory. That structuring of test code actually works quite well and is sufficient for many projects. However, pytest also allows us to group tests with classes.

Let's take a few of the test functions related to Card equality and group them into a class:

ch2/test_classes.py
```
class TestEquality:
    def test_equality(self):
        c1 = Card("something", "brian", "todo", 123)
        c2 = Card("something", "brian", "todo", 123)
        assert c1 == c2
```

```python
def test_equality_with_diff_ids(self):
    c1 = Card("something", "brian", "todo", 123)
    c2 = Card("something", "brian", "todo", 4567)
    assert c1 == c2

def test_inequality(self):
    c1 = Card("something", "brian", "todo", 123)
    c2 = Card("completely different", "okken", "done", 123)
    assert c1 != c2
```

The code looks pretty much the same as it did before, with the exception of some extra white space and each method has to have an initial self argument.

We can now run all of these together by specifying the class:

```
$ cd /path/to/code/ch2
$ pytest -v test_classes.py::TestEquality
========================== test session starts ==========================
collected 3 items

test_classes.py::TestEquality::test_equality PASSED              [ 33%]
test_classes.py::TestEquality::test_equality_with_diff_ids PASSED [ 66%]
test_classes.py::TestEquality::test_inequality PASSED            [100%]

=========================== 3 passed in 0.02s ===========================
```

We can still get at a single method:

```
$ pytest -v test_classes.py::TestEquality::test_equality
========================== test session starts ==========================
collected 1 item

test_classes.py::TestEquality::test_equality PASSED             [100%]

=========================== 1 passed in 0.02s ===========================
```

If you are familiar with object-oriented programming (OOP) and class inheritance with Python, you can utilize test class hierarchies for inherited helper methods. If you are not familiar with OOP and such, don't worry about it. In this book, and in almost all of my own use of test classes, I use them solely for the purpose of grouping tests to easily run them together. I recommend that in production test code, you also use test classes sparingly and primarily for grouping. Getting fancy with test class inheritance will certainly confuse someone, possibly yourself, in the future.

Running a Subset of Tests

In the previous section, we used test classes to be able to run a subset of tests. Running just a small batch of tests is handy while debugging or if you want to limit the tests to a specific section of the code base you are working on at the time.

pytest allows you to run a subset of tests in several ways:

Subset	Syntax
Single test method	pytest path/test_module.py::TestClass::test_method
All tests in a class	pytest path/test_module.py::TestClass
Single test function	pytest path/test_module.py::test_function
All tests in a module	pytest path/test_module.py
All tests in a directory	pytest path
Tests matching a name pattern	pytest -k pattern
Tests by marker	Covered in Chapter 6, Markers, on page 73.

We've used everything but pattern and marker subsets so far. But let's run through examples anyway.

We'll start from the top-level code directory so that we can use ch2 to show the path in the command-line examples:

```
$ cd /path/to/code
```

Running a single test method, test class, or module:

```
$ pytest ch2/test_classes.py::TestEquality::test_equality
$ pytest ch2/test_classes.py::TestEquality
$ pytest ch2/test_classes.py
```

Running a single test function or module:

```
$ pytest ch2/test_card.py::test_defaults
$ pytest ch2/test_card.py
```

Running the whole directory:

```
$ pytest ch2
```

We'll cover markers in Chapter 6, Markers, on page 73, but let's talk about -k here.

The -k argument takes an expression, and tells pytest to run tests that contain a substring that matches the expression. The substring can be part of the test name or the test class name. Let's take a look at using -k in action.

We know we can run the tests in the TestEquality class with:

```
$ pytest ch2/test_classes.py::TestEquality
```

We can also use -k and just specify the test class name:

```
$ cd /path/to/code/ch2
$ pytest -v -k TestEquality
```

```
=========================== test session starts ===========================
collected 24 items / 21 deselected / 3 selected

test_classes.py::TestEquality::test_equality PASSED                  [ 33%]
test_classes.py::TestEquality::test_equality_with_diff_ids PASSED    [ 66%]
test_classes.py::TestEquality::test_inequality PASSED                [100%]

==================== 3 passed, 21 deselected in 0.06s =====================
```

or even just part of the name:

```
$ pytest -v -k TestEq
=========================== test session starts ===========================
collected 24 items / 21 deselected / 3 selected

test_classes.py::TestEquality::test_equality PASSED                  [ 33%]
test_classes.py::TestEquality::test_equality_with_diff_ids PASSED    [ 66%]
test_classes.py::TestEquality::test_inequality PASSED                [100%]

==================== 3 passed, 21 deselected in 0.06s =====================
```

Let's run all the tests with "equality" in their name:

```
$ pytest -v --tb=no -k equality
=========================== test session starts ===========================
collected 24 items / 17 deselected / 7 selected

test_card.py::test_equality PASSED                                   [ 14%]
test_card.py::test_equality_with_diff_ids PASSED                     [ 28%]
test_card.py::test_inequality PASSED                                 [ 42%]
test_card_fail.py::test_equality_fail FAILED                         [ 57%]
test_classes.py::TestEquality::test_equality PASSED                  [ 71%]
test_classes.py::TestEquality::test_equality_with_diff_ids PASSED    [ 85%]
test_classes.py::TestEquality::test_inequality PASSED                [100%]

=============== 1 failed, 6 passed, 17 deselected in 0.08s ================
```

Yikes. One of those is our fail example. We can eliminate that by expanding
the expression:

```
$ pytest -v --tb=no -k "equality and not equality_fail"
=========================== test session starts ===========================
collected 24 items / 18 deselected / 6 selected

test_card.py::test_equality PASSED                                   [ 16%]
test_card.py::test_equality_with_diff_ids PASSED                     [ 33%]
test_card.py::test_inequality PASSED                                 [ 50%]
test_classes.py::TestEquality::test_equality PASSED                  [ 66%]
test_classes.py::TestEquality::test_equality_with_diff_ids PASSED    [ 83%]
test_classes.py::TestEquality::test_inequality PASSED                [100%]

==================== 6 passed, 18 deselected in 0.07s =====================
```

The keywords and, not, or, and parentheses are allowed to create complex expressions. Here's a test run of all tests with "dict" or "ids" in the name, but not ones in the "TestEquality" class:

```
$ pytest -v --tb=no -k "(dict or ids) and not TestEquality"
=========================== test session starts ===========================
collected 24 items / 18 deselected / 6 selected

test_card.py::test_equality_with_diff_ids PASSED              [ 16%]
test_card.py::test_from_dict PASSED                           [ 33%]
test_card.py::test_to_dict PASSED                             [ 50%]
test_classes.py::test_from_dict PASSED                        [ 66%]
test_classes.py::test_to_dict PASSED                          [ 83%]
test_structure.py::test_to_dict PASSED                        [100%]

==================== 6 passed, 18 deselected in 0.08s ====================
```

The keyword flag, -k, along with and, not, and or, add quite a bit of flexibility to selecting exactly the tests you want to run. This really proves quite helpful when debugging failures or developing new tests.

Review

We've covered a lot in this chapter and are well on our way to testing the Cards application.

- The sample code should be downloaded into /path/to/code.

- The Cards application (and pytest) is installed into a virtual environment with the following steps:

  - cd /path/to/code
  - python -m venv venv --prompt cards
  - source venv/bin/activate (or venv\Scripts\activate.bat on Windows)
  - pip install ./cards_proj
  - pip install pytest

- pytest uses assert rewriting, which allows us to use standard Python assert expressions.

- Tests can fail from assertion failures, from calls to fail(), or from any uncaught exception.

- pytest.raises() is used to test for expected exceptions.

- A great way to structure tests is called Given-When-Then or Arrange-Act-Assert.

- Classes can be used to group tests.

- Running small subsets of tests is handy while debugging, and pytest allows you to run a small batch of tests in many ways.

- The -vv command-line flag shows even more information during test failures.

Exercises

We'll use the Cards project in the rest of the book, so it's important you are able to install it and run tests against it.

If you haven't already, download the code from the book's web page[9] and make sure you can install the Cards application locally with pip install /path/to/code/cards_proj.

Navigate to the path/to/code/ch2 directory. Run pytest test_card.py.

You should see something like this:

```
$ pytest test_card.py
========================= test session starts =========================
collected 7 items

test_card.py .......                                          [100%]

========================= 7 passed in 0.07s =========================
```

If you are not able to run pytest, or don't get seven passing tests, something's wrong. Please try to resolve these issues before attempting to go further.

These are things that might have gone wrong:

- You installed pytest in a virtual environment, but forgot to activate the environment.

- You have pytest and cards installed in separate environments.

- pip list --not-required shows all top level packages you have installed. Make sure both pytest and cards show up in the list.

The following exercises are to get you started on playing with some code and thinking about how to extend testing, as well as thinking about missing tests.

1. The file test_card_mod.py in /path/to/code/exercises/ch2 is a copy of test_card.py, but the import statement is replaced with the definition of the Card class. Modify default values in the Card definition. For example, replace some None values with an empty string or a filled-in string. Do the tests catch the changes?

---

9. https://pragprog.com/titles/bopytest2/source_code

2. What happens if we change `compare=False` to `compare=True`?

3. Are there any missing tests? Any functionality not covered? Add some test functions if there is something missing.

4. Try the `-k` option to select a test.

Using the options as they come up in the book will help you to get used to the flexibility of the pytest command line. Even if you don't remember the options, if you use them a couple of times, you'll remember that the functionality is there, and can look for it again in `pytest --help` if you ever need it in the future.

What's Next

An important point discussed in this chapter is the structure of Given-When-Then or Arrange-Act-Assert, which helps us focus on what we are testing with a test function. In the next chapter, you will learn about fixtures, which allow us to focus even more by pushing the "Given" or "Arrange" setup portion into a separate function. Pushing setup and teardown into fixtures is extremely powerful, as it allows for an elegant separation of complex system state and test code and keeps track of external resources.

pytest Fixtures

Now that you've used pytest to write and run test functions, let's turn our attention to test helper functions called *fixtures*, which are essential to structuring test code for almost any non-trivial software system. Fixtures are functions that are run by pytest before (and sometimes after) the actual test functions. The code in the fixture can do whatever you want it to. You can use fixtures to get a data set for the tests to work on. You can use fixtures to get a system into a known state before running a test. Fixtures are also used to get data ready for multiple tests.

In this chapter, you'll learn how to create fixtures and learn how to work with them. You'll learn how to structure fixtures to hold both setup and teardown code. You'll use scope to allow fixtures to run once over many tests, and learn how tests can use multiple fixtures. You'll also learn how to trace code execution through fixtures and test code.

But first, before you learn the ins and outs of fixtures and use them to help test Cards, let's look at a small example fixture and how fixtures and test functions are connected.

Getting Started with Fixtures

Here's a simple fixture that returns a number:

```
ch3/test_fixtures.py
import pytest


@pytest.fixture()
def some_data():
    """Return answer to ultimate question."""
    return 42
```

```
def test_some_data(some_data):
    """Use fixture return value in a test."""
    assert some_data == 42
```

The @pytest.fixture() decorator is used to tell pytest that a function is a fixture. When you include the fixture name in the parameter list of a test function, pytest knows to run it before running the test. Fixtures can do work, and can also return data to the test function.

You don't need to have a complete understanding of Python decorators to use the decorators included with pytest. pytest uses decorators to add functionality and features to other functions. In this case, pytest.fixture() is decorating the some_data() function. The test, test_some_data(), has the name of the fixture, some_data, as a parameter. pytest will see this and look for a fixture with this name.

The term *fixture* has many meanings in the programming and test community, and even in the Python community. I use "fixture," "fixture function," and "fixture method" interchangeably to refer to the @pytest.fixture() decorated functions discussed in this chapter. Fixture can also be used to refer to the resource that is being set up by the fixture functions. Fixture functions often set up or retrieve some data that the test can work with. Sometimes this data is considered a fixture. For example, the Django community often uses *fixture* to mean some initial data that gets loaded into a database at the start of an application.

Regardless of other meanings, in pytest and in this book, test fixtures refer to the mechanism pytest provides to allow the separation of "getting ready for" and "cleaning up after" code from your test functions.

pytest treats exceptions differently during fixtures compared to during a test function. An exception (or assert failure or call to pytest.fail()) that happens during the test code proper results in a "Fail" result. However, during a fixture, the test function is reported as "Error." This distinction is helpful when debugging why a test didn't pass. If a test results in "Fail," the failure is somewhere in the test function (or something the function called). If a test results in "Error," the failure is somewhere in a fixture.

pytest fixtures are one of the unique core features that make pytest stand out above other test frameworks, and are the reason why many people switch to and stay with pytest. There are a lot of features and nuances about fixtures. Once you get a good mental model of how they work, they will seem easy to you. However, you have to play with them a while to get there, so let's do that next.

Using Fixtures for Setup and Teardown

Fixtures are going to help us a lot with testing the Cards application. The Cards application is designed with an API that does most of the work and logic, and a thin CLI. Especially because the user interface is rather thin on logic, focusing most of our testing on the API will give us the most bang for our buck. The Cards application also uses a database, and dealing with the database is where fixtures are going to help out a lot.

Make Sure Cards Is Installed

 Examples in this chapter require having the Cards application installed. If you haven't already installed the Cards application, be sure to install it with cd code; pip install ./cards_proj. See Installing the Sample Application, on page 11 for more information.

Let's start by writing some tests for the count() method that supports the count functionality. As a reminder, let's play with count on the command line:

```
$ cards count
0
$ cards add first item
$ cards add second item
$ cards count
2
```

An initial test, checking that the count starts at zero, might look like this:

```
ch3/test_count_initial.py
from pathlib import Path
from tempfile import TemporaryDirectory
import cards


def test_empty():
    with TemporaryDirectory() as db_dir:
        db_path = Path(db_dir)
        db = cards.CardsDB(db_path)

        count = db.count()
        db.close()

        assert count == 0
```

In order to call count(), we need a database object, which we get by calling cards.CardsDB(db_path). The cards.CardsDB() function is a constructor; it returns a CardsDB object. The db_path parameter needs to be a pathlib.Path object that points to the database directory. The pathlib module was introduced in Python 3.4

and pathlib.Path[1] objects are the standard way to represent file system paths. For testing, a temporary directory works, which we get from tempfile.Temporary-Directory(). There are other ways to get all of this done, but this works for now.

This test function really isn't too painful. It's only a few lines of code. Let's look at the problems anyway. There is code to get the database set up before we call count() that isn't really what we want to test. There is the call to db.close() before the assert statement. It would seem better to place this at the end of the function, but we have to call it before assert, because if the assert statement fails, it won't be called.

These problems are resolved with a pytest fixture:

```
ch3/test_count.py
import pytest


@pytest.fixture()
def cards_db():
    with TemporaryDirectory() as db_dir:
        db_path = Path(db_dir)
        db = cards.CardsDB(db_path)
        yield db
        db.close()


def test_empty(cards_db):
    assert cards_db.count() == 0
```

Right off the bat we can see that the test function itself is way easier to read, as we've pushed all the database initialization into a fixture called cards_db.

The cards_db fixture is "setting up" for the test by getting the database ready. It's then yield-ing the database object. That's when the test gets to run. And then after the test runs, it closes the database.

Fixture functions run before the tests that use them. If there is a yield in the function, it stops there, passes control to the tests, and picks up on the next line after the tests are done. The code above the yield is "setup" and the code after yield is "teardown." The code after the yield, the teardown, is guaranteed to run regardless of what happens during the tests.

In our example, the yield happens within a context manager with block for the temporary directory. That directory stays around while the fixture is in use and the tests run. After the test is done, control passes back to the fixture, the db.close() can run, and then the with block can complete and clean up the directory.

---

1. https://docs.python.org/3/library/pathlib.html#basic-use

Remember: pytest looks at the specific name of the arguments to our test and then looks for a fixture with the same name. We never call fixture functions directly. pytest does that for us.

You can use fixtures in multiple tests. Here's another one:

```
ch3/test_count.py
def test_two(cards_db):
    cards_db.add_card(cards.Card("first"))
    cards_db.add_card(cards.Card("second"))
    assert cards_db.count() == 2
```

test_two() uses the same cards_db fixture. This time, we take the empty database and add two cards before checking the count. We can now use cards_db for any test that needs a configured database to run. The individual tests, such as test_empty() and test_two() can be kept smaller and focus on what we are testing, and not the setup and teardown bits.

The fixture and test function are separate functions. Carefully naming your fixtures to reflect the work being done in the fixture or the object returned from the fixture, or both, will help with readability.

While writing and debugging test functions, it's frequently helpful to visualize when the setup and teardown portions of fixtures run with respect the tests using them. The next section describes --setup-show to help with this visualization.

Tracing Fixture Execution with –setup-show

Now that we have two tests using the same fixture, it would be interesting to know exactly in what order everything is getting called.

Fortunately, pytest provides the command-line flag, --setup-show, which shows us the order of operations of tests and fixtures, including the setup and teardown phases of the fixtures:

```
$ cd /path/to/code/ch3
$ pytest --setup-show test_count.py
========================= test session starts =========================
collected 2 items

test_count.py
        SETUP    F cards_db
        ch3/test_count.py::test_empty (fixtures used: cards_db).
        TEARDOWN F cards_db
        SETUP    F cards_db
        ch3/test_count.py::test_two (fixtures used: cards_db).
        TEARDOWN F cards_db

========================= 2 passed in 0.02s =========================
```

We can see that our test runs, surrounded by the SETUP and TEARDOWN portions of the cards_db fixture. The F in front of the fixture name indicates that the fixture is using function scope, meaning the fixture is called before each test function that uses it, and torn down after each function that uses it. Let's take a look at scope next.

Specifying Fixture Scope

Each fixture has a specific scope, which defines the order of when the setup and teardown run relative to running of all the test function using the fixture. The scope dictates how often the setup and teardown get run when it's used by multiple test functions.

The default scope for fixtures is function scope. That means the setup portion of the fixture will run before each test that needs it runs. Likewise, the teardown portion runs after the test is done, for each test.

However, there may be times when you don't want that to happen. Perhaps setting up and connecting to the database is time-consuming, or you are generating large sets of data, or you are retrieving data from a server or a slow device. Really, you can do anything you want within a fixture, and some of that may be slow.

I could show you an example where I put a time.sleep(1) statement in the fixture when we are connecting to the database to simulate a slow resource, but I think it suffices that you imagine it. So, if we want to avoid that slow connection twice in our example, or imagine 100 seconds for a hundred tests, we can change the scope such that the slow part happens once for multiple tests.

Let's change the scope of our fixture so the database is only opened once, and then talk about different scopes.

It's a one-line change, adding scope="module" to the fixture decorator:

ch3/test_mod_scope.py
```python
@pytest.fixture(scope="module")
def cards_db():
    with TemporaryDirectory() as db_dir:
        db_path = Path(db_dir)
        db = cards.CardsDB(db_path)
        yield db
        db.close()
```

Now let's run it again:

```
$ pytest --setup-show test_mod_scope.py
=========================== test session starts ===========================
collected 2 items

test_mod_scope.py
    SETUP    M cards_db
        ch3/test_mod_scope.py::test_empty (fixtures used: cards_db).
        ch3/test_mod_scope.py::test_two (fixtures used: cards_db).
    TEARDOWN M cards_db

============================ 2 passed in 0.03s ============================
```

Whew! We saved that imaginary one second of setup time for the second test function. The change to module scope allows any test in this module that uses the cards_db fixture to share the same instance of it and not incur extra setup/teardown time.

The fixture decorator scope parameter allows more than function and module. There's also class, package, and session. The default scope is function.

Here's a rundown of each scope value:

scope='function'

> Run once per test function. The setup portion is run before each test using the fixture. The teardown portion is run after each test using the fixture. This is the default scope used when no scope parameter is specified.

scope='class'

> Run once per test class, regardless of how many test methods are in the class.

scope='module'

> Run once per module, regardless of how many test functions or methods or other fixtures in the module use it.

scope='package'

> Run once per package, or test directory, regardless of how many test functions or methods or other fixtures in the package use it.

scope='session'

> Run once per session. All test methods and functions using a fixture of session scope share one setup and teardown call.

Scope is defined with the fixture. I know this is obvious from the code, but it's an important point to make sure you fully grok. The scope is set at the definition of a fixture, and not at the place where it's called. The test functions that use a fixture don't control how often a fixture is set up and torn down.

With a fixture defined within a test module, the session and package scopes act just like module scope. In order to make use of these other scopes, we need to put them in a conftest.py file.

Sharing Fixtures through conftest.py

You can put fixtures into individual test files, but to share fixtures among multiple test files, you need to use a conftest.py file either in the same directory as the test file that's using it or in some parent directory. The conftest.py file is also optional. It is considered by pytest as a "local plugin" and can contain hook functions and fixtures.

Let's start by moving the cards_db fixture out of test_count.py and into a conftest.py file in the same directory:

ch3/a/conftest.py
```python
from pathlib import Path
from tempfile import TemporaryDirectory
import cards
import pytest


@pytest.fixture(scope="session")
def cards_db():
    """CardsDB object connected to a temporary database"""
    with TemporaryDirectory() as db_dir:
        db_path = Path(db_dir)
        db = cards.CardsDB(db_path)
        yield db
        db.close()
```

ch3/a/test_count.py
```python
import cards


def test_empty(cards_db):
    assert cards_db.count() == 0


def test_two(cards_db):
    cards_db.add_card(cards.Card("first"))
    cards_db.add_card(cards.Card("second"))
    assert cards_db.count() == 2
```

And yep, it still works:

```
$ cd /path/to/code/ch3/a/
$ pytest --setup-show test_count.py
========================== test session starts ==========================
collected 2 items

test_count.py
SETUP    S cards_db
```

```
            ch3/a/test_count.py::test_empty (fixtures used: cards_db).
            ch3/a/test_count.py::test_two (fixtures used: cards_db).
TEARDOWN S cards_db

=========================== 2 passed in 0.01s ===========================
```

Fixtures can only depend on other fixtures of their same scope or wider. So a function-scope fixture can depend on other function-scope fixtures (the default, and used in the Cards project so far). A function-scope fixture can also depend on class-, module-, and session-scope fixtures, but you can't go in the reverse order.

Don't Import conftest.py

Although conftest.py is a Python module, it should not be imported by test files. The conftest.py file gets read by pytest automatically, so you don't have import conftest anywhere.

Finding Where Fixtures Are Defined

We've moved a fixture out of the test module and into a conftest.py file. We can have conftest.py files at really every level of our test directory. Tests can use any fixture that is in the same test module as a test function, or in a conftest.py file in the same directory, or in any level of parent directory up to the root of the tests.

That brings up a problem if we can't remember where a particular fixture is located and we want to see the source code. Of course, pytest has our back. Just use --fixtures and we are good to go.

Let's first try it:

```
$ cd /path/to/code/ch3/a/
$ pytest --fixtures -v
...
------------------- fixtures defined from conftest --------------------
cards_db [session scope] -- conftest.py:7
    CardsDB object connected to a temporary database
...
```

pytest shows us a list of all available fixtures our test can use. This list includes a bunch of builtin fixtures that we'll look at in the next chapter, as well as those provided by plugins. The fixtures found in conftest.py files are at the bottom. If you supply a directory, pytest will list the fixtures available to tests in that directory. If you supply a test file name, pytest will include those defined in test modules as well.

pytest also includes the first line of the docstring from the fixture, if you've defined one, and the file and line number where the fixture is defined. It will also include the path if it's not in your current directory.

Adding -v will include the entire docstring. Note that for pytest 6.x, we have to use -v to get the path and line numbers. Those were added to --fixturues without verbose for pytest 7.

You can also use --fixtures-per-test to see what fixtures are used by each test and where the fixtures are defined:

```
$ pytest --fixtures-per-test test_count.py::test_empty
=========================== test session starts ===========================
collected 1 item

---------------------- fixtures used by test_empty ----------------------
-------------------------- (test_count.py:4) --------------------------
cards_db -- conftest.py:7
    CardsDB object connected to a temporary database

=========================== no tests ran in 0.00s ===========================
```

In this example we've specified an individual test, test_count.py::test_empty. However, the flag works for files or directories as well. Armed with --fixtures and --fixtures-per-test, you'll never again wonder where a fixture is defined.

Using Multiple Fixture Levels

There's a little bit of a problem with our test code right now. The problem is the tests both depend on the database being empty to start with, but they use the same database instance in the module-scope and session-scope versions.

The problem becomes very clear if we add a third test:

```
ch3/a/test_three.py
def test_three(cards_db):
    cards_db.add_card(cards.Card("first"))
    cards_db.add_card(cards.Card("second"))
    cards_db.add_card(cards.Card("third"))
    assert cards_db.count() == 3
```

It works fine by itself, but not when it's run after test_count.py::test_two:

```
$ pytest -v test_three.py
=========================== test session starts ===========================
collected 1 item

test_three.py::test_three PASSED                                    [100%]

=========================== 1 passed in 0.01s ===========================
```

```
$ pytest -v --tb=line test_count.py test_three.py
=========================== test session starts ===========================
collected 3 items

test_count.py::test_empty PASSED                                    [ 33%]
test_count.py::test_two PASSED                                      [ 66%]
test_three.py::test_three FAILED                                   [100%]

============================== FAILURES ===============================
/path/to/code/ch3/a/test_three.py:8: assert 5 == 3
======================== short test summary info ========================
FAILED test_three.py::test_three - assert 5 == 3
==================== 1 failed, 2 passed in 0.01s ====================
```

There are five elements in the database because the previous test added two items before test_three ran. There's a time-honored rule of thumb that says tests shouldn't rely on the run order. And clearly, this does. test_three passes just fine if we run it by itself, but fails if it is run after test_two.

If we still want to try to stick with one open database, but start all the tests with zero elements in the database, we can do that by adding another fixture:

ch3/b/conftest.py
```python
@pytest.fixture(scope="session")
def db():
    """CardsDB object connected to a temporary database"""
    with TemporaryDirectory() as db_dir:
        db_path = Path(db_dir)
        db_ = cards.CardsDB(db_path)
        yield db_
        db_.close()


@pytest.fixture(scope="function")
def cards_db(db):
    """CardsDB object that's empty"""
    db.delete_all()
    return db
```

I've renamed the old cards_db to db and made it session scope.

The cards_db fixture has db named in its parameter list, which means it depends on the db fixture. Also, cards_db is function scoped, which is a more narrow scope than db. When fixtures depend on other fixtures, they can only use fixtures that have equal or wider scope.

Let's see if it works:

```
$ cd /path/to/code/ch3/b/
$ pytest --setup-show
```

```
========================= test session starts =========================
collected 3 items

test_count.py
SETUP    S db
        SETUP    F cards_db (fixtures used: db)
        ch3/b/test_count.py::test_empty (fixtures used: cards_db, db).
        TEARDOWN F cards_db
        SETUP    F cards_db (fixtures used: db)
        ch3/b/test_count.py::test_two (fixtures used: cards_db, db).
        TEARDOWN F cards_db
test_three.py
        SETUP    F cards_db (fixtures used: db)
        ch3/b/test_three.py::test_three (fixtures used: cards_db, db).
        TEARDOWN F cards_db
TEARDOWN S db

========================= 3 passed in 0.01s =========================
```

We can see that the setup for db happens first, and has session scope (from
the S). The setup for cards_db happens next, and before each test function call,
and has function scope (from the F). Also, all three tests pass.

Using multiple stage fixtures like this can provide some incredible speed
benefits and maintain test order independence.

Using Multiple Fixtures per Test or Fixture

Another way we can use multiple fixtures is just to use more than one in
either a function or a fixture. As an example, we can put some pre-canned
tasks together to test with as a fixture:

ch3/c/conftest.py
```python
@pytest.fixture(scope="session")
def some_cards():
    """List of different Card objects"""
    return [
        cards.Card("write book", "Brian", "done"),
        cards.Card("edit book", "Katie", "done"),
        cards.Card("write 2nd edition", "Brian", "todo"),
        cards.Card("edit 2nd edition", "Katie", "todo"),
    ]
```

Then we can use both empty_db and some_cards in a test:

ch3/c/test_some.py
```python
def test_add_some(cards_db, some_cards):
    expected_count = len(some_cards)
    for c in some_cards:
        cards_db.add_card(c)
    assert cards_db.count() == expected_count
```

Fixtures can also use multiple other fixtures:

```
ch3/c/conftest.py
@pytest.fixture(scope="function")
def non_empty_db(cards_db, some_cards):
    """CardsDB object that's been populated with 'some_cards'"""
    for c in some_cards:
        cards_db.add_card(c)
    return cards_db
```

The fixture non_empty_db has to be function scope because it uses cards_db, which is function scope. If you try to make non_empty_db module scope or wider, pytest will throw an error. Remember that if you don't specify a scope, you get function-scope fixtures.

And now, tests that need a database with stuff in it can do that easily:

```
ch3/c/test_some.py
def test_non_empty(non_empty_db):
    assert non_empty_db.count() > 0
```

We've discussed how different fixture scopes work and how to use different scopes in different fixtures to our advantage. However, there may be times where you need a scope to be determined at runtime. That's possible with dynamic scoping.

Deciding Fixture Scope Dynamically

Let's say we have the fixture setup as we do now, with db at session scope and cards_db at function scope, but we're worried about it. The cards_db fixture is empty because it calls delete_all(). But what if we don't completely trust that delete_all() function yet, and want to put in place some way to completely set up the database for each test function?

We can do this by dynamically deciding the scope of the db fixture at runtime. First, we change the scope of db:

```
ch3/d/conftest.py
@pytest.fixture(scope=db_scope)
def db():
    """CardsDB object connected to a temporary database"""
    with TemporaryDirectory() as db_dir:
        db_path = Path(db_dir)
        db_ = cards.CardsDB(db_path)
        yield db_
        db_.close()
```

Instead of a specific scope, we've put in a function name, db_scope. So we also have to write that function:

ch3/d/conftest.py
```python
def db_scope(fixture_name, config):
    if config.getoption("--func-db", None):
        return "function"
    return "session"
```

There are many ways we could have figured out which scope to use, but in this case, I chose to depend on a new command-line flag, --func-db. In order to allow pytest to allow us to use this new flag, we need to write a hook function (which I'll cover in more depth in Chapter 15, Building Plugins, on page 205):

ch3/d/conftest.py
```python
def pytest_addoption(parser):
    parser.addoption(
        "--func-db",
        action="store_true",
        default=False,
        help="new db for each test",
    )
```

After all that, the default behavior is the same as before, with session-scope db:

```
$ pytest --setup-show test_count.py
========================= test session starts =========================
collected 2 items

test_count.py
SETUP    S db
        SETUP    F cards_db (fixtures used: db)
        ch3/d/test_count.py::test_empty (fixtures used: cards_db, db).
        TEARDOWN F cards_db
        SETUP    F cards_db (fixtures used: db)
        ch3/d/test_count.py::test_two (fixtures used: cards_db, db).
        TEARDOWN F cards_db
TEARDOWN S db

========================= 2 passed in 0.01s =========================
```

But when we use the new flag, we get a function-scope db fixture:

```
$ pytest --func-db --setup-show test_count.py
========================= test session starts =========================
collected 2 items

test_count.py
        SETUP    F db
        SETUP    F cards_db (fixtures used: db)
        ch3/d/test_count.py::test_empty (fixtures used: cards_db, db).
        TEARDOWN F cards_db
        TEARDOWN F db
        SETUP    F db
        SETUP    F cards_db (fixtures used: db)
        ch3/d/test_count.py::test_two (fixtures used: cards_db, db).
```

```
        TEARDOWN F cards_db
        TEARDOWN F db

=========================== 2 passed in 0.01s ===========================
```

The database is now set up before each test function, and torn down afterwards.

Using autouse for Fixtures That Always Get Used

So far in this chapter, all of the fixtures used by tests were named by the tests or another fixture in a parameter list. However, you can use autouse=True to get a fixture to run all of the time. This works well for code you want to run at certain times, but tests don't really depend on any system state or data from the fixture.

Here's a rather contrived example:

```python
ch3/test_autouse.py
import pytest
import time


@pytest.fixture(autouse=True, scope="session")
def footer_session_scope():
    """Report the time at the end of a session."""
    yield
    now = time.time()
    print("--")
    print(
        "finished : {}".format(
            time.strftime("%d %b %X", time.localtime(now))
        )
    )
    print("-----------------")


@pytest.fixture(autouse=True)
def footer_function_scope():
    """Report test durations after each function."""
    start = time.time()
    yield
    stop = time.time()
    delta = stop - start
    print("\ntest duration : {:0.3} seconds".format(delta))


def test_1():
    """Simulate long-ish running test."""
    time.sleep(1)


def test_2():
    """Simulate slightly longer test."""
    time.sleep(1.23)
```

We want to add test times after each test, and the date and current time at the end of the session. Here's what these look like:

```
$ cd /path/to/code/ch3
$ pytest -v -s test_autouse.py
===================== test session starts =====================
collected 2 items

test_autouse.py::test_1 PASSED
test duration : 1.0 seconds

test_autouse.py::test_2 PASSED
test duration : 1.24 seconds
--
finished : 25 Jul 16:18:27
-----------------
=================== 2 passed in 2.25 seconds ===================
```

I used the -s flag in this example. It's a shortcut flag for --capture=no that tells pytest to turn off output capture. I used it because the new fixtures have print functions in them, and I wanted to see the output. Without turning off output capture, pytest only prints the output of tests that fail.

The autouse feature is good to have around. But it's more of an exception than a rule. Opt for named fixtures unless you have a really great reason not to.

Renaming Fixtures

The name of a fixture, listed in the parameter list of tests and other fixtures using it, is usually the same as the function name of the fixture. However, pytest allows you to rename fixtures with a name parameter to @pytest.fixture():

ch3/test_rename_fixture.py
```python
import pytest

@pytest.fixture(name="ultimate_answer")
def ultimate_answer_fixture():
    return 42

def test_everything(ultimate_answer):
    assert ultimate_answer == 42
```

I've run across a few examples where renaming is desirable. As in this example, some people like to name their fixtures with a _fixture suffix or fixture_ prefix or similar.

One instance where renaming is useful is when the most obvious fixture name already exists as an existing variable or function name:

ch3/test_rename_2.py
```python
import pytest
from somewhere import app


@pytest.fixture(scope="session", name="app")
def _app():
    """The app object"""
    yield app()


def test_that_uses_app(app):
    assert app.some_property == "something"
```

I usually only use fixture renaming with a fixture that lives in the same module as the tests using it, as renaming a fixture can make it harder to find where it's defined. However, remember that there is always --fixtures, which can help you find where a fixture lives.

Review

In this chapter, we covered a lot about fixtures:

- Fixtures are @pytest.fixture() decorated functions.

- Test functions or other fixtures depend on a fixture by putting its name in their parameter list.

- Fixtures can return data using return or yield.

- Code before the yield is the setup code. Code after the yield is the teardown code.

- Fixtures can be set to function, class, module, package, or session scope. The default is function scope. You can even define the scope dynamically.

- Multiple test functions can use the same fixture.

- Multiple test modules can use the same fixture if it's in a conftest.py file.

- Multiple fixtures at different scope can speed up test suites while maintaining test isolation.

- Tests and fixtures can use multiple fixtures.

- Autouse fixtures don't have to be named by the test function.

- You can have the name of a fixture be different than the fixture function name.

We also covered a few new command-line flags:

- pytest --setup-show is used to see the order of execution.
- pytest --fixtures is used to list available fixtures and where the fixture is located.
- -s and --capture=no allow print statements to be seen even in passing tests.

Exercises

Fixtures are often one of the trickier parts of pytest for people to get used to. Going through the following exercises will

- help solidify your understanding of how fixtures work,
- allow you to use different fixture scopes, and
- internalize the run sequence with the visual output of --setup-show.

1. Create a test file called test_fixtures.py.

2. Write a few data fixtures—functions with the @pytest.fixture() decorator—that return some data (perhaps a list, dictionary, or tuple).

3. For each fixture, write at least one test function that uses it.

4. Write two tests that use the same fixture.

5. Run pytest --setup-show test_fixtures.py. Are all the fixtures run before every test?

6. Add scope='module' to the fixture from Exercise 4.

7. Re-run pytest --setup-show test_fixtures.py. What changed?

8. For the fixture from Exercise 6, change return <data> to yield <data>.

9. Add print statements before and after the yield.

10. Run pytest -s -v test_fixtures.py. Does the output make sense?

11. Run pytest --fixtures. Can you see your fixtures listed?

12. Add a docstring to one of your fixtures, if you didn't include them already. Re-run pytest --fixtures to see the description show up.

What's Next

The pytest fixture implementation is flexible enough to use fixtures like building blocks to build up test setup and teardown. Because fixtures are so flexible, I use them heavily to push as much of the setup of my tests into fixtures as I can.

In this chapter, we looked at pytest fixtures you write yourself, but pytest provides loads of useful fixtures for you to use right out of the box. We'll take a closer look at some of the builtin fixtures in the next chapter.

## CHAPTER 4

Builtin Fixtures

In the previous chapter, you learned what fixtures are, how to write them, and how to use them for test data as well as setup and teardown code. You also used conftest.py for sharing fixtures between tests in multiple test files.

Reusing common fixtures is such a good idea that the pytest developers included some commonly used fixtures with pytest. The builtin fixtures that come prepackaged with pytest can help you do some pretty useful things in your tests easily and consistently. For example, pytest includes builtin fixtures that can handle temporary directories and files, access command-line options, communicate between test sessions, validate output streams, modify environment variables, and interrogate warnings. The builtin fixtures are extensions to the core functionality of pytest.

We'll take a look at a few of the builtin fixtures in this chapter:

- tmp_path and tmp_path_factory—for temporary directories

- capsys—for capturing output

- monkeypatch—for changing the environment or application code, like a lightweight form of mocking

This is a good mix that shows you some of the extra capabilities you can get with creative fixture use. I encourage you to read up on other builtin fixtures by reading the output of pytest --fixtures.

Using tmp_path and tmp_path_factory

The tmp_path and tmp_path_factory fixtures are used to create temporary directories. The tmp_path function-scope fixture returns a pathlib.Path instance that points to a temporary directory that sticks around during your test and a bit longer. The tmp_path_factory session-scope fixture returns a TempPathFactory object.

This object has a mktemp() function that returns Path objects. You can use mktemp() to create multiple temporary directories.

You use them like this:

```
ch4/test_tmp.py
def test_tmp_path(tmp_path):
    file = tmp_path / "file.txt"
    file.write_text("Hello")
    assert file.read_text() == "Hello"


def test_tmp_path_factory(tmp_path_factory):
    path = tmp_path_factory.mktemp("sub")
    file = path / "file.txt"
    file.write_text("Hello")
    assert file.read_text() == "Hello"
```

Their usage is almost identical except for the following:

- With tmp_path_factory, you have to call mktemp() to get a directory.
- tmp_path_factory is session scope.
- tmp_path is function scope.

In the previous chapter, we used the standard library tempfile.TemporaryDirectory for our db fixture:

```
ch4/conftest_from_ch3.py
from pathlib import Path
from tempfile import TemporaryDirectory


@pytest.fixture(scope="session")
def db():
    """CardsDB object connected to a temporary database"""
    with TemporaryDirectory() as db_dir:
        db_path = Path(db_dir)
        db_ = cards.CardsDB(db_path)
        yield db_
        db_.close()
```

Let's use one of the new builtins instead. Because our db fixture is session scope, we cannot use tmp_path, as session-scope fixtures cannot use function-scope fixtures. We can use tmp_path_factory:

```
ch4/conftest.py
@pytest.fixture(scope="session")
def db(tmp_path_factory):
    """CardsDB object connected to a temporary database"""
    db_path = tmp_path_factory.mktemp("cards_db")
    db_ = cards.CardsDB(db_path)
    yield db_
    db_.close()
```

Nice. Notice that this also allows us to remove two import statements, as we don't need to import pathlib or tempfile.

Following are two related builtin fixtures:

- *tmpdir*—Similar to tmp_path, but returns a py.path.local object. This fixture was available in pytest long before tmp_path. py.path.local predates pathlib, which was added in Python 3.4. py.path.local is being phased out slowly in pytest in favor of the stdlib pathlib version. Therefore, I recommend using tmp_path.

- *tmpdir_factory*—Similar to tmp_path_factory, except its mktemp function returns a py.path.local object instead of a pathlib.Path object

The base directory for all of the pytest temporary directory fixtures is system- and user-dependent, and includes a pytest-NUM part, where NUM is incremented for every session. The base directory is left as-is immediately after a session to allow you to examine it in case of test failures. pytest does eventually clean them up. Only the most recent few temporary base directories are left on the system.

You can also specify your own base directory if you need to with pytest --basetemp=mydir.

Using capsys

Sometimes the application code is supposed to output something to stdout, stderr, and so on. As it happens, the Cards sample project has a command-line interface that should be tested.

The command, cards version, is supposed to output the version:

```
$ cards version
1.0.0
```

The version is also available from the API:

```
$ python -i
>>> import cards
>>> cards.__version__
'1.0.0'
```

One way to test this would be to actually run the command with subprocess.run(), grab the output, and compare it to the version from the API:

ch4/test_version.py
```
import subprocess


def test_version_v1():
```

```
    process = subprocess.run(
        ["cards", "version"], capture_output=True, text=True
    )
    output = process.stdout.rstrip()
    assert output == cards.__version__
```

The rstrip() is used to remove the newline. (I started with this example because sometimes calling a subprocess and reading the output is your only option. However, it makes a lousy capsys example.)

The capsys fixture enables the capturing of writes to stdout and stderr. We can call the method that implements this in the CLI directly, and use capsys to read the output:

ch4/test_version.py
```
import cards


def test_version_v2(capsys):
    cards.cli.version()
    output = capsys.readouterr().out.rstrip()
    assert output == cards.__version__
```

The capsys.readouterr() method returns a namedtuple that has out and err. We're just reading the out part and then stripping the newline with rstrip().

Another feature of capsys is the ability to temporarily disable normal output capture from pytest. pytest usually captures the output from your tests and the application code. This includes print statements.

Here's a small example:

ch4/test_print.py
```
def test_normal():
    print("\nnormal print")
```

If we run it, we don't see any output:

```
$ cd /path/to/code/ch4
$ pytest test_print.py::test_normal
======================= test session starts =======================
collected 1 item

test_print.py .                                             [100%]

======================= 1 passed in 0.00s =======================
```

pytest captures all the output. It helps keep the command-line session cleaner.

However, there may be times when we want to see all the output, even on passing tests. We can use the -s or --capture=no flag for that:

```
$ pytest -s test_print.py::test_normal
======================= test session starts =======================
collected 1 item

test_print.py
normal print
.

======================= 1 passed in 0.00s =======================
```

pytest will then show the output for tests that fail, at the end.

Here's a simple failing test:

ch4/test_print.py
```
def test_fail():
    print("\nprint in failing test")
    assert False
```

The output is shown:

```
$ pytest test_print.py::test_fail
======================= test session starts =======================
collected 1 item

test_print.py F                                             [100%]

=========================== FAILURES ===========================
_____ test_fail _____

    def test_fail():
        print("\nprint in failing test")
>       assert False
E       assert False

test_print.py:9: AssertionError
---------------------- Captured stdout call ----------------------

print in failing test
==================== short test summary info ====================
FAILED test_print.py::test_fail - assert False
======================= 1 failed in 0.04s =======================
```

Another way to always include output is with capsys.disabled():

ch4/test_print.py
```
def test_disabled(capsys):
    with capsys.disabled():
        print("\ncapsys disabled print")
```

The output in the with block will always be displayed, even without the -s flag:

```
$ pytest test_print.py::test_disabled
======================= test session starts =======================
collected 1 item
```

```
test_print.py
capsys disabled print
.                                                          [100%]

======================= 1 passed in 0.00s =======================
```

Following are related builtin fixtures:

- *capfd*—Like capsys, but captures file descriptors 1 and 2, which usually is the same as stdout and stderr

- *capsysbinary*—Where capsys captures text, capsysbinary captures bytes.

- *capfdbinary*—Captures bytes on file descriptors 1 and 2

- *caplog*—Captures output written with the logging package

Using monkeypatch

During the previous discussion of capsys, we used this code to test the output of the Cards project:

ch4/test_version.py
```
import cards


def test_version_v2(capsys):
    cards.cli.version()
    output = capsys.readouterr().out.rstrip()
    assert output == cards.__version__
```

That made a decent example of how to use capsys, but it's still not how I prefer to test the CLI. The Cards application uses a library called Typer[1] that includes a runner feature that allows us to test more of our code, makes it look more like a command-line test, remains in process, and provides us with output hooks. It's used like this:

ch4/test_version.py
```
from typer.testing import CliRunner


def test_version_v3():
    runner = CliRunner()
    result = runner.invoke(cards.app, ["version"])
    output = result.output.rstrip()
    assert output == cards.__version__
```

We'll use this method of output testing as a starting point for the rest of the tests we do of the Cards CLI.

---

1.   https://pypi.org/project/typer

I started the CLI testing by testing cards version. Starting with cards version is nice because it doesn't use the database. In order to test the rest of the CLI, we need to redirect the database to a temporary directory, like we did when testing the API in Using Fixtures for Setup and Teardown, on page 33. We'll use monkeypatch for that.

A "monkey patch" is a dynamic modification of a class or module during runtime. During testing, "monkey patching" is a convenient way to take over part of the runtime environment of the application code and replace either input dependencies or output dependencies with objects or functions that are more convenient for testing. The monkeypatch builtin fixture allows you to do this in the context of a single test. It is used to modify objects, dictionaries, environment variables, the python search path, or the current directory. It's like a mini version of mocking. And when the test ends, regardless of pass or fail, the original unpatched code is restored, undoing everything changed by the patch.

This is all very hand-wavy until we jump into some examples. After looking at the API, we'll look at how monkeypatch is used in test code.

The monkeypatch fixture provides the following functions:

- setattr(target, name, value, raising=True)—Sets an attribute
- delattr(target, name, raising=True)—Deletes an attribute
- setitem(dic, name, value)—Sets a dictionary entry
- delitem(dic, name, raising=True)—Deletes a dictionary entry
- setenv(name, value, prepend=None)—Sets an environment variable
- delenv(name, raising=True)—Deletes an environment variable
- syspath_prepend(path)—Prepends path to sys.path, which is Python's list of import locations
- chdir(path)—Changes the current working directory

The raising parameter tells pytest whether or not to raise an exception if the item doesn't already exist. The prepend parameter to setenv() can be a character. If it is set, the value of the environment variable will be changed to value + prepend + <old value>.

We can use monkeypatch to redirect the CLI to a temporary directory for the database in a couple of ways. Both methods involve knowledge of the application code. Let's look at the cli.get_path() method:

cards_proj/src/cards/cli.py
```python
def get_path():
    db_path_env = os.getenv("CARDS_DB_DIR", "")
    if db_path_env:
        db_path = pathlib.Path(db_path_env)
    else:
        db_path = pathlib.Path.home() / "cards_db"
    return db_path
```

This is the method that tells the rest of the CLI code where the database is. We can either patch the whole function, patch pathlib.Path().home(), or set the environment variable CARDS_DB_DIR.

We'll test these modifications with the cards config command, which conveniently returns the database location:

```
$ cards config
/Users/okken/cards_db
```

Before we jump in, we're going to be calling runner.invoke() to call cards several times, so let's put that code into a helper function called run_cards():

ch4/test_config.py
```python
from typer.testing import CliRunner
import cards


def run_cards(*params):
    runner = CliRunner()
    result = runner.invoke(cards.app, params)
    return result.output.rstrip()


def test_run_cards():
    assert run_cards("version") == cards.__version__
```

Notice that I included a test function for our helper function, just to make sure I got it right.

First, let's try patching the entire get_path function:

ch4/test_config.py
```python
def test_patch_get_path(monkeypatch, tmp_path):
    def fake_get_path():
        return tmp_path

    monkeypatch.setattr(cards.cli, "get_path", fake_get_path)
    assert run_cards("config") == str(tmp_path)
```

Like mocking, monkey-patching requires a bit of a mind shift to get everything set up right. The function, get_path is an attribute of cards.cli. We want to replace it with fake_get_path. Because get_path is a callable function, we have to replace it with another callable function. We can't just replace it with tmp_path, which is a pathlib.Path object that is not callable.

If we want to instead replace the home() method in pathlib.Path, it's a similar patch:

```
ch4/test_config.py
def test_patch_home(monkeypatch, tmp_path):
    full_cards_dir = tmp_path / "cards_db"

    def fake_home():
        return tmp_path

    monkeypatch.setattr(cards.cli.pathlib.Path, "home", fake_home)
    assert run_cards("config") == str(full_cards_dir)
```

Because cards.cli is importing pathlib, we have to patch the home attribute of cards.cli.pathlib.Path.

Seriously, if you start using monkey-patching and/or mocking more, a couple things will happen:

- You'll start to understand this.
- You'll start to avoid mocking and monkey-patching whenever possible.

Let's hope the environment variable patch is less complicated:

```
ch4/test_config.py
def test_patch_env_var(monkeypatch, tmp_path):
    monkeypatch.setenv("CARDS_DB_DIR", str(tmp_path))
    assert run_cards("config") == str(tmp_path)
```

Well, look at that. It is less complicated. However, I cheated. I've set the code up so that this environment variable is essentially part of the Cards API so that I could use it during testing.

Design for Testability

Designing for testability is a concept borrowed from hardware designers, specifically those developing integrated circuits. The concept is simply that you add functionality to software to make it easier to test. In some cases, it may mean undocumented API or parts of the API that are turned off for release. In other cases, the API is extended and made public.

In the case of the Cards config command that returns the database location and the support of CARDS_DB_DIR environment variable, these were added expressly to make the code easier to test. They may also be useful to end users. At the very least, they are not harmful for users to know about, so they were left as part of the public API.

Remaining Builtin Fixtures

In this chapter, we've looked at the tmp_path, tmp_path_factory, capsys, and monkeypatch builtin fixtures. There are quite a few more. Some we will discuss in other parts of the book. Others are left as an exercise for the reader to research if you find the need for them.

Here's a list of the remaining builtin fixtures that come with pytest, as of the writing of this edition:

- capfd, capfdbinary, capsysbinary—Variants of capsys that work with file descriptors and/or binary output

- caplog—Similar to capsys and the like; used for messages created with Python's logging system

- cache—Used to store and retrieve values across pytest runs. The most useful part of this fixture is that it allows for --last-failed, --failed-first, and similar flags.

- doctest_namespace—Useful if you like to use pytest to run doctest-style tests

- pytestconfig—Used to get access to configuration values, pluginmanager, and plugin hooks

- record_property, record_testsuite_property—Used to add extra properties to the test or test suite. Especially useful for adding data to an XML report to be used by continuous integration tools

- recwarn—Used to test warning messages

- request—Used to provide information on the executing test function. Most commonly used during fixture parametrization

- pytester, testdir—Used to provide a temporary test directory to aid in running and testing pytest plugins. pytester is the pathlib based replacement for the py.path based testdir.

- tmpdir, tmpdir_factory—Similar to tmp_path and tmp_path_factory; used to return a py.path.local object instead of a pathlib.Path object

We will take a look at many of these fixtures in the remaining chapters. You can find the full list of builtin fixtures by running pytest --fixtures, which also gives pretty good descriptions. You can also find more information in the online pytest documentation.[2]

---

2.   https://docs.pytest.org/en/latest/reference/fixtures.html

Review

In this chapter, we looked at the tmp_path, tmp_path_factory, capsys, and monkeypatch builtin fixtures:

- The tmp_path and tmp_path_factory fixtures are used to for temporary directories. tmp_path is function scope, and tmp_path_factory is session scope. Related fixtures not covered in the chapter are tmpdir and tmpdir_factory.

- capsys can be used to capture stdout and stderr. It can also be used to temporarily turn off output capture. Related fixtures are capsysbinary, capfd, capfdbinary, and caplog.

- monkeypatch can be used to change the application code or the environment. We used it with the Cards application to redirect the database location to a temporary directory created with tmp_path.

- You can read about these and other fixtures with pytest --fixtures.

Exercises

Reaching for builtin fixtures whenever possible is a great way to simplify your own test code. The exercises below are designed to give you experience using tmp_path and monkeypatch, two super handy and common builtin fixtures.

Take a look at this script that writes to a file:

```python
ch4/hello_world.py
def hello():
    with open("hello.txt", "w") as f:
        f.write("Hello World!\n")


if __name__ == "__main__":
    hello()
```

1. Write a test without fixtures that validates that hello() writes the correct content to hello.txt.

2. Write a second test using fixtures that utilizes a temporary directory and monkeypatch.chdir().

3. Add a print statement to see where the temporary directory is located. Manually check the hello.txt file after a test run. pytest leaves the temporary directories around for a while after test runs to help with debugging.

4. Comment out the calls to hello() in both tests and re-run. Do they both fail? If not, why not?

What's Next

So far all of the test functions we've used only run once. In the next chapter, we're going to explore a few ways to have test functions run a bunch of times with different data or with different environments. It's a fantastic way to test more thoroughly without writing more tests.

## CHAPTER 5

Parametrization

In the last couple of chapters, we looked at custom and builtin fixtures. In this chapter, we return to test functions. We'll look at how to turn one test function into many test cases to test more thoroughly with less work. We'll do this with *parametrization*.

Parametrized testing refers to adding parameters to our test functions and passing in multiple sets of arguments to the test to create new test cases. We'll look at three ways to implement parametrized testing in pytest in the order in which they should be selected:

- Parametrizing functions
- Parametrizing fixtures
- Using a hook function called pytest_generate_tests

We'll compare them side by side by solving the same parametrization problem using all three methods; however, as you'll see, there are times when one solution is preferred over the others.

Before we really jump in to how to use parametrization, though, we'll take a look at the redundant code we are avoiding with parametrization. Then we'll look at three methods of parametrization. When we're done, you'll be able to write concise, easy-to-read test code that tests a huge number of test cases.

Parametrize or Parameterize?

 The English language offers many spellings of this word: parametrize, parameterize, parametrise, parameterise. The difference being "s" vs "z" and whether or not to have an "e" between "t" and "r."

Parametrize or Parameterize?

pytest uses one spelling: parametrize. However, if you forget and use one of the other forms, pytest will generate an error message such as:

"E Failed: Unknown 'parameterize' mark, did you mean 'parametrize'?"

That's helpful.

Testing Without Parametrize

Sending some values through a function and checking the output to make sure it's correct is a common pattern in software testing. However, calling a function once with one set of values and one check for correctness isn't enough to fully test most functions. Parametrized testing is a way to send multiple sets of data through the same test and have pytest report if any of the sets failed.

To help understand the problem parametrized testing is trying to solve, let's write some tests for the finish() API method:

cards_proj/src/cards/api.py
```python
def finish(self, card_id: int):
    """Set a card state to 'done'."""
    self.update_card(card_id, Card(state="done"))
```

The states used in the application are "todo," "in prog," and "done," and this method sets a card's state to "done."

To test this, we could

- create a Card object and add it to the database, so we have a Card to work with,

- call finish(), and

- make sure the end state is "done."

One variable is the start state of the Card. It could be "todo," "in prog," or even already "done."

Let's test all three. Here's a start:

ch5/test_finish.py
```python
from cards import Card


def test_finish_from_in_prog(cards_db):
    index = cards_db.add_card(Card("second edition", state="in prog"))
    cards_db.finish(index)
```

```
    card = cards_db.get_card(index)
    assert card.state == "done"

def test_finish_from_done(cards_db):
    index = cards_db.add_card(Card("write a book", state="done"))
    cards_db.finish(index)
    card = cards_db.get_card(index)
    assert card.state == "done"

def test_finish_from_todo(cards_db):
    index = cards_db.add_card(Card("create a course", state="todo"))
    cards_db.finish(index)
    card = cards_db.get_card(index)
    assert card.state == "done"
```

The test functions are very similar. The only difference is the starting state and the summary. Because we only have three states, it's not overly terrible to write essentially the same code three times, but it does seem like a waste.

Let's run it:

```
$ cd /path/to/code/ch5
$ pytest -v test_finish.py
========================= test session starts =========================
collected 3 items

test_finish.py::test_finish_from_todo PASSED                    [ 33%]
test_finish.py::test_finish_from_in_prog PASSED                 [ 66%]
test_finish.py::test_finish_from_done PASSED                    [100%]

========================= 3 passed in 0.05s =========================
```

One way to reduce the redundant code is to combine them into the same function, like this:

ch5/test_finish_combined.py
```
from cards import Card

def test_finish(cards_db):
    for c in [
        Card("write a book", state="done"),
        Card("second edition", state="in prog"),
        Card("create a course", state="todo"),
    ]:
        index = cards_db.add_card(c)
        cards_db.finish(index)
        card = cards_db.get_card(index)
        assert card.state == "done"
```

This sorta works, but has problems. Check out this test:

```
$ pytest test_finish_combined.py
========================== test session starts ==========================
collected 1 item

test_finish_combined.py .                                        [100%]

========================= 1 passed in 0.01s =========================
```

It passes, and we have eliminated the redundant code. Woohoo! But, there are other problems:

- We have one test case reported instead of three.

- If one of the test cases fails, we really don't know which one without looking at the traceback or some other debugging information.

- If one of the test cases fails, the test cases following the failure will not be run. pytest stops running a test when an assert fails.

pytest parametrization is a great fit to solve this kind of testing problem. We'll start with function parametrization, then fixture parametrization, and finish up with pytest_generate_tests.

Parametrizing Functions

To parametrize a test function, add parameters to the test definition and use the @pytest.mark.parametrize() decorator to define the sets of arguments to pass to the test, like this:

```
ch5/test_func_param.py
import pytest
from cards import Card

@pytest.mark.parametrize(
    "start_summary, start_state",
    [
        ("write a book", "done"),
        ("second edition", "in prog"),
        ("create a course", "todo"),
    ],
)
def test_finish(cards_db, start_summary, start_state):
    initial_card = Card(summary=start_summary, state=start_state)
    index = cards_db.add_card(initial_card)

    cards_db.finish(index)

    card = cards_db.get_card(index)
    assert card.state == "done"
```

The test_finish() function now has its original cards_db fixture as a parameter, but also two new parameters: start_summary and start_state. These match directly to the first argument to @pytest.mark.parametrize().

The first argument to @pytest.mark.parametrize() is a list of names of the parameters. They are strings and can be an actual list of strings, as in ["start_summary", "start_state"], or they can be a comma-separated string, as in "start_summary, start_state". The second argument to @pytest.mark.parametrize() is our list of test cases. Each element in the list is a test case represented by a tuple or list that has one element for each argument that gets sent to the test function.

pytest will run this test once for each (start_summary, start_state) pair and report each as a separate test:

```
$ pytest -v test_func_param.py::test_finish
========================= test session starts =========================
collected 3 items

test_func_param.py::test_finish[write a book-done] PASSED       [ 33%]
test_func_param.py::test_finish[second edition-in prog] PASSED  [ 66%]
test_func_param.py::test_finish[create a course-todo] PASSED    [100%]

========================= 3 passed in 0.05s =========================
```

This use of parametrize() works for our purposes. However, changing the summary for each test case doesn't really matter for this test. Therefore, changing it with each test case really is an extra bit of complexity that is not necessary.

Let's change the parametrization to just start_state, and see how the syntax changes:

ch5/test_func_param.py
```
@pytest.mark.parametrize("start_state", ["done", "in prog", "todo"])
def test_finish_simple(cards_db, start_state):
    c = Card("write a book", state=start_state)
    index = cards_db.add_card(c)
    cards_db.finish(index)
    card = cards_db.get_card(index)
    assert card.state == "done"
```

It's still mostly the same test. The "list" of parameters is just one parameter, "start_state". The list of test cases now contains just values for the single parameter. The function definition no longer includes a start_summary parameter. We've just hard-coded the start summary into the Card("write a book", state=start_state) call.

Now when we run it, it focuses on the change we care about:

```
$ pytest -v test_func_param.py::test_finish_simple
========================= test session starts =========================
collected 3 items

test_func_param.py::test_finish_simple[done] PASSED            [ 33%]
test_func_param.py::test_finish_simple[in prog] PASSED         [ 66%]
test_func_param.py::test_finish_simple[todo] PASSED            [100%]

========================= 3 passed in 0.05s =========================
```

Looking at the difference in the output of the two examples, we see that now we only have the starting state listed, "todo," "in prog," and "done." In the first example, pytest displayed the values of both parameters, separated by a dash (-). No dash is needed when there's only one parameter changing.

In both the test code and the output, we've focused attention on the different starting states. In the test code, it's subtle, and I'm often tempted to add more parameters than necessary. The output change, however, is dramatic. It's very clear from the output the differences in the test cases. This clarity in the output is extremely helpful when a test case fails. It'll allow you to more quickly zero in on the changes that matter to the test failure.

We can write the same test using fixture parametrization instead of function parametrization. It works mostly the same, but the syntax is different.

Parametrizing Fixtures

When we used function parametrization, pytest called our test function once each for every set of argument values we provided. With fixture parametrization, we shift those parameters to a fixture. pytest will then call the fixture once each for every set of values we provide. Then downstream, every test function that depends on the fixture will be called, once each for every fixture value.

Also, the syntax is different:

```
ch5/test_fix_param.py
@pytest.fixture(params=["done", "in prog", "todo"])
def start_state(request):
    return request.param


def test_finish(cards_db, start_state):
    c = Card("write a book", state=start_state)
    index = cards_db.add_card(c)
    cards_db.finish(index)
    card = cards_db.get_card(index)
    assert card.state == "done"
```

What happens is pytest ends up calling start_state() three times, once each for all values in params. Each value of params is saved to request.param for the fixture to use. Within start_state() we could have code that depends on the parameter value. However, in this case, we're just returning the parameter value.

The test_finish() function is identical to the test_finish_simple() function we used in function parametrization, but with no parametrize decorator. Because it has start_state as a parameter, pytest will call it once for each value passed to the start_state() fixture. And after all of that, the output looks the same as before:

```
$ pytest -v test_fix_param.py
========================= test session starts =========================
collected 3 items

test_fix_param.py::test_finish[done] PASSED                    [ 33%]
test_fix_param.py::test_finish[in prog] PASSED                 [ 66%]
test_fix_param.py::test_finish[todo] PASSED                    [100%]

========================= 3 passed in 0.05s =========================
```

That's cool. It looks just like the function parametrization example.

At first glance, fixture parametrization serves just about the same purpose as function parametrization, but with a bit more code. There are times where there is benefit to fixture parametrization.

Fixture parametrization has the benefit of having a fixture run for each set of arguments. This is useful if you have setup or teardown code that needs to run for each test case—maybe a different database connection, or different contents of a file, or whatever.

It also has the benefit of many test functions being able to run with the same set of parameters. All tests that use the start_state fixture will all be called three times, once for each start state.

Fixture parametrization is also a different way to think about the same problem. Even in the case of testing finish(), if I'm thinking about it in terms of "same test, different data," I often gravitate toward function parametrization. But if I'm thinking about it as "same test, different start state," I gravitate toward fixture parametrization.

Parametrizing with pytest_generate_tests

The third way to parametrize is by using a hook function called pytest_generate_tests. Hook functions are often used by plugins to alter the normal operation flow of pytest. But we can use many of them in test files and conftest.py files.

Implementing the same flow as before with pytest_generate_tests looks like this:

ch5/test_gen.py
```python
from cards import Card


def pytest_generate_tests(metafunc):
    if "start_state" in metafunc.fixturenames:
        metafunc.parametrize("start_state", ["done", "in prog", "todo"])


def test_finish(cards_db, start_state):
    c = Card("write a book", state=start_state)
    index = cards_db.add_card(c)
    cards_db.finish(index)
    card = cards_db.get_card(index)
    assert card.state == "done"
```

The test_finish() function hasn't changed. We've just changed the way pytest fills in the value for initial_state every time the test gets called.

The pytest_generate_tests function we provide will get called by pytest when it's building its list of tests to run. The metafunc object has a lot of information,[1] but we're using it just to get the parameter name and to generate the parametrizations.

This form looks familiar when we run it:

```
$ pytest -v test_gen.py
========================= test session starts =========================
collected 3 items

test_gen.py::test_finish[done] PASSED                          [ 33%]
test_gen.py::test_finish[in prog] PASSED                       [ 66%]
test_gen.py::test_finish[todo] PASSED                          [100%]

========================= 3 passed in 0.06s =========================
```

The pytest_generate_tests function is actually super powerful. This example is a simple case to match functionality of previous parametrization methods. However, pytest_generate_tests is especially useful if we want to modify the parametrization list at test collection time in interesting ways.

Here are a few possibilities:

- We could base our parametrization list on a command-line flag, since metafunc gives us access to metafunc.config.getoption("--someflag"). Maybe we add a --excessive flag to test more values, or a --quick flag to test just a few.

---

1. https://docs.pytest.org/en/latest/reference.html#metafunc

- The parametrization list of a parameter could be based on the presence of another parameter. For example, for test functions asking for two related parameters, we can parametrize them both with a different set of values than if the test is just asking for one of the parameters.

- We could parametrize two related parameters at the same time with metafunc.parametrize("planet, moon", [('Earth', 'Moon'), ('Mars', 'Deimos'), ('Mars', 'Phobos'), ...]), for example.

Now we've seen three ways to parametrize tests. Although we're using it to just create three test cases from one test function in the finish() example, parametrization has the possibility of generating a large number of test cases. In the next section, we'll look at how to use the -k flag to select a subset.

Using Keywords to Select Test Cases

Parametrization techniques are quite effective at creating large numbers of test cases. As such, it's often beneficial to be able to run a subset of the tests. We first looked at -k in Running a Subset of Tests, on page 25, but let's use it here, as we've got quite a few test cases in this chapter:

```
$ pytest -v
========================== test session starts ==========================
collected 16 items

test_finish.py::test_finish_from_in_prog PASSED                  [  6%]
test_finish.py::test_finish_from_done PASSED                     [ 12%]
test_finish.py::test_finish_from_todo PASSED                     [ 18%]
test_finish_combined.py::test_finish PASSED                      [ 25%]
test_fix_param.py::test_finish[done] PASSED                      [ 31%]
test_fix_param.py::test_finish[in prog] PASSED                   [ 37%]
test_fix_param.py::test_finish[todo] PASSED                      [ 43%]
test_func_param.py::test_finish[write a book-done] PASSED        [ 50%]
test_func_param.py::test_finish[second edition-in prog] PASSED   [ 56%]
test_func_param.py::test_finish[create a course-todo] PASSED     [ 62%]
test_func_param.py::test_finish_simple[done] PASSED              [ 68%]
test_func_param.py::test_finish_simple[in prog] PASSED           [ 75%]
test_func_param.py::test_finish_simple[todo] PASSED              [ 81%]
test_gen.py::test_finish[done] PASSED                            [ 87%]
test_gen.py::test_finish[in prog] PASSED                         [ 93%]
test_gen.py::test_finish[todo] PASSED                            [100%]

========================== 16 passed in 0.05s ==========================
```

We can run all of the "todo" cases with -k todo:

```
$ pytest -v -k todo
========================== test session starts ==========================
collected 16 items / 11 deselected / 5 selected
```

```
test_finish.py::test_finish_from_todo PASSED                    [ 20%]
test_fix_param.py::test_finish[todo] PASSED                     [ 40%]
test_func_param.py::test_finish[create a course-todo] PASSED    [ 60%]
test_func_param.py::test_finish_simple[todo] PASSED             [ 80%]
test_gen.py::test_finish[todo] PASSED                           [100%]

=================== 5 passed, 11 deselected in 0.02s ===================
```

If we want to eliminate the test cases with "play" or "create," we can further zoom in:

```
$ pytest -v -k "todo and not (play or create)"
========================= test session starts =========================
collected 16 items / 12 deselected / 4 selected

test_finish.py::test_finish_from_todo PASSED                    [ 25%]
test_fix_param.py::test_finish[todo] PASSED                     [ 50%]
test_func_param.py::test_finish_simple[todo] PASSED             [ 75%]
test_gen.py::test_finish[todo] PASSED                           [100%]

=================== 4 passed, 12 deselected in 0.02s ===================
```

We can select a single test function, and that will run all of the parametrizations of it:

```
$ pytest -v "test_func_param.py::test_finish"
========================= test session starts =========================
collected 3 items

test_func_param.py::test_finish[write a book-done] PASSED       [ 33%]
test_func_param.py::test_finish[second edition-in prog] PASSED  [ 66%]
test_func_param.py::test_finish[create a course-todo] PASSED    [100%]

========================= 3 passed in 0.02s =========================
```

We can also just select one test case:

```
$ pytest -v "test_func_param.py::test_finish[write a book-done]"
========================= test session starts =========================
collected 1 item

test_func_param.py::test_finish[write a book-done] PASSED       [100%]

========================= 1 passed in 0.01s =========================
```

Use Quotes

 It's a really good idea to include quotes when selecting a parametrized test to run, as the dashes and brackets and spaces can mess with command shells.

It's nice to see that all of the normal subset tools work with parametrized tests. These aren't new techniques, but I find I use them frequently when running and debugging parametrized tests.

Review

In this chapter, we looked at three ways to parametrize tests:

- We can parametrize test functions, creating many test cases, when we apply the @pytest.mark.parametrize() decorator.

- We can parametrize fixtures with @pytest.fixture(params=()). This is helpful if the fixture needs to do different work based on the parameter values.

- We can generate complex parametrization sets with pytest_generate_tests.

We also looked at how we can run subsets of parametrized test cases using pytest -k.

However, while the techniques for parametrization covered in this chapter are quite powerful, when you start using parametrization in your own testing, you may run into more complex parameter set needs, such as needing to

- parametrize multiple parameters with all three techniques,

- combine techniques,

- use lists and generators for parametrization,

- create custom identifiers (which is especially useful when parametrizing with object values), or

- use indirect parametrization.

We'll cover these advanced scenarios in Chapter 16, Advanced Parametrization, on page 221.

Exercises

When people start working with parametrization, I've noticed that many tend to favor the technique they learned first—usually function parametrization—and seldom use the other methods.

Working through these exercises will help you learn how easy all three techniques are. Then later, in your own testing, you'll be able to chose from three tools and select which is most useful to you at the time.

We've tested finish() already. But there's another similar API method that needs testing, start():

cards_proj/src/cards/api.py
```python
def start(self, card_id: int):
    """Set a card state to 'in prog'."""
    self.update_card(card_id, Card(state="in prog"))
```

Let's build some parametrized tests for it:

1. Write out three test functions that make sure any start state results in "in prog" when start() is called:

   - test_start_from_done()
   - test_start_from_in_prog()
   - test_start_from_todo()

2. Write a test_start() function that uses function parametrization to test the three test cases.

3. Rewrite test_start() using fixture parametrization.

4. Rewrite test_start() using pytest_generate_tests.

For Exercise 3 and Exercise 4, you can re-use the start_state fixture and the pytest_generate_tests implementation if you put the test_start() function in the same file as test_finish().

Shared fixtures, even parametrized ones, and pytest_generate_tests can also be placed in conftest.py and shared between many test files. However, in our case, if we try to put a start_state fixture in conftest.py and a pytest_generate_tests hook function that parametrizes start_state, it won't work. pytest will notice the collision and give us a duplicate 'start_state' error. This, of course, is not a problem normally, as we don't usually use two methods for parametrizing the same parameter.

What's Next

The focus of this chapter was on parametrization. And the first technique you learned was using @pytest.mark.parametrize. parametrize is just one of many builtin markers pytest provides. You'll learn about a bunch more in the next chapter as well as how to use markers to select a subset of tests to run. You've used several techniques so far to run subsets of tests. You can name a specific test, class, file, or directory of tests to run them. You've also just learned how to use keywords to select tests. Markers are another way.

## CHAPTER 6

Markers

In pytest, *markers* are a way to tell pytest there's something special about a particular test. You can think of them like tags or labels. If some tests are slow, you can mark them with @pytest.mark.slow and have pytest skip those tests when you're in a hurry. You can pick a handful of tests out of a test suite and mark them with @pytest.mark.smoke and run those as the first stage of a testing pipeline in a continuous integration system. Really, for any reason you might have for separating out some tests, you can use markers.

pytest includes a handful of builtin markers that modify the behavior of how tests are run. We've used one already, @pytest.mark.parametrize, in Parametrizing Functions, on page 64. In addition to the custom tag-like markers we can create and add to our tests, the builtin markers tell pytest to do something special with the marked tests.

In this chapter, we're going to explore both types of markers: the builtins that change behavior, and the custom markers we can create to select which tests to run. We can also use markers to pass information to a fixture used by a test. We'll take a look at that, too.

Using Builtin Markers

pytest's builtin markers are used to modify the behavior of how tests run. We explored @pytest.mark.parametrize() in the last chapter. Here's the full list of the builtin markers included in pytest as of pytest 6:

- @pytest.mark.filterwarnings(warning): This marker adds a warning filter to the given test.

- @pytest.mark.skip(reason=None): This marker skips the test with an optional reason.

- @pytest.mark.skipif(condition, ..., *, reason): This marker skips the test if any of the conditions are True.

- @pytest.mark.xfail(condition, ..., *, reason, run=True, raises=None, strict=xfail_strict): This marker tells pytest that we expect the test to fail.

- @pytest.mark.parametrize(argnames, argvalues, indirect, ids, scope): This marker calls a test function multiple times, passing in different arguments in turn.

- @pytest.mark.usefixtures(fixturename1, fixturename2, ...): This marker marks tests as needing all the specified fixtures.

These are the most commonly used of these builtins:

- @pytest.mark.parametrize()
- @pytest.mark.skip()
- @pytest.mark.skipif()
- @pytest.mark.xfail()

We used parametrize() in the last chapter. Let's go over the other three with some examples to see how they work.

Skipping Tests with pytest.mark.skip

The skip marker allows us to skip a test. Let's say we're thinking of adding the ability to sort in a future version of the Cards application, so we'd like to have the Card class support comparisons. We write a test for comparing Card objects with < like this:

ch6/builtins/test_less_than.py
```python
from cards import Card


def test_less_than():
    c1 = Card("a task")
    c2 = Card("b task")
    assert c1 < c2


def test_equality():
    c1 = Card("a task")
    c2 = Card("a task")
    assert c1 == c2
```

And it fails:

```
$ cd /path/to/code/ch6/builtins
$ pytest --tb=short test_less_than.py
========================= test session starts =========================
collected 2 items

test_less_than.py F.                                          [100%]
```

```
============================== FAILURES ==============================
_____ test_less_than _____
test_less_than.py:6: in test_less_than
    assert c1 < c2
E   TypeError: '<' not supported between instances of 'Card' and 'Card'
======================= short test summary info =====================
FAILED test_less_than.py::test_less_than - TypeError: '<' not support...
==================== 1 failed, 1 passed in 0.13s ====================
```

Now the failure isn't a shortfall of the software; it's just that we haven't finished this feature yet. So what do we do with this test?

One option is to skip it. Let's do that:

ch6/builtins/test_skip.py
```
import pytest
```

➤
```
@pytest.mark.skip(reason="Card doesn't support < comparison yet")
def test_less_than():
    c1 = Card("a task")
    c2 = Card("b task")
    assert c1 < c2
```

The @pytest.mark.skip() marker tells pytest to skip the test. The reason is optional, but it's important to list a reason to help with maintenance later.

When we run skipped tests, they show up as s:

```
$ pytest test_skip.py
========================= test session starts =======================
collected 2 items

test_skip.py s.                                          [100%]

==================== 1 passed, 1 skipped in 0.03s ===================
```

Or as SKIPPED in verbose:

```
$ pytest -v -ra test_skip.py
========================= test session starts =======================
collected 2 items

test_skip.py::test_less_than SKIPPED (Card doesn't support <...) [ 50%]
test_skip.py::test_equality PASSED                        [100%]

======================= short test summary info =====================
SKIPPED [1] test_skip.py:6: Card doesn't support < comparison yet
==================== 1 passed, 1 skipped in 0.03s ===================
```

The extra line at the bottom lists the reason we gave in the marker, and is there because we used the -ra flag in the command line. The -r flag tells pytest to report reasons for different test results at the end of the session. You give it a single character that represents the kind of result you want more information on. The default display is the same as passing in -rfE: f for failed tests; E for errors. You can see the whole list with pytest --help.

The a in -ra stands for "all except passed." The -ra flag is therefore the most useful, as we almost always want to know the reason why certain tests did not pass.

We can also be more specific and only skip the test if certain conditions are met. Let's look at that next.

Skipping Tests Conditionally with pytest.mark.skipif

Let's say we know we won't support sorting in the 1.x.x versions of the Cards application, but will in version 2.x.x. We can tell pytest to skip the test for all versions of Cards lower than than 2.x.x like this:

```
ch6/builtins/test_skipif.py
import cards
from packaging.version import parse

@pytest.mark.skipif(
    parse(cards.__version__).major < 2,
    reason="Card < comparison not supported in 1.x",
)
def test_less_than():
    c1 = Card("a task")
    c2 = Card("b task")
    assert c1 < c2
```

The skipif marker allows you to pass in as many conditions as you want and if any of them are true, the test is skipped. In our case, we are using packaging.version.parse to allow us to isolate the major version and compare it against the number 2.

This example uses a third-party package called packaging. If you want to try the example, pip install packaging first. version.parse is just one of the many handy utilities found there. See the packaging documentation[1] for more information.

With both the skip and the skipif markers, the test is not actually run. If we want to run the test anyway, we can use xfail.

Another reason we might want to use skipif is if we have tests that need to be written differently on different operating systems. We can write separate tests for each OS and skip on the inappropriate OS.

---

1. https://packaging.pypa.io/en/latest/version.html

Expecting Tests to Fail with pytest.mark.xfail

If we want to run all tests, even those that we know will fail, we can use the xfail marker.

Here's the full signature for xfail:

```
@pytest.mark.xfail(condition, ..., *, reason, run=True,
raises=None, strict=xfail_strict)
```

The first set of parameters to this fixture are the same as skipif. The test is run anyway, by default, but the run parameter can be used to tell pytest to not run the test by setting run=False. The raises parameter allows you to provide an exception type or a tuple of exception types that you want to result in an xfail. Any other exception will cause the test to fail. strict tells pytest if passing tests should be marked as XPASS (strict=False) or FAIL, strict=True.

Let's look at an example:

```
ch6/builtins/test_xfail.py
@pytest.mark.xfail(
    parse(cards.__version__).major < 2,
    reason="Card < comparison not supported in 1.x",
)
def test_less_than():
    c1 = Card("a task")
    c2 = Card("b task")
    assert c1 < c2


@pytest.mark.xfail(reason="XPASS demo")
def test_xpass():
    c1 = Card("a task")
    c2 = Card("a task")
    assert c1 == c2


@pytest.mark.xfail(reason="strict demo", strict=True)
def test_xfail_strict():
    c1 = Card("a task")
    c2 = Card("a task")
    assert c1 == c2
```

We have three tests here: one we know will fail and two we know will pass. These tests demonstrate both the failure and passing cases of using xfail and the effect of using strict. The first example also uses the optional condition parameter, which works like the conditions of skipif.

Here's what they look like when run:

```
$ pytest -v -ra test_xfail.py
========================== test session starts ==========================
collected 3 items

test_xfail.py::test_less_than XFAIL (Card < comparison not s...) [ 33%]
test_xfail.py::test_xpass XPASS (XPASS demo)                     [ 66%]
test_xfail.py::test_xfail_strict FAILED                         [100%]

============================== FAILURES ==============================
_____ test_xfail_strict _____
[XPASS(strict)] strict demo
====================== short test summary info ======================
XFAIL test_xfail.py::test_less_than
  Card < comparison not supported in 1.x
XPASS test_xfail.py::test_xpass XPASS demo
FAILED test_xfail.py::test_xfail_strict
=============== 1 failed, 1 xfailed, 1 xpassed in 0.11s ===============
```

For tests marked with xfail:

- Failing tests will result in XFAIL.
- Passing tests (with no strict setting) will result in XPASSED.
- Passing tests with strict=true will result in FAILED.

When a test fails that is marked with xfail, pytest knows exactly what to tell you: "You were right, it did fail," which is what it's saying with XFAIL. For tests marked with xfail that actually pass, pytest is not quite sure what to tell you. It could result in XPASSED, which roughly means, "Good news, the test you thought would fail just passed." Or it could result in FAILED, or, "You thought it would fail, but it didn't. You were wrong."

So you have to decide. Should your passing xfail tests result in XFAIL? If yes, leave strict alone. If you want them to be FAILED, then set strict. You can either set strict as an option to the xfail marker like we did in this example, or you can set it globally with the xfail_strict=true setting in pytest.ini, which is the main configuration file for pytest.

A pragmatic reason to always use xfail_strict is because we tend to look closely at all failed tests. Setting strict makes you look into the the cases where your test expectations don't match the code behavior.

There are a couple additional reasons why you might want to use xfail:

- You're writing tests first, test-driven development style, and are in the test writing zone, writing a bunch of test cases you know aren't implemented yet but that you plan on implementing shortly. You can mark the new behaviors with xfail and remove the xfail gradually as you implement the behavior. This is really my favorite use of xfail. Try to keep the xfail tests on the feature branch where the feature is being implemented.

Or

- Something breaks, a test (or more) fails, and the person or team that needs to fix the break can't work on it right away. Marking the tests as xfail, strict=true, with the reason written to include the defect/issue report ID is a decent way to keep the test running, not forget about it, and alert you when the bug is fixed.

There are also bad reasons to use use xfail or skip. Here's one:

Suppose you're just brainstorming behaviors you may or may not want in future versions. You can mark the tests as xfail or skip just to keep them around for when you do want to implement the feature. Um, no.

In this case, or similar, try to remember YAGNI ("Ya Aren't Gonna Need It"), which comes from Extreme Programming and states: "Always implement things when you actually need them, never when you just foresee that you need them."[2] It can be fun and useful to peek ahead and write tests for bits of functionality you are just about to implement. However, it's a waste of time to try to look too far into the future. Don't do it. Our ultimate goal is to have all tests pass, and skip and xfail are not passing.

The builtin markers skip, skipif, and xfail are quite handy when you need them, but can quickly become overused. Just be careful.

Now let's switch gears and look at markers that we create ourselves to mark tests we want to run or skip as a group.

Selecting Tests with Custom Markers

Custom markers are markers we make up ourselves and apply to tests. Think of them like tags or labels. Custom markers can be used to select tests to run or skip.

To see custom markers in action, let's take a look at a couple of tests for the "start" behavior:

ch6/smoke/test_start_unmarked.py
```python
import pytest
from cards import Card, InvalidCardId


def test_start(cards_db):
```

---

2. http://c2.com/xp/YouArentGonnaNeedIt.html

```
"""
start changes state from "todo" to "in prog"
"""
i = cards_db.add_card(Card("foo", state="todo"))
cards_db.start(i)
c = cards_db.get_card(i)
assert c.state == "in prog"


def test_start_non_existent(cards_db):
    """
    Shouldn't be able to start a non-existent card.
    """
    any_number = 123  # any number will be invalid, db is empty
    with pytest.raises(InvalidCardId):
        cards_db.start(any_number)
```

Let's say we want to mark some of our tests, in particular happy path test cases, with "smoke." Segmenting a subset of tests into a smoke test suite is a common practice to be able to run a representative set of tests that will tell us if anything is horribly broken with any of the main systems. Further, we'll mark some of our tests with "exception"—those that check for expected exceptions. Well, the choice is pretty easy for this test file, as there are only two tests. Let's mark test_start with "smoke" and test_start_non_existent with "exception."

We'll start with "smoke," and add @pytest.mark.smoke to test_start():

`ch6/smoke/test_start.py`

```
@pytest.mark.smoke
def test_start(cards_db):
    """
    start changes state from "todo" to "in prog"
    """
    i = cards_db.add_card(Card("foo", state="todo"))
    cards_db.start(i)
    c = cards_db.get_card(i)
    assert c.state == "in prog"
```

Now we should be able to select just this test by using the -m smoke flag:

```
$ cd /path/to/code/ch6/smoke
$ pytest -v -m smoke test_start.py
========================= test session starts =========================
collected 2 items / 1 deselected / 1 selected

test_start.py::test_start PASSED                                 [100%]

========================== warnings summary ==========================
test_start_smoke.py:6
  /path/to/code/ch6/tests/test_start.py:6:
    PytestUnknownMarkWarning: Unknown pytest.mark.smoke - is this a typo?
```

```
    You can register custom marks to avoid this warning
    ...
    @pytest.mark.smoke
  ...
=============== 1 passed, 1 deselected, 1 warning in 0.01s ===============
```

Well, it certainly worked to run just one test, but we also got a warning:
Unknown pytest.mark.smoke - is this a typo?

Although possibly annoying at first, this warning is a lifesaver. It helps keep
you from making mistakes like marking tests with smok, somke, soke, or whatever, when you really meant smoke. pytest wants us to register custom markers
so that it can help us avoid typos. Cool. No problem. We register custom
markers by adding a markers section to pytest.ini. Each marker listed is in the
form, <marker_name>: <description> as shown here:

ch6/reg/pytest.ini
```
[pytest]
markers =
    smoke: subset of tests
```

Now pytest won't warn us about an unknown marker:

```
$ cd /path/to/code/ch6/reg
$ pytest -v -m smoke test_start.py
========================== test session starts ==========================
collected 2 items / 1 deselected / 1 selected

test_start.py::test_start PASSED                              [100%]

==================== 1 passed, 1 deselected in 0.01s ====================
```

Let's do the same thing with the "exception" marker for test_start_non_existent.
First, register the marker in pytest.ini:

ch6/reg/pytest.ini
```
[pytest]
markers =
    smoke: subset of tests
    exception: check for expected exceptions
```

Second, add the marker to the test:

ch6/reg/test_start.py
```
@pytest.mark.exception
def test_start_non_existent(cards_db):
    """
    Shouldn't be able to start a non-existent card.
    """
    any_number = 123  # any number will be invalid, db is empty
    with pytest.raises(InvalidCardId):
        cards_db.start(any_number)
```

Third, run it with -m exception:

```
$ pytest -v -m exception test_start.py
========================= test session starts =========================
collected 2 items / 1 deselected / 1 selected

test_start.py::test_start_non_existent PASSED                    [100%]

==================== 1 passed, 1 deselected in 0.01s ====================
```

Using markers to select one test, as we've done twice now, isn't really where markers shine. It starts getting fun when we have more files involved.

Marking Files, Classes, and Parameters

With the tests in test_start.py, we added @pytest.mark.<marker_name> decorators to test functions. We can also add markers to entire files or classes to mark multiple tests, or zoom in to parametrized tests and mark individual parametrizations. We can even put multiple markers on a single test. How fun. We'll use all the mentioned marker types with test_finish.py.

Let's start with file-level markers:

ch6/multiple/test_finish.py
```python
import pytest
from cards import Card, InvalidCardId

pytestmark = pytest.mark.finish
```

If pytest sees a pytestmark attribute in a test module, it will apply the marker(s) to all the tests in that module. If you want to apply more than one marker to the file, you can use a list form: pytestmark = [pytest.mark.marker_one, pytest.mark.marker_two].

Another way to mark multiple tests at once is to have tests in a class and use class-level markers:

ch6/multiple/test_finish.py
```python
@pytest.mark.smoke
class TestFinish:
    def test_finish_from_todo(self, cards_db):
        i = cards_db.add_card(Card("foo", state="todo"))
        cards_db.finish(i)
        c = cards_db.get_card(i)
        assert c.state == "done"

    def test_finish_from_in_prog(self, cards_db):
        i = cards_db.add_card(Card("foo", state="in prog"))
        cards_db.finish(i)
        c = cards_db.get_card(i)
        assert c.state == "done"
```

```
    def test_finish_from_done(self, cards_db):
        i = cards_db.add_card(Card("foo", state="done"))
        cards_db.finish(i)
        c = cards_db.get_card(i)
        assert c.state == "done"
```

The test class TestFinish is marked with @pytest.mark.smoke. Marking a test class like this effectively marks each test method in the class with the same marker. You can also mark individual tests, but we haven't done that in this example.

Marking a file or a class adds markers to multiple tests at a time. We can also zoom in and only mark specific test cases, parametrizations, of a parametrized test:

ch6/multiple/test_finish.py
```
@pytest.mark.parametrize(
    "start_state",
    [
        "todo",
        pytest.param("in prog", marks=pytest.mark.smoke),
        "done",
    ],
)
def test_finish_func(cards_db, start_state):
    i = cards_db.add_card(Card("foo", state=start_state))
    cards_db.finish(i)
    c = cards_db.get_card(i)
    assert c.state == "done"
```

The function test_finish_func() isn't marked directly, but one of its parametrizations is marked: pytest.param("in prog", marks=pytest.mark.smoke). You can use more than one marker by using the list form: marks=[pytest.mark.one, pytest.mark.two]. If you do want to mark all the test cases of a parametrized test, just add the mark like you would a regular function, either above or below the parametrize decorator.

The previous example was for function parametrization. You can also mark fixture parametrizations in the same way:

ch6/multiple/test_finish.py
```
@pytest.fixture(
    params=[
        "todo",
        pytest.param("in prog", marks=pytest.mark.smoke),
        "done",
    ]
)
def start_state_fixture(request):
    return request.param
```

```
def test_finish_fix(cards_db, start_state_fixture):
    i = cards_db.add_card(Card("foo", state=start_state_fixture))
    cards_db.finish(i)
    c = cards_db.get_card(i)
    assert c.state == "done"
```

If you want to add more than one marker to a function, no problem, just stack them up. For example, test_finish_non_existent() is marked with both @pytest.mark.smoke and @pytest.mark.exception:

ch6/multiple/test_finish.py
```
@pytest.mark.smoke
@pytest.mark.exception
def test_finish_non_existent(cards_db):
    i = 123  # any number will do, db is empty
    with pytest.raises(InvalidCardId):
        cards_db.finish(i)
```

We've added a couple of markers a lot of different ways to test_finish.py.

Let's use the markers to select tests to run, but instead of targeting one test file, we'll just let pytest pick from both test files.

Using -m exception should just pick out the two exception tests:

```
$ cd /path/to/code/ch6/multiple
$ pytest -v -m exception
========================= test session starts =========================
collected 12 items / 10 deselected / 2 selected

test_finish.py::test_finish_non_existent PASSED                 [ 50%]
test_start.py::test_start_non_existent PASSED                   [100%]

==================== 2 passed, 10 deselected in 0.06s ====================
```

Excellent.

Now we marked a bunch of stuff with smoke. Let's see what all we get with -m smoke:

```
$ pytest -v -m smoke
========================= test session starts =========================
collected 12 items / 5 deselected / 7 selected

test_finish.py::TestFinish::test_finish_from_todo PASSED        [ 14%]
test_finish.py::TestFinish::test_finish_from_in_prog PASSED     [ 28%]
test_finish.py::TestFinish::test_finish_from_done PASSED        [ 42%]
test_finish.py::test_finish_func[in prog] PASSED               [ 57%]
test_finish.py::test_finish_fix[in prog] PASSED                [ 71%]
test_finish.py::test_finish_non_existent PASSED                [ 85%]
test_start.py::test_start PASSED                               [100%]

==================== 7 passed, 5 deselected in 0.03s ====================
```

Nice. The -m smoke flag picked up all the TestFinish class test methods, one parametrization each from the parametrized tests, and one test from test_start.py.

Last, the -m finish should grab everything in the test_finish.py:

```
$ pytest -v -m finish
========================= test session starts =========================
collected 12 items / 2 deselected / 10 selected

test_finish.py::TestFinish::test_finish_from_todo PASSED        [ 10%]
test_finish.py::TestFinish::test_finish_from_in_prog PASSED     [ 20%]
test_finish.py::TestFinish::test_finish_from_done PASSED        [ 30%]
test_finish.py::test_finish_func[todo] PASSED                   [ 40%]
test_finish.py::test_finish_func[in prog] PASSED               [ 50%]
test_finish.py::test_finish_func[done] PASSED                   [ 60%]
test_finish.py::test_finish_fix[todo] PASSED                    [ 70%]
test_finish.py::test_finish_fix[in prog] PASSED                [ 80%]
test_finish.py::test_finish_fix[done] PASSED                    [ 90%]
test_finish.py::test_finish_non_existent PASSED                [100%]

==================== 10 passed, 2 deselected in 0.03s ====================
```

In this particular case, marking a single file with a marker just for that file may seem kind of silly. However, once we have some CLI-level tests, we may want to have the ability to either group tests by CLI vs API, or group by functionality. Markers give us that ability to group tests regardless of where the tests are in the directory/file structure.

Using "and," "or," "not," and Parentheses with Markers

We can combine markers and use a bit of logic to help select tests, just like we did with -k keywords in Using Keywords to Select Test Cases, on page 69.

We can run the "finish" tests that deal with exceptions with -m "finish and exception":

```
$ pytest -v -m "finish and exception"
========================= test session starts =========================
collected 12 items / 11 deselected / 1 selected

test_finish.py::test_finish_non_existent PASSED                [100%]

==================== 1 passed, 11 deselected in 0.01s ====================
```

We can find all the finish tests that are not included in the smoke tests:

```
$ pytest -v -m "finish and not smoke"
========================= test session starts =========================
collected 12 items / 8 deselected / 4 selected

test_finish.py::test_finish_func[todo] PASSED                  [ 25%]
test_finish.py::test_finish_func[done] PASSED                  [ 50%]
test_finish.py::test_finish_fix[todo] PASSED                   [ 75%]
```

```
test_finish.py::test_finish_fix[done] PASSED                          [100%]

==================== 4 passed, 8 deselected in 0.02s ====================
```

We can also get fancy and use "and," "or," "not," and parentheses to be very specific about the markers:

```
$ pytest -v -m "(exception or smoke) and (not finish)"
========================== test session starts ==========================
collected 12 items / 10 deselected / 2 selected

test_start.py::test_start PASSED                                      [ 50%]
test_start.py::test_start_non_existent PASSED                        [100%]

==================== 2 passed, 10 deselected in 0.01s ===================
```

We can also combine markers and keywords for selection. Let's run the smoke tests that are not part of the TestFinish class:

```
$ pytest -v -m smoke -k "not TestFinish"
========================== test session starts ==========================
collected 12 items / 8 deselected / 4 selected

test_finish.py::test_finish_func[in prog] PASSED                     [ 25%]
test_finish.py::test_finish_fix[in prog] PASSED                      [ 50%]
test_finish.py::test_finish_non_existent PASSED                     [ 75%]
test_start.py::test_start PASSED                                     [100%]

==================== 4 passed, 8 deselected in 0.02s ====================
```

One thing to keep in mind when using markers and keywords is that marker names have to be complete in the -m <marker_name> flag, whereas keywords are more of a substring thing in -k <keyword>. For example, -k "not TestFini" works fine, but -m smok would not.

So what happens if you misspell a marker? That brings us to the topic of --strict-markers.

Being Strict with Markers

Let's say we want to add the "smoke" marker to test_start_non_existent, like we did for test_finish_non_existent. However, we happen to misspell "smoke" as "smok" like this:

```
ch6/bad/test_start.py
@pytest.mark.smok
@pytest.mark.exception
def test_start_non_existent(cards_db):
    """
    Shouldn't be able to start a non-existent card.
    """
    any_number = 123  # any number will be invalid, db is empty
```

```
    with pytest.raises(InvalidCardId):
        cards_db.start(any_number)
```

If we try to run this "smoke" test, we'll get a familiar warning:

```
$ cd /path/to/code/ch6/bad
$ pytest -m smoke
========================= test session starts =========================
collected 12 items / 5 deselected / 7 selected

test_finish.py ......                                        [ 85%]
test_start.py .                                              [100%]

========================== warnings summary ==========================
test_start.py:17
  /path/to/code/ch6/bad/test_start.py:17:
    PytestUnknownMarkWarning:
      Unknown pytest.mark.smok - is this a typo?  ...
    @pytest.mark.smok
    ...
=============== 7 passed, 5 deselected, 1 warning in 0.06s =============
```

However, if we want that warning to be an error instead, we can use the --strict-markers flag:

```
$ pytest --strict-markers -m smoke
========================= test session starts =========================
collected 10 items / 1 error / 4 deselected / 5 selected

================================ ERRORS ===============================
_____ ERROR collecting test_start.py _____
'smok' not found in `markers` configuration option
======================= short test summary info ======================
ERROR test_start.py
!!!!!!!!!!!!!!!!! Interrupted: 1 error during collection !!!!!!!!!!!!!!!!
==================== 4 deselected, 1 error in 0.15s ===================
```

So, what's the difference? First, the error is issued at collection time, not at run time. If you have a test suite longer than a second or two, you will appreciate getting that feedback fast. Second, errors are sometimes easier to catch than warnings, especially in continuous integration systems. I recommend always using --strict-markers. Instead of typing it all the time, you can add --strict-markers to your addopts section of pytest.ini:

ch6/strict/pytest.ini
```
[pytest]
markers =
    smoke: subset of tests
    exception: check for expected exceptions
    finish: all of the "cards finish" related tests
➤ addopts =
➤     --strict-markers
```

Having strict markers turned on is something that I always want but hardly ever think about, so I try to always put it in my pytest.ini files.

Combining Markers with Fixtures

Markers can be used in conjunction with fixtures. They also can be used in conjunction with plugins and hook functions (but that's a topic for Chapter 15, Building Plugins, on page 205). Here, we'll combine markers and fixtures to help test the Cards application.

The builtin markers took parameters, while the custom ones we've used so far do not. Let's create a new marker called num_cards that we can pass to the cards_db fixture.

The cards_db fixture currently cleans out the database for each test that wants to use it:

ch6/combined/test_three_cards.py
```
@pytest.fixture(scope="function")
def cards_db(session_cards_db):
    db = session_cards_db
    db.delete_all()
    return db
```

If we want to, say, have three cards in the database when our test starts, we could just write a different but similar fixture:

ch6/combined/test_three_cards.py
```
@pytest.fixture(scope="function")
def cards_db_three_cards(session_cards_db):
    db = session_cards_db
    # start with empty
    db.delete_all()
    # add three cards
    db.add_card(Card("Learn something new"))
    db.add_card(Card("Build useful tools"))
    db.add_card(Card("Teach others"))
    return db
```

Then we could use the original fixture for tests that expect an empty database, and the new fixture for tests that expect the database to include three cards:

ch6/combined/test_three_cards.py
```
def test_zero_card(cards_db):
    assert cards_db.count() == 0


def test_three_card(cards_db_three_cards):
    cards_db = cards_db_three_cards
    assert cards_db.count() == 3
```

Well, great. Now we have the option of either having zero or three cards in the database when we start. What if we want one card, or four cards, or 20 cards? Do we write a fixture for each? Nah. It'd be so much nicer if we could just tell the fixture how many cards we want right from the test. Markers make this possible.

We'd like to be able to write this:

```
ch6/combined/test_num_cards.py
@pytest.mark.num_cards(3)
def test_three_cards(cards_db):
    assert cards_db.count() == 3
```

In order to do that, we need to first declare a marker, modify the cards_db fixture to detect if the marker is used, and then read the value supplied as a marker parameter to figure out how many cards to prefill. Also, hard-coding the card information isn't going to work very well, so we'll enlist the help of a Python package called Faker[3] that conveniently includes a pytest fixture that creates fake data.

First, we need to install Faker:

```
$ pip install Faker
```

Then we need to declare our marker:

```
ch6/combined/pytest.ini
[pytest]
markers =
    smoke: subset of tests
    exception: check for expected exceptions
    finish: all of the "cards finish" related tests
    num_cards: number of cards to prefill for cards_db fixture
```

Now we need to modify the cards_db fixture:

```
ch6/combined/conftest.py
@pytest.fixture(scope="function")
def cards_db(session_cards_db, request, faker):
    db = session_cards_db
    db.delete_all()

    # support for `@pytest.mark.num_cards(<some number>)`

    # random seed
    faker.seed_instance(101)
    m = request.node.get_closest_marker("num_cards")
    if m and len(m.args) > 0:
        num_cards = m.args[0]
```

---

3.   https://faker.readthedocs.io

```
        for _ in range(num_cards):
            db.add_card(
                Card(summary=faker.sentence(), owner=faker.first_name())
            )
    return db
```

There are a lot of changes here, so let's walk through them.

We added request and faker to the cards_db parameter list. We use request for the line m = request.node.get_closest_marker('num_cards'). The term request.node is pytest's representation of a test. get_closest_marker('num_cards') returns a Marker object if the test is marked with num_cards, otherwise it returns None. The name of the function get_closest_marker() seems weird at first. There's only one marker. What makes it the closest one? Well, remember that we can place markers on tests, classes, and even files. get_closest_marker('num_cards') returns the marker closest to the test, which is usually what we want.

The expression, m and len(m.args) > 0 will be true if the test is marked with num_cards, and an argument is provided. The extra len check is done so that if someone accidentally uses just pytest.mark.num_cards without specifying the number of cards, then we skip this part. We could also raise an exception or assert something, which would very much alert users that they've done something wrong. However, we'll assume it's the same as them saying num_cards(0).

Once we know how many cards to create, we let Faker create some data for us. Faker provides the faker fixture. The call to faker.seed_instance(101) seeds the randomness of Faker so that we get the same data every time. We're not using Faker for random data, we're using it to avoid making up data ourselves. For the summary field, the method faker.sentence() will work. And faker.first_name() works for the owner. There are tons of other capabilities you can utilize with Faker. I encourage you to search the Faker documentation for other capabilities for your own projects.

That's it...really. Now all of our old tests that don't use the marker will still work the same, and new tests that want some initial cards in the database work as well, with the same fixture:

ch6/combined/test_num_cards.py
```python
import pytest


def test_no_marker(cards_db):
    assert cards_db.count() == 0


@pytest.mark.num_cards
def test_marker_with_no_param(cards_db):
    assert cards_db.count() == 0
```

```
@pytest.mark.num_cards(3)
def test_three_cards(cards_db):
    assert cards_db.count() == 3
    # just for fun, let's look at the cards Faker made for us
    print()
    for c in cards_db.list_cards():
        print(c)


@pytest.mark.num_cards(10)
def test_ten_cards(cards_db):
    assert cards_db.count() == 10
```

One more thing: I'm often curious about what the fake data looks like, so I added some print statements to test_three_cards().

Let's run these to make sure it works right, and see an example of this fake data:

```
$ cd /path/to/code/ch6/combined
$ pytest -v -s test_num_cards.py
========================= test session starts =========================
collected 4 items

test_num_cards.py::test_no_marker PASSED
test_num_cards.py::test_marker_with_no_param PASSED
test_num_cards.py::test_three_cards
Card(summary='Suggest training much grow any me own true.',
     owner='Todd', state='todo', id=1)
Card(summary='Forget just effort claim knowledge.',
     owner='Amanda', state='todo', id=2)
Card(summary='Line for PM identify decade.',
     owner='Russell', state='todo', id=3)
PASSED
test_num_cards.py::test_ten_cards PASSED

========================= 4 passed in 0.06s =========================
```

These sentences are oddballs and meaningless. However, they do the trick to test the code. Using Faker and our marker/fixture combination allows us to create a large database of unique cards, if we want to.

This last example of using markers and fixtures and a third-party package was included kinda for the fun of it, but also to demonstrate the massive power of combining different features of pytest, which may be simple on their own, into a behavior that's larger than the sum of parts. With very little effort, we transformed the cards_db fixture from database access with zero entries into a database with any number of entries we want by simply adding @pytest.mark.num_cards(<any number>) to a test. That's pretty cool, and pretty simple to use.

Listing Markers

We've covered a lot of markers in this chapter. We used the builtin markers skip, skipif, and xfail. We created our own markers, smoke, exception, finish, and num_cards. There are also a few more builtin markers. And as we start using pytest plugins, those plugins may also include some markers.

To list all the markers available, including descriptions and parameters, run pytest --markers:

```
$ cd /path/to/code/ch6/multiple
$ pytest --markers
@pytest.mark.smoke: subset of tests

@pytest.mark.exception: check for expected exceptions

@pytest.mark.finish: all of the "cards finish" related tests

@pytest.mark.num_cards: number of cards to prefill for cards_db fixture

...

@pytest.mark.skip(reason=None): skip the given test function with
 an optional reason. ...

@pytest.mark.skipif(condition, ..., *, reason=...): skip the given test
 function if any of the conditions evaluate to True. ...

@pytest.mark.xfail(condition, ..., *, reason=..., run=True,
  raises=None, strict=xfail_strict): mark the test function as an expected
  failure if any of the conditions evaluate to True. ...

@pytest.mark.parametrize(argnames, argvalues): call a test function multiple
 times passing in different arguments in turn. ...
...
```

This is a super handy feature to let us look up markers quickly, and a good reason to include useful descriptions with our own markers.

Review

In this chapter, we looked at custom markers, builtin markers, and how to use markers to pass data to fixtures. We also covered a few new options and changes to pytest.ini.

Here's an example pytest.ini file:

```
[pytest]
markers =
    <marker_name>: <marker_description>
    <marker_name>: <marker_description>
```

```
addopts =
    --strict-markers
    -ra
xfail_strict = true
```

- Custom markers are declared with the markers section.

- The --strict-markers flag tells pytest to raise an error if it sees us using an undeclared marker. The default is a warning.

- The -ra flag tells pytest to list the reason for any test that isn't passing. This includes fail, error, skip, xfail, and xpass.

- Setting xfail_strict = true turns any passing tests marked with xfail into failed tests since our understanding of the system behavior was wrong. Leave this out if you want xfail tests that pass to result in XPASS.

- Custom markers can be used to select a subset of tests to run with -m <marker name> or not run with -m "not <marker name>".

- Markers are placed on tests using the syntax, @pytest.mark.<marker_name>.

- Markers on classes also use the @pytest.mark.<marker_name> syntax and will result in each class test method being marked.

- Files can have markers, using pytestmark = pytest.mark.<marker_name> or pytestmark = [pytest.mark.<marker_one>, pytest.mark.<marker_two>].

- For parametrized tests, an individual parametrization can be marked with pytest.param(<actual parameter>, marks=pytest.mark.<marker_name>). Like the file version, the parametrized version can accept a list of markers.

- The -m flag can use logic operators and, or, not, and parentheses.

- pytest --markers lists all available markers.

- Builtin markers provide extra behavior functionality, and we discussed skip, skipif, and xfail.

- Tests can have more than one marker, and a marker can be used on more than one test.

- From a fixture, you can access markers using request.node.get_closest_marker(<marker_name>).

- Markers can have parameters that can be accessed with .args and .kwargs attributes.

- Faker is a handy Python package that provides a pytest fixture called faker to generate fake data.

Exercises

Using markers for test selection is a powerful pytest capability to help run a subset of tests. Walking through these exercises will help you get comfortable with them.

The directory /path/to/code/ch6/exercises has a couple of files:

```
exercises/ch6
├── pytest.ini
└── test_markers.py
```

test_markers.py includes seven test cases:

```
$ cd ch6/exercises
$ pytest -v
========================= test session starts =========================
collected 7 items

test_markers.py::test_one PASSED                             [ 14%]
test_markers.py::test_two PASSED                             [ 28%]
test_markers.py::test_three PASSED                           [ 42%]
test_markers.py::TestClass::test_four PASSED                 [ 57%]
test_markers.py::TestClass::test_five PASSED                 [ 71%]
test_markers.py::test_param[6] PASSED                        [ 85%]
test_markers.py::test_param[7] PASSED                        [100%]
```

1. Modify pytest.ini to register three markers, odd, testclass, and all.

2. Mark all the odd test cases with odd.

3. Use a file level marker to add the all marker.

4. Mark the test class with the testclass marker.

5. Run all the tests using the all marker.

6. Run the odd tests.

7. Run the odd tests that are not marked with testclass.

8. Run the odd tests that are parametrized. (Hint: Use both marker and keyword flags.)

What's Next

So far in this book you've learned about all of the primary powers of pytest. Now you are ready to unleash these powers onto an unsuspecting project...bwahahaha!

Actually, in the next part of the book, we're going to build a full test suite for the Cards project and learn lots of skills related to testing real projects. We are going to take a look at testing strategy and build a test suite, use code coverage to see if we missed anything, use mocks to test the user interface, learn how to debug test failures, set up a development workflow with tox, learn how pytest plays nice with continuous integration systems, and learn about how to tell pytest where your code is if you are testing something other than an installable Python package.

Whew! That's a lot. But it's going to be fun.

Part II

Working with Projects

## CHAPTER 7

Strategy

So far in this book we've been talking about the mechanics of pytest—the "how to write tests" part of software testing—including writing test functions, using fixtures, and implementing parametrized testing. In this chapter, we're going to use all that you've learned about pytest so far to create a test strategy for the Cards project—the "what tests to write" part of software testing.

We'll start by defining goals for our test suite. We'll then look at how the software architecture of Cards has influence on our test strategy and is influenced by the need for tests. Then we can start selecting and prioritizing which features to test. Once we know what features need tests, we can generate a list of test cases needed. All of this methodical planning really doesn't take long, and will help to generate a pretty decent initial test suite.

Although this isn't a comprehensive look at software testing strategy as a whole—that'd be a book in itself—looking at a possible testing strategy for a single project can help you determine the best testing strategies for your own projects.

Determining Test Scope

Different projects have different test goals and requirements. Critical systems like heart monitoring systems, air traffic control systems, and smart braking systems require exhaustive testing at all levels. And then there are tools to make animated gifs. Most software is somewhere in between.

We will almost always want to test the behavior of the user visible functionality. However, there are quite a few other questions we need to consider when determining how much testing we need to do:

- Is security a concern? This is especially important if you save any confidential information.

- Performance? Do interactions need to be fast? How fast?

- Loading? Can you handle lots of people with lots of requests? Are you expecting to need to? If so, you should test for that.

- Input validation? For really any system that accepts input from users, we should validate the data before acting on it.

The Cards project is intended for use by an individual or a small team. Even so, in reality, all of the concerns above apply to this project, especially as it grows. So for an initial test suite, how much testing should we do? Here's a reasonable start:

- Test the behavior of user visible functionality.

- Postpone security, performance, and load testing for the current design. The current design is to have the database stored in the users home directory. When/if that moves to a shared location with multiple users, these concerns will definitely be more important.

- Input validation is also less important while Cards is a single user application. However, I also don't want stack traces to occur while using the app, so we should test wacky input, at least at the CLI level.

All projects will need to have functionality or feature testing. However, even with functionality testing alone, we need to decide which features need testing and at what priority. Then for each feature, we need to decide on test cases.

Using a methodical approach makes all of this fairly straightforward. We'll go through all of this for the Cards project as an example. We'll begin by prioritizing features and then generating test cases. But first, let's take a look at how your project's software architecture can influence the testing strategy you choose.

Testing Enough to Sleep at Night

 The idea of testing enough so that you can sleep at night may have come from software systems where developers have to be on call to fix software if it stops working in the middle of the night. It's been extended to include sleeping soundly, knowing that your software is well tested. Although it's a very informal concept, the idea is helpful as we evaluate what features to test and what test cases are needed in the following sections.

Considering Software Architecture

How your application is set up—its software architecture—is an important consideration when determining a testing strategy. Software architecture pertains to how your project's software is organized, what APIs are available, what the interfaces are, where code complexity lives, modularity, and so much more. In relation to testing, we need to know how much of the system we need to test and what the entry points are.

As a simple example, let's say we're testing code that exists in one module, is intended to be used on the command line, has no interactive components other than print output, and has no API. Also, it's not written in Python. We have no choices then. Our only option is to test it as a black box. We'll have our test code call it with different parameters and state and watch the output.

If the code is written in Python and is importable, and we can test the different parts of it by calling functions within the module, we then have choices. We can still test it as before, as a black box. But we can also test the functions inside separately if we want to.

This concept scales well. If the software under test is designed as a Python package with lots of submodules, we can still test at the CLI level, or we can zoom in a bit and test the modules, or we can zoom in further and test the functions within the modules. Scaling up one more, we have larger systems that are designed as interacting subsystems, each possibly with multiple packages and modules.

All of this affects our testing strategy in many ways:

- At what level should we be testing? The top user interface? Something lower? Subsystem? All levels?

- How easy is it to test at different levels? UI testing is often the most difficult, but can also be easier to tie to customer features. Testing for individual functions might be easier to implement, but harder to tie to customer requirements.

- Who is responsible for the different levels and the testing of each? If you are supplying a subsystem, are you only responsible for that subsystem? Is someone else doing the system testing? If so, it's an easy choice: test your own subsystem. However, it would be good to be involved at least with knowing what's being tested at the system level.

Let's simplify things a bit. Let's say you and your team are responsible for the whole shebang, and your software is built up in layers. You've got a UI at the top that's super thin on logic, calls an API layer, and calls whatever else is in the system. The rest of the code could be a huge single file or well-designed subsystems and modules.

You can then essentially do system testing against the API, and do some minimal testing of the UI to make sure it calls the API correctly. Then you could do some high-level tests at the UI level as system tests and focus your testing effort on the API.

That simplified system is what we have with Cards. The Cards project is implemented in three layers: (1) the CLI that lives in cli.py, (2) the API that lives in api.py, and (3) a database layer in db.py.

The CLI is implemented in cli.py. It depends on two third-party packages: Typer,[1] which is a tool for building CLIs, and Rich,[2] which does lots of great rich text terminal stuff, but we're just using it for nice tables. The CLI is intentionally as thin as possible, with almost all logic passed off to the API.

The interaction with the underlying database is handled in db.py. It has a third-party dependency, TinyDB,[3] which is the underlying database. It's also as thin as possible.

Both cli.py and db.py are as thin as possible for a few reasons:

- Testing through the API tests most of the system and logic.
- Third-party dependencies are isolated to a single file.

Isolating third-party packages brings several benefits. If anything needs to change due to interface changes in those dependencies, the changes will be isolated to a single file. This may even include swapping out the dependency for something else. If we ever want to try a different database backend, for example, we could create a test suite using db.py as an entry point, change the database, and make any adapter modifications necessary in db.py.

In Cards, the primary reason for keeping cli.py thin is to allow most of the testing to be directed at the API. For db.py, the primary reason is to allow isolated testing of our expectations of any underlying database.

How does this relate to testing strategy? A few ways:

- Because the CLI is thin on logic, we can test most everything through the API.

---

1. https://pypi.org/project/typer
2. https://pypi.org/project/rich
3. https://pypi.org/project/tinydb

- Testing the CLI enough to verify it calls the correct API entry point should be sufficient.

- Because the database interactions are isolated to db.py, we can add subsystem testing at that layer if we feel it's necessary.

Even if we test through the API, we want to focus testing effort on visible enduser behavior, instead of getting lost in testing implementation. Therefore, here's a workable testing strategy for Cards:

- Test features that are accessible to users—features that are visible in the CLI.

- Test those features through the API, not through the CLI.

- Test the CLI enough to verify it's connected to the API correctly.

That seems like a decent place to start. We can hold off on isolated testing of the database for now. Next, let's take a look at the user-visible features to decide what to test.

Evaluating the Features to Test

Before we create the cases we want to test, we first need to evaluate what features to test. When you have a lot of functionality and features to test, you have to prioritize the order of developing tests. At least a rough idea of order helps.

I generally prioritize features to test based on the following factors:

- *Recent*—New features, new areas of code, new functionality that has been recently repaired, refactored, or otherwise modified

- *Core*—Your product's unique selling propositions (USPs). The essential functions that must continue to work in order for the product to be useful

- *Risk*—Areas of the application that pose more risk, such as areas important to customers but not used regularly by the development team or parts that use third-party code you don't quite trust

- *Problematic*—Functionality that frequently breaks or often gets defect reports against it

- *Expertise*—Features or algorithms understood by a limited subset of people

Cards has a limited feature set. Here are the features visible to the end user:

```
$ cards --help
Usage: cards [OPTIONS] COMMAND [ARGS]...

  Cards is a small command line task tracking application.

Options:
  --help  Show this message and exit.

Commands:
  add      Add a card to db.
  config   List the path to the Cards db.
  count    Return number of cards in db.
  delete   Remove card in db with given id.
  finish   Set a card state to 'done'.
  list     List cards in db.
  start    Set a card state to 'in prog'.
  update   Modify a card in db with given id with new info.
  version  Return version of cards application
```

Because we're treating the Cards project as a legacy system needing testing, some of these criteria are more helpful than others:

- *Core*

  - add, count, delete, finish, list, start, and update all seem like core functionality.
  - config and version seem less important.
- *Risk*

  - The third-party packages are Typer for the CLI and TinyDB for the database. Having some focused tests around our use of these components would be prudent. Our use of Typer will be tested when we test the CLI. Our use of TinyDB will be tested really in all of the other tests, and since db.py is isolating our interaction with TinyDB, we can create tests focused at that layer if necessary.

And because the feature set is small, we'll actually test all of the Cards project. However, even this quick analysis of features helps us come up with our strategy:

- Test core features thoroughly.
- Test non-core features with at least one test case.
- Test the CLI in isolation.

Now let's take this plan and generate test cases.

Creating Test Cases

As with determining the goals and scope of your test strategy, generating test cases is also easier if you take a methodical approach. For generating an initial set of test cases, these criteria will be helpful:

- Start with a non-trivial, "happy path" test case.

- Then look at test cases that represent

    - interesting sets of input,
    - interesting starting states,
    - interesting end states, or
    - all possible error states.

Some of these test cases will overlap. If a test case satisfies more than one of the above criteria, that's fine. Let's go through a few of the Cards features to get the hang of it.

For count, a happy path test case might be, "For an empty database, count returns 0." However, I'd also consider this a trivial example. It just doesn't seem like it tests much. What if count is hard-coded to return 0? Therefore, for a decent non-trivial, happy path example, let's say:

- For a database with three elements, count returns 3.

What are the interesting sets of inputs? None. count doesn't take any parameters.

What are the interesting starting states? I would say:

- Empty database
- One item
- More than one item

Interesting ending states? None. count doesn't modify the database.

Error states? Also none that I can think of.

So, for count we've got these test cases:

- count from an empty database
- count with one item
- count with more than one item

Because the last test satisfies our happy path test case, we can just leave it at these three.

Actually, the happy path is often satisfied by one of the other test cases generated by the other criteria. So why should we specifically think of a non-trivial, happy path test case? We should for a couple of reasons. First, if we are in a hurry, we could create only non-trivial, happy path test cases, one for each feature we are testing. That's not a thorough test suite. However, it's quite effective in testing a large portion of the system with minimal work. Many times I have started here and built out more test cases during development.

The second reason to start with the happy path is that it makes thinking about the other criteria pretty easy. If you start with everything that could go wrong, you may forget to test the cases where it goes right.

Let's now look at add and delete.

For add, here's the help text:

```
$ cards add --help
Usage: cards add [OPTIONS] SUMMARY...

  Add a card to db.

Arguments:
  SUMMARY...  [required]

Options:
  -o, --owner TEXT
  --help            Show this message and exit.
```

A non-trivial, happy path case could be to add a card to a non-empty database. A summary is required, and an owner passed in is optional. So we should test both summary alone and test summary plus owner. What if we don't pass in a summary? That would fall under the error conditions. As would empty text for an owner. What if we add a card who's summary and owner match an already existing card? Should that be allowed or rejected as an error state? This question highlights some of the value in writing tests during development, or at the very least, before the behavior and API are too far along to easily change without disrupting existing users. What should the behavior be? The Cards app allows duplicates. But either answer would be reasonable. Still, we should test for it.

Here are the test cases we have for add:

- add to an empty database, with summary
- add to a non-empty database, with summary
- add a card with both summary and owner set
- add a card with a missing summary
- add a duplicate card

Now for delete, here's the help text:

```
cards delete --help
Usage: cards delete [OPTIONS] CARD_ID

  Remove card in db with given id.

Arguments:
  CARD_ID  [required]

Options:
  --help  Show this message and exit.
```

For a non-trivial, happy path test case, let's start with more than one card and delete one. The only input is the card ID. Interesting options could be an ID that exists and a non-existent ID. Interesting starting states could be empty, non-empty with the card we are deleting, and non-empty without the card. Ending states finally make an appearance as a useful criteria, since the action of deleting could bring us from non-empty to empty. For error conditions, I think the non-existent card deletion is really the only one.

Here are the test cases we have for delete:

- delete one from a database with more than one
- delete the last card
- delete a non-existent card

So far we have test cases for add, delete, and count. Let's take a look at start and finish together. Because these functions change the state of a single card, looking at the card state is more interesting than looking at the database state. The possible states of cards are "todo," "in prog," and "done." All seem interesting. Like delete, you pass in an ID of a card you want to start or finish. We should test existing IDs and non-existent IDs. This brings us these new test cases:

- start from "todo," "in prog," and "done" states
- start an invalid ID
- finish from "todo," "in prog," and "done" states
- finish an invalid ID

We've got update, list, config, and version left. If you would like practice with this technique, I encourage you to try them yourself now before reading on, and see if your list is different than mine.

Here's what I came up with for the remaining features:

- update the owner of a card
- update the summary of a card

- update owner and summary of a card at the same time
- update a non-existent card
- list from an empty database
- list from a non-empty database
- config returns the correct database path
- version returns the correct version

That's a reasonably good set of test cases to start with. Note that these aren't detailed test descriptions. As we implement the test cases, questions might come up regarding what the correct behavior really is. That's great. These questions often trigger communication, design clarity, and API completeness. They can also help determine holes in documentation.

The initial list of test cases is also not complete. As we work through the test writing, we'll inevitably come up with more test cases. This is also a great time to get feedback from a team, if you are working with a team. The informal nature of the test cases at this stage allows for a discussion of behavior without getting lost in the details of the code.

There may still be some missing information that will be needed to complete the test writing. For example, if an exception is expected, what specific exception will it be? Missing information is okay, especially if the API for the code being tested isn't finalized. If you discuss the test case list with domain experts on the team at this stage, they will be ready for questions about specifics when you run into them while writing the tests.

After this planning work of examining the features to test and generating an initial test case list, you may want to jump right in to writing tests. However, it's a good idea to pause and write down what we've worked on so far.

Writing a Test Strategy

Earlier in the chapter we decided that most of our testing will be through the API. The CLI will be tested enough to make sure it calls the API correctly. We're going to punt on database testing for now. We can pick it up later if we want to have a set of tests useful for migrating to a new database package.

Even with this quick summary of our testing strategy, it's easy to forget the details once we are in the thick of testing. Therefore, I really like to write a testing strategy down so I can refer to it later. Writing it down is especially important if you are working with teams, even if there are just two of you.

Here's the current Cards testing strategy:

- Test the behaviors and features that are accessible through the end user interface, the CLI.

- Test those features through the API as much as possible.

- Test the CLI enough to verify the API is getting properly called for all features.

- Test the following core features thoroughly: add, count, delete, finish, list, start, and update.

- Include cursory tests for config and version.

- Test our use of TinyDB with subsystem tests against db.py.

Also, we won't list it here, but if you are sharing the strategy with a team in a document or an internal wiki or something, definitely include the initial test case list.

We know we'll probably extend this initial strategy as the testing progresses. Whenever we feel it needs to change, that's a great time to discuss the changes with the team.

Taking the time to write down the features to test, an initial list of test cases, and a test strategy is up-front time, but it pays for itself quickly as we blast through implementing the tests, which is the next step.

Test Case Implementation

 The tests written for the test cases generated in previous sections are included in the code download under code/ch7. None of the code is complicated and uses only pytest features we've covered in previous chapters. Feel free to look through the code.

Review

In this chapter, we looked at developing an initial test suite and a test strategy for the Cards project. We started by looking at at the system architecture and deciding at what layer we should test. We then looked at features to test, prioritizing based on:

- *Recent*—New features, new areas of code, new functionality that has been recently repaired, refactored, or otherwise modified

- *Core*—Your product's unique selling propositions (USPs). The essential functions that must continue to work in order for the product to be useful

- *Risk*—Areas of the application that pose more risk, such as areas important to customers but not used regularly by the development team or parts that use third-party code you don't quite trust

- *Problematic*—Functionality that frequently breaks or often gets defect reports against it

- *Expertise*—Features or algorithms understood by a limited subset of people

Then for each feature, we listed test cases using these criteria:

- Start with a non-trivial, happy path test case.

- Then look at test cases that represent

  - interesting sets of input,
  - interesting starting states,
  - interesting end states, or
  - all possible error states.

Finally, we wrote down the features we're testing, the list of initial test cases, and the overall test strategy so that we can discuss it and refer to it later.

Exercises

When writing automated tests, these are common mistakes:

- Only writing happy path test cases
- Spending too much time thinking about how things can go wrong
- Ignoring how behaviors change based on system or component state

Like many complex activities, the hardest part of writing a thorough yet efficient test suite is just getting started and getting the initial list of test cases. The methods covered in this chapter should be practiced so they become second nature to you.

The cool thing about these strategies is that you can practice on really any project. Going through these exercises will help you learn how to think about behavior. Going through them with even two to three projects you use but didn't build will help you when you need to come up with test cases for your own software.

1. Pick a software project you are familiar with. This could be something you wrote or helped write, or it could be some software that you use regularly.

2. Describe one or two user accessible features.

3. Write down test cases for these features. What are the interesting starting states? Are there possible error cases? Does the ending state matter? What input should you try?

4. If the project is one of your own, or a Python package that's installable with pip, try to write these test cases.

What's Next

The test cases developed in this chapter were used to create an initial test suite. In the next chapter, we'll put these tests into a directory layout, along with pytest's configuration files. We'll discuss the effect file structure has on testing, as well as the role of each configuration file.

## CHAPTER 8

Configuration Files

Configuration files—those non-test files that affect how pytest runs—save time and duplicated work. If you find yourself always using certain flags in your tests, like --verbose or --strict-markers, you can tuck those away in a config file and not have to type them all the time. In addition to configuration files, a handful of other files are useful when using pytest to make work of writing and running tests easier. We'll cover all of them in this chapter.

Understanding pytest Configuration Files

Let's run down the non-test files relevant to pytest:

- *pytest.ini*: This is the primary pytest configuration file that allows you to change pytest's default behavior. Its location also defines the pytest root directory, or rootdir.

- *conftest.py*: This file contains fixtures and hook functions. It can exist at the rootdir or in any subdirectory.

- *_init_.py*: When put into test subdirectories, this file allows you to have identical test file names in multiple test directories.

- *tox.ini*, *pyproject.toml*, and *setup.cfg*: These files can take the place of pytest.ini. If you already have one of these files in a project, you can use it to save pytest settings.

  - tox.ini is used by tox, the command-line automated testing tool we take a look at in Chapter 11, tox and Continuous Integration, on page 151.

  - pyproject.toml is used for packaging Python projects and can be used to save settings for various tools, including pytest.

  - setup.cfg is also used for packaging, and can be used to save pytest settings.

Let's look at some of these files in the context of an example project directory structure:

```
cards_proj
├── ... top level project files, src dir, docs, etc ...
├── pytest.ini
└── tests
    ├── conftest.py
    ├── api
    │   ├── __init__.py
    │   ├── conftest.py
    │   └── ... test files for api ...
    └── cli
        ├── __init__.py
        ├── conftest.py
        └── ... test files for cli ...
```

In the case of the Cards project we've been using so far for testing against, there is no tests directory. However, in either open-source or closed-source projects, the tests usually exist in a tests directory of the project.

We'll refer to this structure while talking about the various files in the rest of this section.

Saving Settings and Flags in pytest.ini

Let's look at an example pytest.ini file:

```
ch8/project/pytest.ini
[pytest]
addopts =
    --strict-markers
    --strict-config
    -ra

testpaths = tests

markers =
    smoke: subset of tests
    exception: check for expected exceptions
```

The file starts with [pytest] to denote the start of the pytest settings. It may seem weird that we have to include this notation, given that it's strictly a pytest configuration file. However, including [pytest] allows the pytest ini parsing to treat pytest.ini and tox.ini identically. After that are the individual settings, each on their own line (or multiple lines) in the form of <setting> = <value>.

Configuration settings that allow more than one value often allow values to be written on either one line or on multiple lines. For instance, we could have written the options all on one line like this:

addopts = --strict-markers --strict-config -ra

Splitting them up into one line per flag is a style thing. Markers are different, and only one marker per line is allowed.

This example is a basic pytest.ini file that includes items I almost always have set. Let's run through the options and settings briefly:

- addopts = --strict-markers --strict-config -ra

  - The addopts setting enables us to list the pytest flags we always want to run in this project.

  - --strict-markers tells pytest to raise an error for any unregistered marker encountered in the test code as opposed to a warning. Turn this on to avoid marker-name typos.

  - --strict-config tells pytest to raise an error for any difficulty in parsing configuration files. The default is a warning. Turn this on to avoid configuration-file typos going unnoticed.

  - -ra tells pytest to display extra test summary information at the end of a test run. The default is to show extra information on only test failures and errors. The a part of -ra tells pytest to show information on everything except passing tests. This adds skipped, xfailed, and xpassed to the failure and error tests.

- testpaths = tests

  - The testpaths setting tells pytest where to look for tests if you haven't given a file or directory name on the command line. Setting testpaths to tests tells pytest to look in the tests directory.

  - At first glance, setting testpaths to tests may seem redundant because pytest will look there anyway, and we don't have any test_ files in our src or docs directories. However, specifying a testpaths directory can save a bit of startup time, especially if our docs or src or other directories are quite large.

- markers = ...

  - The markers setting is used to declare markers, as we did in Selecting Tests with Custom Markers, on page 79.

You can specify many more configuration settings and command-line options in configuration files, and you can see all of them by running pytest --help.

Using tox.ini, pyproject.toml, or setup.cfg in place of pytest.ini

If you are writing tests for a project that already has a pyproject.toml, tox.ini, or setup.cfg file in place, you can still use pytest.ini to store your pytest configuration settings. Or you can store your configuration settings in one of these alternate configuration files. The syntax is a little different in the two non-ini files, so we'll take a look at each one.

tox.ini

A tox.ini file contains settings for tox, which is covered in more detail in Chapter 11, tox and Continuous Integration, on page 151. It can also include a [pytest] section. And because it's also an .ini file, the tox.ini example below is almost identical to the pytest.ini example shown earlier. The only difference is that there will also be a [tox] section.

A sample tox.ini file looks like this:

```
ch8/alt/tox.ini
[tox]
; tox specific settings

[pytest]
addopts =
    --strict-markers
    --strict-config
    -ra

testpaths = tests

markers =
    smoke: subset of tests
    exception: check for expected exceptions
```

pyproject.toml

The pyproject.toml file started as a file intended for packaging Python projects; however, the Poetry[1] and Flit[2] projects use pyproject.toml for defining a project settings. The Setuptools library, which has been the standard packaging tool before Flit and Poetry came around, hasn't traditionally used pyproject.toml.

---

1. https://python-poetry.org
2. https://flit.readthedocs.io

However, you can now use Setuptools with pyproject.toml.[3] In 2018, a Python code formatter named Black[4] started to gain popularity. The only way to configure Black is to use pyproject.toml. Since then, more and more tools have started to support storing configuration in pyproject.toml, including pytest.

Because TOML[5] is a different configuration file standard than .ini files, the format is a little different, but fairly easy to get used to. The format looks like this:

```
ch8/alt/pyproject.toml
[tool.pytest.ini_options]
addopts = [
    "--strict-markers",
    "--strict-config",
    "-ra"
    ]

testpaths = "tests"

markers = [
        "smoke: subset of tests",
        "exception: check for expected exceptions"
]
```

Instead of [pytest], you start the section with [tool.pytest.ini_options]. The setting values need quotes around them, and lists of setting values need to be lists of strings in brackets.

setup.cfg

The setup.cfg file format is more like .ini. Here's what our configuration example looks like as a setup.cfg file:

```
ch8/alt/setup.cfg
[tool:pytest]
addopts =
    --strict-markers
    --strict-config
    -ra

testpaths = tests

markers =
    smoke: subset of tests
    exception: check for expected exceptions
```

---

3. https://setuptools.readthedocs.io/en/latest/build_meta.html
4. https://pypi.org/project/black
5. https://toml.io/en

Here, the only noticeable difference between this and pytest.ini is the section specifier of [tool:pytest].

However, the pytest documentation warns that the .cfg parser is different then the .ini file parser, and that difference may cause problems that are hard to track down.[6]

Determining a Root Directory and Config File

Even before it starts looking for test files to run, pytest reads the configuration file—the pytest.ini file or the tox.ini, setup.cfg, or pyproject.toml files that contain a pytest section.

If you've passed in a test directory, pytest starts looking there. If you've passed in multiple files or directories, pytest starts at the common ancestor of all of them. If you don't pass in a file or directory, it starts at the current directory. If pytest finds a configuration file at the starting directory, that's the root. If not, pytest goes up the directory tree until it finds a configuration file that has a pytest section in it. Once pytest finds a configuration file, it marks the directory where it found it as the root directory, or rootdir. This root directory is also the relative root of test node IDs. It also tells you where it found a configuration file.

The rules around which configuration file to use and where the root directory is can seem confusing at first. However, having a well-defined rootdir search process and having pytest display what the rootdir is allows us to run tests at various levels and be assured that pytest will find the correct configuration file. For instance, even if you change directories into a test subdirectory deep inside the tests directory, pytest will still find your configuration file at the top of the project.

Even if you don't need any configuration settings, it's still a great idea to place an empty pytest.ini at the top of your project. If you don't have any configuration files, pytest will keep searching to the root of your file system. At best, this will just cause a slight delay while pytest is looking. At worst, it will find one along the way that has nothing to do with your project.

Once it locates a configuration file, pytest will print out which rootdir and configuration file it's using at the top of a test run:

```
$ cd /path/to/code/ch8/project
$ pytest
```

---

6. https://docs.pytest.org/en/latest/reference/customize.html#setup-cfg

```
========================= test session starts =========================
platform darwin -- Python 3.x.y, pytest-x.y.z, py-1.x.y, pluggy-0.x.y
rootdir: /path/to/code/ch8/project, configfile: pytest.ini, testpaths: tests
collected 28 items

tests/api/test_add.py .....                                  [ 17%]
tests/api/test_config.py .                                   [ 21%]
...
tests/api/test_update.py ....                                [ 96%]
tests/api/test_version.py .                                  [100%]

========================= 28 passed in 0.14s =========================
```

It also shows the testpaths if you have it set, which we do. That's nice.

Note that for most of the examples in this book, you won't see this header information, as it's been removed for the sole purpose of making the examples shorter and easier to read.

Sharing Local Fixtures and Hook Functions with conftest.py

The conftest.py file is used to store fixtures and hook functions. (Fixtures are described in Chapter 3, pytest Fixtures, on page 31, and hook functions are discussed in Chapter 15, Building Plugins, on page 205.) You can have as many conftest.py files as you want in a project, even one per test subdirectory. Anything defined in a conftest.py file applies to tests in that directory and all subdirectories.

If you have one top conftest.py file at the tests level, fixtures defined there can be used with all tests in the top-level tests directory and below. Then if there are specific fixtures that only apply to a subdirectory, they can be defined in another conftest.py file in that subdirectory. For instance, the GUI tests might need different fixtures than the API tests, and they might also want to share some.

However, it's a good idea to try to stick to one conftest.py file so that you can find fixture definitions easily. Even though you can always find where a fixture is defined by using pytest --fixtures -v, it's still easier if you know it's either in the test file you are looking at or in one other file, the conftest.py file.

Avoiding Test File Name Collision

The _init_.py file affects pytest in one way and one way only: it allows you to have duplicate test file names.

If you have _init_.py files in every test subdirectory, you can have the same test file name show up in multiple directories. That's it—the only reason to have a _init_.py file.

Here's an example:

```
$ cd /path/to/code/ch8/dup
$ tree tests_with_init
tests_with_init
├── api
│   ├── __init__.py
│   └── test_add.py
├── cli
│   ├── __init__.py
│   └── test_add.py
└── pytest.ini
```

We might want to test some add functionality both through the API and through the CLI, so having a test_add.py in both seems reasonable.

As long as we also have a _init_.py file in both the api and cli directories, this test will work fine:

```
$ pytest -v tests_with_init
========================= test session starts =========================
collected 2 items

tests_with_init/api/test_add.py::test_add PASSED                [ 50%]
tests_with_init/cli/test_add.py::test_add PASSED                [100%]

========================= 2 passed in 0.02s =========================
```

However, if we leave out the _init_.py files, it won't work. Here's the same directory, without the _init_.py files:

```
$ tree tests_no_init
tests_no_init
├── api
│   └── test_add.py
├── cli
│   └── test_add.py
└── pytest.ini
```

When we try to run the test, we get an error:

```
$ pytest -v tests_no_init
========================= test session starts =========================
collected 1 item / 1 error
```

```
================================ ERRORS ================================
_____ ERROR collecting cli/test_add.py _____
import file mismatch:
imported module 'test_add' has this __file__ attribute:
  /path/to/code/ch8/dup/tests_no_init/api/test_add.py
which is not the same as the test file we want to collect:
  /path/to/code/ch8/dup/tests_no_init/cli/test_add.py
HINT: remove __pycache__ / .pyc files and/or use a unique basename for
      your test file modules
======================= short test summary info ========================
ERROR tests_no_init/cli/test_add.py
!!!!!!!!!!!!!!!!! Interrupted: 1 error during collection !!!!!!!!!!!!!!!!!
=========================== 1 error in 0.07s ===========================
```

The error message highlights that we have two files named the same, and recommends changing the file names. Changing the file names would work to avoid this error, but you can also add _init_.py files and leave them as they are.

Duplicated file names is such a confusing error when you run into it that it's a decent habit to just stick _init_.py files in subdirectories and be done with it.

Review

In this chapter, we looked at all the files related to tests that are not test files:

- You can have pytest settings in one primary configuration file per project: pytest.ini, pyproject.toml, tox.ini, or setup.cfg.

- pytest calls the primary configuration file location the root directory or rootdir.

- Settings live in the configuration file, including options and flags defined by the addopts configuration setting.

- The conftest.py file is used for fixtures and hook functions shared by all tests in the same directory or lower.

- The _init_.py files in test subdirectories allow you to duplicate test file names.

Exercises

Getting used to adding and editing configuration files now will help you understand just how simple and powerful they can be. These exercises focus on the primary configuration files.

The following exercises are based around the /path/to/code/exercises/ch8 directory, which looks like this:

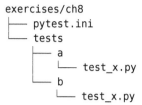

```
exercises/ch8
├── pytest.ini
└── tests
    ├── a
    │   └── test_x.py
    └── b
        └── test_x.py
```

1. Go to /path/to/code/exercises/ch8 and run pytest.

   - What is the root directory?
   - What is the configuration file in use?
   - You should also see an error message. What does it say?

2. In the pytest.ini file, set testpaths to tests/a.

   - Does that fix the error?

3. Change the testpaths from tests/a to tests. Add __init__.py files to a and b.

   - Does that fix the error?

4. Set addopts to -v and re-run pytest.

   - What was the behavior change?

5. Create a tests/pyproject.toml file.

   - Set addopts to "-v".

   - Run pytest from the exercises/ch8 directory and once from the exercises/ch8/tests directory.

   - Was the root directory and configuration file different?

   - If so, why?

What's Next

When writing tests for a software project, it can be useful to understand how much of the application code is being tested and if there are any untested parts. In the next chapter, we'll use the code coverage tools coverage.py and pytest-cov to see how much of the source code for the Cards project is being tested by the test suite developed in Chapter 7, Strategy, on page 99.

## CHAPTER 9

Coverage

In Chapter 7, Strategy, on page 99, we generated an initial list of test cases based on a test strategy by analyzing the user-facing features of the Cards project. The tests in the ch7 directory of the book's source code[1] are an implementation of those test cases, which test Cards through the API. But how do we know if these tests are thoroughly testing our code? That's where code coverage comes in.

Tools that measure code coverage watch your code while a test suite is being run and keep track of which lines are hit and which are not. That measurement—called *line coverage*—is calculated by dividing the total number of lines run divided by the total lines of code. Code coverage tools can also tell you if all paths are taken in control statements, a measurement called *branch coverage*.

Code coverage cannot tell you if your test suite is good; it can only tell you how much of the application code is getting hit by your test suite. But that in itself is useful information.

Coverage.py[2] is the preferred Python coverage tool that measures code coverage. And pytest-cov[3] is a popular pytest plugin often used in conjunction with coverage.py that makes the command line a little shorter. In this chapter, we'll use both tools to see if we missed anything important in the test suite we developed in the last chapter for the Cards project.

Using coverage.py with pytest-cov

Both coverage.py and pytest-cov are third-party packages that need to be installed before use:

---

1. https://pragprog.com/titles/bopytest2/source_code
2. https://coverage.readthedocs.io
3. https://pytest-cov.readthedocs.io

```
$ pip install coverage
$ pip install pytest-cov
```

To run tests with coverage.py, you need to add the --cov flag and provide either a path to the code you want to measure, or the installed package you are testing. In our case, the Cards project is an installed package, so we'll test it using --cov=cards.

The normal pytest output is followed by the coverage report, as shown here:

```
$ cd /path/to/code
$ pytest --cov=cards ch7
=========================== test session starts ============================
collected 27 items

ch7/test_add.py .....                                              [ 18%]
ch7/test_config.py .                                               [ 22%]
ch7/test_count.py ...                                              [ 33%]
ch7/test_delete.py ...                                             [ 44%]
ch7/test_finish.py ....                                            [ 59%]
ch7/test_list.py ..                                                [ 66%]
ch7/test_start.py ....                                             [ 81%]
ch7/test_update.py ....                                            [ 96%]
ch7/test_version.py .                                              [100%]

---------- coverage: platform darwin, python 3.x.y -----------
Name                                               Stmts   Miss  Cover
----------------------------------------------------------------------
venv/lib/python3.x/site-packages/cards/__init__.py     3      0   100%
venv/lib/python3.x/site-packages/cards/api.py         72      3    96%
venv/lib/python3.x/site-packages/cards/cli.py         86     53    38%
venv/lib/python3.x/site-packages/cards/db.py          23      0   100%
----------------------------------------------------------------------
TOTAL                                                184     56    70%

=========================== 27 passed in 0.12s =============================
```

The previous output was produced by the report capabilities of coverage, even though we didn't call coverage directly. The command, pytest --cov=cards ch7 told the pytest-cov plugin to

- run coverage with --source set to cards while running pytest with the tests in ch7, and

- run coverage report for the terminal line-coverage report.

We can do this all ourselves using coverage directly. Without pytest-cov, the commands would look like this:

```
$ coverage run --source=cards -m pytest ch7
$ coverage report
```

The resulting output report is the same, which is a little surprising. Even though the source code for cards is in /path/to/code/cards_proj/src/cards, the coverage report is for the installed package within the virtual environment. The virtual environment path to the Cards source files is annoyingly long, but still useful. The virtual environment path is the correct path, as that's where the code is running during the tests. However, the code is also in the local cards_proj directory. Having coverage list the local cards_proj directory would be nice. Luckily, there is a workaround to tell coverage that the local cards_proj code is the same as the installed code, and to use the local location instead.

If you try the same commands using the book's source code, you'll get a different result. The reason is because the source code includes a .coveragerc file with the following content:

```
.coveragerc
[paths]
source =
    cards_proj/src/cards
    */site-packages/cards
```

This file is the coverage.py configuration file, and the source setting tells coverage to treat the cards_proj/src/cards directory as if it's the same as the installed cards within */site-packages/cards. The asterisk (*) is a wildcard there to save us a bit of typing, and also makes the path work for multiple versions of Python. Typing out the whole /path/to/venv/lib/python3.x/site-packages/cards path will only match one particular Python version.

Here's what the modified output looks like after the .coveragerc changes:

```
$ pytest --cov=cards ch7
============================ test session starts ============================
collected 27 items

...actual test run omitted...

---------- coverage: platform darwin, python 3.x.y ----------
Name                               Stmts   Miss  Cover
cards_proj/src/cards/__init__.py       3      0   100%
cards_proj/src/cards/api.py           72      3    96%
cards_proj/src/cards/cli.py           86     53    38%
cards_proj/src/cards/db.py            23      0   100%
----------------------------------------------------
TOTAL                                184     56    70%

============================ 27 passed in 0.12s ============================
```

The report now lists the local files instead of the installed location. The shorter path helps to focus our attention on the important part: the coverage report. But does the report make sense knowing what we know about the test code?

The _init_.py and db.py files are at 100% coverage, which means our test suite is hitting every line in those files. It doesn't tell us that it's sufficiently tested or that the tests will catch failure possibilities. But it does at least tell us that every line has been run during the test suite, and that's a nice feeling.

The cli.py file is at 38% coverage. This might seem surprisingly high as we aren't testing the CLI at all yet. The short answer to the question why is that cli.py is getting imported by _init_.py, so all of the function definitions are run, but none of the function *contents* are being run.

What we really care about now is the api.py file. It is tested at 96% coverage. Is this good? Bad? We don't know yet. We need to look at the actual code to see which lines are being missed to know if testing them is important or not. We can find out what was missed either through the *terminal report* or through an *HTML report*.

To add missing lines to the terminal report, we can either re-run the tests and add the --cov-report=term-missing flag like this:

```
$ pytest --cov=cards --cov-report=term-missing ch7
```

Or we can run coverage report --show-missing like this:

```
$ coverage report --show-missing
Name                              Stmts   Miss  Cover   Missing
-------------------------------------------------------------------
cards_proj/src/cards/__init__.py      3      0   100%
cards_proj/src/cards/api.py          72      3    96%   75, 79, 81
cards_proj/src/cards/cli.py          86     53    38%   20, 28-31,
38-42, 53-65, 75-80, 87-91, 98-102, 109-110, 117-118, 126-127,
131-136, 143-146
cards_proj/src/cards/db.py           23      0   100%
-------------------------------------------------------------------
TOTAL                               184     56    70%
```

It's important to know that even if you run coverage with pytest-cov, you still have access to the report using coverage directly.

Now that we have line numbers of what lines haven't been tested, we can open the files in an editor and look at missed lines. However, looking at the HTML report is easier.

Generating HTML Reports

With coverage.py, we are able to generate HTML reports to help view coverage data in more detail. The report is generated either by using the --cov-report=html flag, or by running coverage html after running a previous coverage run:

```
$ cd /path/to/code
$ pytest --cov=cards --cov-report=html ch7
```

or

```
$ pytest --cov=cards ch7
$ coverage html
```

Either command asks coverage.py to generate an HTML report. The report, called htmlcov/, is placed in the directory from which you ran the command.

Open htmlcov/index.html with a browser and you'll see:

Module	statements	missing	excluded	coverage
Coverage report: 70%				
cards_proj/src/cards/__init__.py	3	0	0	100%
cards_proj/src/cards/api.py	72	3	0	96%
cards_proj/src/cards/cli.py	86	53	0	38%
cards_proj/src/cards/db.py	23	0	0	100%
Total	**184**	**56**	**0**	**70%**

Clicking the api.py file shows a report for that file, as shown here:

Coverage for cards_proj/src/cards/api.py: 96%

72 statements | 69 run | 3 missing | 0 excluded

```
1  """
2  API for the cards project
3  """
4  from dataclasses import asdict
5  from dataclasses import dataclass
6  from dataclasses import field
7  from typing import List
8  import cards
9
10 from .db import DB
11
12 __all__ = [
13     "Card",
```

The top of the report shows the percentage of lines covered (96%), the total number of statements (72), and how many statements were run (69), missed (3), and excluded (0). Scroll down and you can see the highlighted lines that were missed:

```
cards_proj/src/cards/api.py: 96%   69    3    0

70
71        def list_cards(self, owner=None, state=None):
72            """Return a list of cards."""
73            all = self._db.read_all()
74            if (owner is not None) and (state is not None):
75                return [Card.from_dict(t)
76                        for t in all
77                        if (t['owner'] == owner and t['state']== state)]
78            elif owner is not None:
79                return [Card.from_dict(t) for t in all if t['owner'] == owner]
80            elif state is not None:
81                return [Card.from_dict(t) for t in all if t['state'] == state]
82            else:
83                return [Card.from_dict(t) for t in all]
84
```

Looks like the list_cards() function has a couple of optional parameters—owner and state—that allow the list to be filtered. These lines are not being tested by our test suite.

Should we add tests to exercise these lines? If we go back to our test strategy, remember that we decided to test user-visible functionality through the API. It's visible to the user if it's also visible in the CLI. So let's check that:

```
$ cards list --help
Usage: cards list [OPTIONS]

  List cards in db.

Options:
  -o, --owner TEXT
  -s, --state TEXT
  --help            Show this message and exit.
```

Yep. The cards list command allows for these to be passed in. Looks like we missed that bit of functionality when generating the initial test case list. Therefore, we need to add at least these test cases to our list:

- list with owner to filter by owner
- list with state to filter by state
- list with owner and state to filter by both

Those test cases should hit the three lines we're missing, which is good, as they seem like important features to test.

Excluding Code from Coverage

In the HTML reports generated in the previous section, notice the inclusion of a column that indicates "0 excluded." This refers to a feature of coverage that allows us to exclude some lines from being tested. In Cards, we aren't excluding anything. But it's not unusual to exclude some code from being part of the coverage calculation.

As an example, a module that can be either imported or run directly might include a block like this:

```
if __name__ == '__main__':
    main()
```

This command tells Python to run main() if we call the module directly, like python some_module.py, but not to run the code if the module is imported.

These types of blocks are frequently excluded from testing with a simple pragma statement:

```
if __name__ == '__main__':  # pragma: no cover
    main()
```

This tells coverage to exclude either a single line or a block of code. In this sample case, you don't have to put the pragma on both lines of code. Having it on the if statement counts for the rest of the block.

Beware of Coverage-Driven Development

The coverage report generated with coverage.py in Generating HTML Reports, on page 127 indicates which lines of our code were not run by our test suite, which helps us determine if there was functionality that wasn't tested but should have been. In our case, the report indicated that there were three legitimate missing test cases. However, if the filter feature had not been visible to the user, and therefore, not part of our test strategy, we would have had different decisions to make, such as:

- Should we add the functionality to the CLI?

- Should we remove the functionality from the API?

- Should we add test cases because we plan to add this functionality to the CLI soon?

- Should we just be okay with less than 100% coverage?

- Should we pretend the code isn't there with # pragma: no cover?

- Should we add test cases just to cover these lines and let us hit 100%?

I would argue that the last option is the worst.

For the three missing lines in Cards specifically, the pragma option is just as bad. However, there are times where excluding makes sense, such as when the _name_ == '_main_' block is used, as discussed earlier in Excluding Code from Coverage, on page 129.

The others are legitimate options depending on the circumstances.

The problem with adding tests just to hit 100% is that doing so will mask the fact that these lines aren't being used and therefore are not needed by the application. It also adds test code and coding time that is not necessary.

Running Coverage on Tests

In addition to using coverage to determine if our test suite is hitting every line of our application code. Let's add our test directory to the coverage report:

```
$ pytest --cov=cards --cov=ch7 ch7
=========================== test session starts ============================
collected 27 items

...actual test run omitted...

---------- coverage: platform darwin, python 3.x.y ----------
Name                              Stmts   Miss  Cover
-----------------------------------------------------
cards_proj/src/cards/__init__.py      3      0   100%
cards_proj/src/cards/api.py          71      3    96%
cards_proj/src/cards/cli.py          71     39    45%
cards_proj/src/cards/db.py           23      0   100%
ch7/conftest.py                      22      0   100%
ch7/test_add.py                      31      0   100%
ch7/test_config.py                    2      0   100%
ch7/test_count.py                     9      0   100%
ch7/test_delete.py                   28      0   100%
ch7/test_finish.py                   13      0   100%
ch7/test_list.py                     11      0   100%
ch7/test_start.py                    13      0   100%
ch7/test_update.py                   21      0   100%
ch7/test_version.py                   5      0   100%
-----------------------------------------------------
TOTAL                               323     42    87%

=========================== 27 passed in 0.14s =============================
```

The --cov=cards command tells coverage to watch the cards package. The --cov=ch7 command tells coverage to watch the ch7 directory, where our tests are located.

Why would we do this? Of course we're going to hit all of our tests, right? Not always. A common error in all programming, and especially in coding tests, is to add a new test function with copy/paste/modify. For a new test function, we might copy an existing function, paste it as a new function, and modify the code to meet a new test case. If we forget to change the function name, then two functions will have the same name, and only the last one in the file will be run. The problem of duplicate named tests is easily caught by including your test code in the sources for coverage.

A similar problem can happen with large test modules when we just forget all of the function names and accidentally name a second test function with the same name as a previous one.

A third problem is more subtle. coverage has the ability to combine reports from several test sessions. This is necessary, for example, to test on different hardware in continuous integration. Some tests may be specific to certain hardware and be skipped on others. The combined report, if we include tests, will help us make sure all of our tests eventually got run on at least some hardware. It also helps with finding unused fixtures, or dead code inside fixtures.

Running Coverage on a Directory

We've been running coverage on an installed package, cards. But there's a lot more to the Python world than just building installable packages. In addition to packages, we can ask coverage to pay attention to directories and files as well. Let's take a look at running coverage on a directory.

In the ch9/some_code directory, we have a couple source code modules and a test module:

```
$ tree ch9/some_code
ch9/some_code
├── bar_module.py
├── foo_module.py
└── test_some_code.py
```

To demonstrate pointing coverage at a path instead package, let's stay in the top-level code directory and run the tests from there:

```
$ pytest --cov=ch9/some_code ch9/some_code/test_some_code.py
========================= test session starts =========================
collected 2 items

ch9/some_code/test_some_code.py ..                          [100%]

---------- coverage: platform darwin, python 3.x.y ----------
Name                                    Stmts   Miss  Cover
-----------------------------------------------------------
ch9/some_code/bar_module.py                 4      1    75%
```

```
ch9/some_code/foo_module.py            2      0   100%
ch9/some_code/test_some_code.py        6      0   100%
------------------------------------------------------
TOTAL                                 12      1    92%

========================= 2 passed in 0.03s =========================
```

We passed the directory with --cov=ch9/some_code. We can also run everything right from the ch9 directory:

```
$ cd /path/to/code/ch9
$ pytest --cov=some_code some_code/test_some_code.py
```

or even just:

```
$ pytest --cov=some_code some_code
```

Because test_some_code.py is the only test file, these two pytest commands are equivalent.

Now let's look at an odd corner case: a single file.

Running Coverage on a Single File

A lot of lovely single-file Python applications could use a little test coverage. Single-file applications, sometimes called *scripts*, are often not packaged or deployed, but just shared as single files. In those cases, it's handy to put the test code right into the script.

Here's a small example:

ch9/single_file.py

```python
def foo():
    return "foo"


def bar():
    return "bar"


def baz():
    return "baz"


def main():
    print(foo(), baz())


if __name__ == "__main__":  # pragma: no cover
    main()

# test code, requires pytest


def test_foo():
    assert foo() == "foo"
```

```
def test_baz():
    assert baz() == "baz"

def test_main(capsys):
    main()
    captured = capsys.readouterr()
    assert captured.out == "foo baz\n"
```

Here's what it looks like to run:

```
$ cd /path/to/code/ch9
$ python single_file.py
foo baz
```

We can run the tests on it just by swapping the python for pytest:

```
$ pytest single_file.py
```

But what about coverage? If this script is sitting in a directory with a bunch of other stuff, we can't simply pass the directory to coverage because we only want to measure this single file.

In this case, we treat the file as a package, even though nothing is getting imported, and use --cov=single_file with no .py extension:

```
$ pytest --cov=single_file single_file.py
========================== test session starts ==========================
collected 3 items

single_file.py ...                                              [100%]

---------- coverage: platform darwin, python 3.x.y -----------
Name             Stmts   Miss  Cover
----------------------------------------
single_file.py      16      1    94%
----------------------------------------
TOTAL               16      1    94%

========================== 3 passed in 0.02s ==========================
```

One of the beautiful things about pytest is that we don't even need to import pytest. To add tests to a script, we can just add them. If we do need to use parametrization or markers, however, you can stick the import in the else block of the if __name__ == '__main__' block:

```
if __name__ == '__main__': # pragma: no cover
    main()
else:
    import pytest
```

That way it's there when you are running the tests, but not required for anyone just using your script as a script.

Review

In this chapter, we used coverage.py and pytest-cov to measure code coverage and used quite a few commands and options.

For running coverage with pytest-cov, use:

- pytest --cov=cards <test path> to run with a simple report
- pytest --cov=cards --cov-report=term-missing <test path> to show which lines weren't run
- pytest --cov=cards --cov-report=html <test path> to generate an HTML report

For running coverage by itself, use:

- coverage run --source=cards -m pytest <test path> to run the test suite with coverage
- coverage report to show a simple terminal report
- coverage report --show-missing to show which lines weren't run
- coverage html to generate an HTML report

Even if you ran coverage from pytest --cov=..., you can run different reports or generate HTML using coverage report and coverage html.

The --cov and --source flags tell coverage what code to watch, and can either be the name of an installed package, or the path to the application code.

There's a lot more to coverage.py and pytest-cov than we've *covered* here. (Get it? Ha! Okay, I'll stop.) Read up on combining coverage from multiple runs, branch coverage, and much more at the respective documentation for both tools.

Exercises

Running coverage a few times will help you learn how easy and powerful it is. We'll start out easy and get a little more exciting with these exercises.

1. Coverage for single_file.py showed 94%.

    - Add a command-line flag to include which lines are missing in the terminal report.

    - *Bonus:* Add or change a test to get to 100%.

2. The example for some_code showed the coverage at 92%.

    - Generate an HTML report to find out what code is missing.

    - *Bonus:* Add or change a test to get to 100%.

3. For Cards, we found a few missing lines in api.py related to filtering the list command.

   - Run a coverage report and make sure you see the three missing lines of code in api.py.

   - Extend ch7/test_list.py by writing three new test functions to satisfy the new test cases:
     - list with owner to filter by owner
     - list with state to filter by state
     - list with owner and state to filter by both
   - Run coverage reports to see if you've hit the missing lines.

What's Next

So far we've mostly ignored the user interface of Cards—the CLI. In the next chapter, we'll write tests for the CLI using mocking. You'll also learn about various ways to use and abuse mocks during testing.

## CHAPTER 10

Mocking

In the last chapter, we tested the Cards project through the API. In this chapter, we're going to test the CLI. When we wrote the test strategy for the Cards project in Writing a Test Strategy, on page 108, we included the following statement:

- Test the CLI enough to verify the API is getting properly called for all features.

We're going to use the mock package to help us with that. Shipped as part of the Python standard library as unittest.mock as of Python 3.3,[1] the mock package is used to swap out pieces of the system to isolate bits of our application code from the rest of the system. *Mock objects* are sometimes called *test doubles*, *spies*, *fakes*, or *stubs*. Between pytest's own monkeypatch fixture (covered in Using monkeypatch, on page 54) and mock, you should have all the test double functionality you need.

In this chapter, we'll take a look at using mock to help us test the Cards CLI. We'll also look at using the CliRunner provided by Typer to assist in testing.

Isolating the Command-Line Interface

The Cards CLI uses the Typer library[2] to handle all of the command-line parts, and then it passes the real logic off to the Cards API. In testing the Cards CLI, the idea is that we'd like to test the code within cli.py and cut off access to the rest of the system. To do that, we have to look at cli.py to see how it's accessing the rest of Cards.

The cli.py module accesses the rest of the Cards system through an import of cards:

---

1. https://docs.python.org/3/library/unittest.mock.html
2. https://pypi.org/project/typer

cards_proj/src/cards/cli.py
```
import cards
```

Through this cards namespace, cli.py accesses:

- cards._version_ (a string)
- cards.CardDB (a class representing the main API methods)
- cards.InvalidCardID (an exception)
- cards.Card (the primary data type for use between the CLI and API)

Most of the API access is through a context manager that creates a cards.CardsDB object:

cards_proj/src/cards/cli.py
```
@contextmanager
def cards_db():
    db_path = get_path()
    db = cards.CardsDB(db_path)
    yield db
    db.close()
```

Most of the functions work through that object. For example, the start command accesses db.start() through db, a CardsDB instance:

cards_proj/src/cards/cli.py
```
@app.command()
def start(card_id: int):
    """Set a card state to 'in prog'."""
    with cards_db() as db:
        try:
            db.start(card_id)
        except cards.InvalidCardId:
            print(f"Error: Invalid card id {card_id}")
```

Both add and update also use the cards.Card data structure we've played with before:

cards_proj/src/cards/cli.py
```
db.add_card(cards.Card(summary, owner, state="todo"))
```

And the version command looks up cards._version_:

cards_proj/src/cards/cli.py
```
@app.command()
def version():
    """Return version of cards application"""
    print(cards.__version__)
```

For the sake of what to mock for testing the CLI, let's mock both _version_ and CardsDB.

The version command looks pretty simple. It just accesses cards._version_ and prints that. We'll start there. But first, let's look at how Typer helps us with testing.

Testing with Typer

A great feature of Typer is that it provides a testing interface. With it, we can call our application without having to resort to using subprocess.run, which is good, because we can't mock stuff running in a separate process. (We looked at a short example of using subprocess.run with test_version_v1 in Using capsys, on page 51.) We just need to give the runner's invoke function our app—cards.app—and a list of strings that represents the command.

Here's an example of invoking the version function:

```
ch10/test_typer_testing.py
from typer.testing import CliRunner
from cards.cli import app

runner = CliRunner()


def test_typer_runner():
    result = runner.invoke(app, ["version"])
    print()
    print(f"version: {result.stdout}")

    result = runner.invoke(app, ["list", "-o", "brian"])
    print(f"list:\n{result.stdout}")
```

In the example test:

- To run cards version, we run runner.invoke(app, ["version"]).
- To run cards list -o brian, we run runner.invoke(app, ["list", "-o", "brian"]).

We don't have to include "cards" in the list to send to the app, and the rest of the string is split into a list of strings.

Let's run this code and see what happens:

```
$ cd /path/to/code/ch10
$ pytest -v -s test_typer_testing.py::test_typer_runner
========================= test session starts =========================
collected 1 item

test_typer_testing.py::test_typer_runner
version: 1.0.0

list:
  ID   state   owner   summary
```

```
  3     todo     brian    Finish second edition
PASSED
========================= 1 passed in 0.05s =========================
```

Looks like it works, and is running against the live database.

However, before we move on, let's write a helper function called cards_cli. We know we're going to invoke the app plenty of times during testing the CLI, so let's simplify it a bit:

ch10/test_typer_testing.py
```python
import shlex


def cards_cli(command_string):
    command_list = shlex.split(command_string)
    result = runner.invoke(app, command_list)
    output = result.stdout.rstrip()
    return output


def test_cards_cli():
    result = cards_cli("version")
    print()
    print(f"version: {result}")

    result = cards_cli("list -o brian")
    print(f"list:\n{result}")
```

This allows us to let shlex.split() turn "list -o brian" into ["list", "-o", "brian"] for us, as well as grab the output and return it.

Now we're ready to get back to mocking.

Mocking an Attribute

Most of the Cards API is accessed through a CardsDB object, but one entry point is just an attribute, cards._version_. Let's look at how we can use mocking to make sure the value from cards._version_ is correctly reported through the CLI.

There are several patch methods within the mock package. We'll be using patch.object. We'll use it primarily in its context manager form. Here's what it looks like to mock _version_:

ch10/test_mock.py
```python
from unittest import mock

import cards
import pytest
from cards.cli import app
from typer.testing import CliRunner
```

```
runner = CliRunner()

def test_mock_version():
    with mock.patch.object(cards, "__version__", "1.2.3"):
        result = runner.invoke(app, ["version"])
        assert result.stdout.rstrip() == "1.2.3"
```

In our test code, we import cards. The resulting cards object is what we're going to be patching. The call to mock.patch.object() used as a context manager within a with block returns a mock object that is cleaned up after the with block.

In this case, the _version_ attribute of cards is replaced with "1.2.3" for the duration of the with block. We then use invoke to call our application with the "version" command. The print statement within the version() method will add a newline, which we are stripping with result.stdout.rstrip() to make the comparison easier.

When the version() method is called from the CLI code, the _version_ attribute isn't the original string, it's the string we replaced with patch.object().

Mock is replacing part of our system with something else, namely mock objects. With mock objects, we can do lots of stuff, like setting attribute values, return values for callables, and even look at how callables are called.

If that last bit was confusing, you're not alone. This weirdness is one of the reasons many people avoid mocking altogether. Once you get your head around that, the rest kinda sorta makes sense.

In the upcoming sections, we'll look at mocking classes and methods of classes.

Mocking a Class and Methods

Let's take a look at how to test config:

cards_proj/src/cards/cli.py
```
@app.command()
def config():
    """List the path to the Cards db."""
    with cards_db() as db:
        print(db.path())
```

The cards_db() is a context manager that returns a cards.CardsDB object. The returning object is then used as db to call db.path(). So we have two things to mock: cards.CardsDB and one of its methods, path().

We'll start with the class:

```
ch10/test_mock.py
def test_mock_CardsDB():
    with mock.patch.object(cards, "CardsDB") as MockCardsDB:
        print()
        print(f"        class:{MockCardsDB}")
        print(f"return_value:{MockCardsDB.return_value}")
        with cards.cli.cards_db() as db:
            print(f"       object:{db}")
```

This is an exploratory test function to see if we have the mocking set up right.

This time, we want to have CardsDB be a mock object.

If someone calls a mock object, a new mock object is returned. The mock object returned is also accessible as the return_value attribute of the original object. This seems strange, but it's very convenient.

Let's look at the objects involved before moving on:

```
$ pytest -v -s test_mock.py::test_mock_CardsDB
========================= test session starts =========================
collected 1 item

test_mock.py::test_mock_CardsDB
       class:<MagicMock name='CardsDB' id='140410645302384'>
return_value:<MagicMock name='CardsDB()' id='140410647097840'>
      object:<MagicMock name='CardsDB()' id='140410647097840'>
PASSED

========================= 1 passed in 0.03s =========================
```

When someone calls CardsDB(), they won't get a new CardsDB object, they will get the mock object that is assigned to the attribute return_value of the original.

It's this second mock object, the return value from CardsDB(), where we can change the path attribute. Specifically, we also don't really want to change the path attribute, but change the *behavior* when someone calls path(), so again, we modify the return_value:

```
ch10/test_mock.py
def test_mock_path():
    with mock.patch.object(cards, "CardsDB") as MockCardsDB:
        MockCardsDB.return_value.path.return_value = "/foo/"
        with cards.cli.cards_db() as db:
            print()
            print(f"{db.path=}")
            print(f"{db.path()=}")
```

Let's make sure it really works:

```
$ pytest -v -s test_mock.py::test_mock_path
========================= test session starts =========================
```

```
collected 1 item

test_mock.py::test_mock_path
db.path=<MagicMock name='CardsDB().path' id='140712512496016'>
db.path()='/foo/'
PASSED

========================= 1 passed in 0.03s =========================
```

Cool. We have almost all of the pieces in place.

The last thing we need to do before we really start testing the CLI is push the mock for the database into a fixture—because we're going to need it in lots of test methods:

ch10/test_mock.py
```python
@pytest.fixture()
def mock_cardsdb():
    with mock.patch.object(cards, "CardsDB", autospec=True) as CardsDB:
        yield CardsDB.return_value
```

This fixture mocks the CardsDB object and returns the return_value so that tests can use it to replace things like path:

ch10/test_mock.py
```python
def test_config(mock_cardsdb):
    mock_cardsdb.path.return_value = "/foo/"
    result = runner.invoke(app, ["config"])
    assert result.stdout.rstrip() == "/foo/"
```

And hey, look at that. We have are first CLI test done, and it's not too scary-looking.

Notice, though, that the fixture added one more component, autospec=True. Let's talk about that.

Keeping Mock and Implementation in Sync with Autospec

Mock objects are typically intended to be objects that are used in place of the real implementation. However, by default, they will accept any access. For example, if the real object allows .start(index), we want our mock objects to allow .start(index) as well. There's a problem, however. Mock objects are too flexible by default. They will also accept star() happily, any misspelled methods, any additional parameters, really anything.

Now initially, we won't do that; we'll test with the real method names and proper parameters, hopefully. But then *mock drift* can happen. Mock drift occurs when the interface you are mocking changes, and your mock in your test code doesn't.

This form of mock drift is cured by adding autospec=True to the mock during creation, as we did for CardsDB. Without it, a mock will allow you to call any function with any parameters, even if it doesn't make sense for the real thing being mocked.

For example, let's try to call .path() with an argument and try to call .not_valid(), a function that doesn't exist:

ch10/test_mock.py
```python
def test_bad_mock():
    with mock.patch.object(cards, "CardsDB") as CardsDB:
        db = CardsDB("/some/path")
        db.path()  # good
        db.path(35)  # invalid arguments
        db.not_valid()  # invalid function
```

This will pass just fine:

```
$ pytest -v -k bad_mock test_mock.py
========================= test session starts =========================
collected 7 items / 6 deselected / 1 selected

test_mock.py::test_bad_mock PASSED                            [100%]

=================== 1 passed, 6 deselected in 0.03s ===================
```

However, we don't want that. Lots of normal mistakes are hidden by mocks without a spec:

- Misspelling a method in the source code, maybe .pth() instead of .path()

- Adding or removing a parameter to an API method and forgetting to change the calling code in the CLI

- Changing a method name during refactoring, and again, forgetting to change it everywhere

If we add that little extra code, autospec=True, these mistakes are caught by the tests:

ch10/test_mock.py
```python
def test_good_mock():
    with mock.patch.object(cards, "CardsDB", autospec=True) as CardsDB:
```

And pytest and mock will catch our mistakes with lines like:

```
E    TypeError: too many positional arguments
```

or

```
E    AttributeError: Mock object has no attribute 'not_valid'
```

We want this protection. So always autospec when you can. Really the only time you can't is if the class or object being mocked is naturally dynamic with methods or if attributes are being added at runtime. The Python documentation has a great section on autospec.[3]

Making Sure Functions Are Called Correctly

So far we've utilized return values from a mocked method to make sure our application code is dealing with the return values correctly. But sometimes there is not any useful return value. In those cases, we can actually ask the mock object if it was called correctly.

The config command calls .path() and prints the return value. So we can mock the return value of .path() and and test what config prints. The count command prints the output of db.count(), so we can test that a lot like config.

But there are a bunch of other commands where we can't test the behavior by checking the output, because there is no output. For instance, cards add some tasks -o brian.

After calling cards_cli("add some tasks -o brian"), instead of using the API to check if that item made it to the database, we'll use a mock to make sure the CLI called the right API method correctly.

The add command implementation ends up calling db.add_card() with a Card object:

cards_proj/src/cards/cli.py
```
db.add_card(cards.Card(summary, owner, state="todo"))
```

To make sure it was called correctly, we can ask the mock:

ch10/test_cli.py
```
def test_add_with_owner(mock_cardsdb):
    cards_cli("add some task -o brian")
    expected = cards.Card("some task", owner="brian", state="todo")
    mock_cardsdb.add_card.assert_called_with(expected)
```

If the add_card() isn't called, or is called with the wrong type or wrong object contents, the test will fail. For example, if we capitalize the "B" in Brian in the expectation, but not in the CLI call, we will get something like this:

```
...
E    AssertionError: expected call not found.
E    Expected: add_card(Card(summary='some task', owner='Brian', ...
E    Actual: add_card(Card(summary='some task', owner='brian', ...
...
```

---

3. https://docs.python.org/3/library/unittest.mock.html#autospeccing

There are quite a few variants of assert_called(). Read the documentation[4] for a full list and description. When the only way to test is to make sure something was called correctly, the various assert_called methods do the trick.

Creating Error Conditions

Now let's check to make sure the Cards CLI deals with error conditions correctly. For example, here's the delete command implementation:

cards_proj/src/cards/cli.py

```
@app.command()
def delete(card_id: int):
    """Remove card in db with given id."""
    with cards_db() as db:
        try:
            db.delete_card(card_id)
        except cards.InvalidCardId:
            print(f"Error: Invalid card id {card_id}")
```

To test the CLI's handling of an error condition, we can pretend that delete_card generates an exception by assigning the exception to the mock object side_effect attribute, like this:

ch10/test_cli.py

```
def test_delete_invalid(mock_cardsdb):
    mock_cardsdb.delete_card.side_effect = cards.api.InvalidCardId
    out = cards_cli("delete 25")
    assert "Error: Invalid card id 25" in out
```

That's pretty much all we need to test the CLI. We've talked about mocking return values, asserting how mock functions were called, and mocking exceptions. For many applications, including the Cards CLI, that's all the mocking techniques we need. However, there's quite a bit more to mocking that we haven't covered, so be sure to read the documentation if you wish to make a lot of use of mocking.

> ## Mocking Tests Implementation, Not Behavior
>
> One of the biggest problems when using mocks is that when we are using mocks in a test, we are no longer testing behavior, but testing *implementation*. Focusing tests on testing implementation is dangerous and time-consuming. A completely valid refactoring, say changing a variable name, might break tests if that particular variable was being mocked.
>
> We have a name for tests that break during valid refactoring: *change detector tests*. We want most of our tests to fail only when valid breaks in behavior occur. When

---

4.   https://docs.python.org/3/library/unittest.mock.html#unittest.mock.Mock.assert_called

tests fail whenever the code changes, they are change detector tests, and are usually more trouble than they are worth.

Are there any benefits to mocking? Of course. There are times when it's the simplest way to generate exceptions or error conditions, and make sure your code handles those correctly. There are also times where testing behavior is unreasonable, like accessing payment API or sending email. In those cases, making sure your code calls a particular API method when its supposed to, with the correct parameters, is a decent option for testing. However, it's good to know what you are getting into when testing implementation over behavior.

Testing at Multiple Layers to Avoid Mocking

Our initial Cards testing strategy statement, "Test the CLI enough to verify the API is getting properly called for all features," can be taken literally as checking the API calls, as we did with mocks. However, we can satisfy this statement in other ways.

While testing the CLI, we could also use the API. We won't be testing the API, but using it to check the behavior of actions made through the CLI. Let's look at an example:

```
ch10/test_cli_alt.py
def test_add_with_owner(cards_db):
    """
    A card shows up in the list with expected contents.
    """
    cards_cli("add some task -o brian")
    expected = cards.Card("some task", owner="brian", state="todo")
    all_cards = cards_db.list_cards()
    assert len(all_cards) == 1
    assert all_cards[0] == expected
```

For comparison, here's the mock version:

```
ch10/test_cli.py
def test_add_with_owner(mock_cardsdb):
    cards_cli("add some task -o brian")
    expected = cards.Card("some task", owner="brian", state="todo")
    mock_cardsdb.add_card.assert_called_with(expected)
```

Mocking tested the implementation of the CLI, making sure a specific API call was called with specific parameters. The mixed-layer approach tests the behavior, making sure the outcome is what we want. This kind of approach is much less of a change detector and has a greater chance of remaining valid during refactoring.

The rest of ch10/test_cli_alt.py demonstrates completely replacing mocking with mixed-layer testing. Interestingly, it's about twice as fast:

```
$ pytest test_cli.py
========================= test session starts =========================
collected 17 items

test_cli.py .................                                  [100%]

========================= 17 passed in 0.26s =========================
$ pytest test_cli_alt.py
========================= test session starts =========================
collected 17 items

test_cli_alt.py .................                              [100%]

========================= 17 passed in 0.11s =========================
```

We could also avoid mocking in another way. We could test behavior completely through the CLI. This would involve possibly parsing the cards list output to verify correct database contents.

In the API, add_card() returns an index and provides a get_card(index) method, which helps with testing. Neither of those are present in the CLI, but conceptually, they could be. We could maybe add cards get index or cards info index commands to allow us to retrieve one card instead of having to use cards list for everything. list also already supports filtering. Perhaps filtering on index would work instead of adding a new command. And we could add an output to cards add to say something such as, "Card added at index 3". These modifications would fall into the "Design for Testability" category of changes. They also don't seem like deep intrusions to the interface, and perhaps should be considered in future versions.

Using Plugins to Assist Mocking

This chapter has focused on using unittest.mock directly. However, there are many plugins that help with mocking, such as pytest-mock, which is a general-purpose plugin that provides a mocker fixture that acts as a thin wrapper around unittest.mock. One benefit of using pytest-mock is that the fixture cleans up after itself, so you don't have to use a with block, as we did in our examples.

There are also several special-purpose mocking libraries that should be considered if their focus matches what you are testing:

- For mocking database access, try pytest-postgresql, pytest-mongo, pytest-mysql, and pytest-dynamodb.

- For mocking HTTP servers, try pytest-httpserver.

- For mocking requests, try responses and betamax.

And there are even more tools, such as pytest-rabbitmq, pytest-solr, pytest-elasticsearch, and pytest-redis.

This is just a short sampling. Lots of people like to use mock to isolate parts of their system. If you are using a third-party service, there's a decent chance someone has made a pytest plugin or other package to help mock it. It may save you time to do a quick search before rolling your own mocks.

Review

In this chapter, we looked at how to test a layer of code in isolation using mocks and mock objects. Mocks allow us to swap out pieces of the application code with mock objects or other code. In addition:

- Mock objects can simulate return values, raise exceptions, and record how they were called.

- Using autospec=True when mocking objects, such as CardsDB, can help avoid mock drift and make sure our use of the mock in tests is the same as the API of the object being mocked.

- Return values can be simulated with mock_object.return_value = <new value>.

- Exceptions can be simulated with mock_object.side_effect = Exception.

Mock objects return new mock objects when called as a function, unless you've set their return_value.

Mocking has some drawbacks, the most important of which is that using mocks during testing means that you are testing implementation instead of testing behavior.

Testing at multiple layers is one way of avoiding the need for mocking.

Adding functionality that makes testing easier is part of "design for testability" and can be used to allow testing at multiple levels or testing at a higher level.

Exercises

Mocking is a powerful tool for testing, and it's important to know how to use it. Spending a bit of time now to play with mocks will help solidify the concepts and help you recognize places in your testing future where you may want to use mocks.

For the exercise, we'll use a small script called my_info.py:

exercises/ch10/my_info.py

```python
from pathlib import Path

def home_dir():
    return str(Path.home())

if __name__ == "__main__":
    print(home_dir())
```

The home_dir() function utilizes pathlib to get a users home directory. Just to show you how it works, the _name_ == "_main_" allows us to see it in action. This is what it looks like for me:

```
$ cd /path/to/code/exercises/ch10
$ python my_info.py
/Users/okken
```

Obviously, everyone's home directory is different, so this is going to be hard to test.

1. In test_my_info.py, write a test that uses mock and changes the return value of Path.home() to "/users/fake_user", and checks the return value of home_dir().

2. Write another test that also calls home_dir(), but instead of checking the value, just asserts that Path.home() is called by home_dir().

What's Next

With the testing done for both the API and the CLI, the application has 100% coverage and all is well with the world. Let's keep it that way. In the next chapter, you'll learn how to keep your tests running with every change to your code to make sure nothing breaks.

tox and Continuous Integration

When working with a team of people who are all working on the same code-base, continuous integration (CI) offers an amazing productivity boost. CI refers to the practice of merging all developers' code changes into a shared repository on a regular basis—often several times a day. CI is also quite helpful even when working on a project alone.

Most tools used for CI run on a server (GitHub Actions is one example). tox is an automation tool that works a lot like a CI tool but can be run both locally and in conjunction with other CI tools on a server.

In this chapter, we take a look at tox and how to set it up in the Cards application to help us with testing Cards locally. Then we'll set up testing on GitHub using GitHub Actions. First, let's review what exactly CI is and how it fits into the testing universe.

What Is Continuous Integration?

In software engineering, the name "continuous integration" only makes sense in the context of history. Before the implementation of CI, software teams used version control to keep track of code updates, and different developers would add a feature or fix a bug on the separate code branches. At some point, the code was merged, built, and (hopefully) tested. The frequency of this merge varied from "when your code is ready, merge it" to regularly scheduled merges, maybe weekly or every other week. This merge phase was called integration because the code is being integrated together.

With this sort of version control, code conflicts happened often. Therefore, some teams had dedicated people to do the merge and debug merge conflicts, sometimes pulling in other developers to help with decisions. Some errors in merging were not found until testing. And some merge errors were not found until much later.

This is obviously not a fun way to write software. Thus, CI was born.

CI tools build and run tests all on their own, usually triggered by a merge request. Because the build and test stages are automated, developers can integrate more frequently, even several times a day. This frequency makes it so the code change between branches is smaller, reducing the chance of merge conflicts. Combining that with the advances in automated merging present in tools like Git, we get the "continuous" part of the continuous integration process.

CI tools traditionally automate the process of build and test. The actual merge to the final main code branch can sometimes be handled by the CI systems. However, more frequently, the tools stop after test. The software team can then continue with a code review and manually click a "merge" button in the revision control system.

At first glance, CI seems to be most helpful for teams of people. However, the automation, convenience, and consistency that CI brings to a project are also valuable to single-person projects.

Introducing tox

tox[1] is a command-line tool that allows you to run your complete suite of tests in multiple environments. tox is a great starting point when learning about CI. Although it strictly is not a CI system, it acts a lot like one, and can run locally. We're going to use tox to test the Cards project in multiple versions of Python. However, tox is not limited to just Python versions. You can use it to test with different dependency configurations and different configurations for different operating systems.

In gross generalities, here's a mental model for how tox works:

tox uses project information in either setup.py or pyproject.toml for the package under test to create an installable distribution of your package. It looks in tox.ini for a list of environments, and then for each environment, tox

1. creates a virtual environment in a .tox directory,
2. pip installs some dependencies,
3. builds your package,
4. pip installs your package, and
5. runs your tests.

---

1. https://tox.wiki

After all environments are tested, tox reports a summary of how they all did. This makes a lot more sense when you see it in action, so let's look at how to set up the Cards project to use tox.

tox Alternatives

Although tox is used by many projects, there are alternatives that perform similar functions. Two alternatives to tox are nox and invoke. This chapter focuses on tox mostly because it's the tool I use.

Setting Up tox

Up to now we've had the cards_proj code in one directory and the tests in our chapter directories. Now we'll combine them into one project and add a tox.ini file.

Here's the abbreviated code layout:

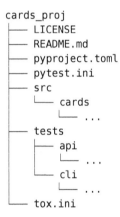

```
cards_proj
├── LICENSE
├── README.md
├── pyproject.toml
├── pytest.ini
├── src
│   └── cards
│       └── ...
├── tests
│   ├── api
│   │   └── ...
│   └── cli
│       └── ...
└── tox.ini
```

You can explore the full project at /path/to/code/ch11/cards_proj. This is a typical layout for many package projects.

Let's take a look at a basic tox.ini file in the Cards project:

ch11/cards_proj/tox.ini
```
[tox]
envlist = py310
isolated_build = True

[testenv]
deps =
  pytest
  faker
commands = pytest
```

Under [tox], we have envlist = py310. This is shorthand to tell tox to run our tests using Python version 3.10. We'll add more versions of Python shortly, but using one for now helps to understand the flow of tox. Note also the line, isolated_build = True. The Cards project configures the build instructions to Python in a pyproject.toml file. For all pyproject.toml-configured packages, we need to set isolated_build = True. For setup.py-configured projects using the setuptools library, this line can be left out.

Under [testenv], the deps section lists pytest and faker. This tells tox that we need to install both of these tools for testing. You can specify which version to use, if you wish, such as pytest == 6.2.4 or pytest >= 6.2.4.

Finally, the commands setting tells tox to run pytest in each environment.

Running tox

Before running tox, you have to make sure you install it:

```
$ pip install tox
```

This can be done within a virtual environment.

Then to run tox, just run, well... tox:

```
$ cd /path/to/code/ch11/cards_proj
$ tox
py310 recreate: /path/to/code/ch11/cards_proj/.tox/py310
py310 installdeps: pytest, faker
py310 inst: /path/to/code/ch11/cards_proj/
            .tox/.tmp/package/1/cards-1.0.0.tar.gz
py310 installed: ...
py310 run-test: commands[0] | pytest
========================= test session starts =========================
collected 51 items

tests/api/test_add.py .....                                    [  9%]
tests/api/test_config.py .                                     [ 11%]
...
tests/cli/test_update.py .                                     [ 98%]
tests/cli/test_version.py .                                    [100%]

========================= 51 passed in 0.32s =========================
_____ summary _____
  py310: commands succeeded
  congratulations :)
```

At the end, tox gives you a nice summary of all the test environments (just py310 for now) and their outcomes:

```
_____ summary _____
py310: commands succeeded
congratulations :)
```

Doesn't that give you a nice warm, happy feeling? We got a "congratulations" *and* a smiley face.

Testing Multiple Python Versions

Let's extend envlist in tox.ini to add more Python versions:

ch11/cards_proj/tox_multiple_pythons.ini
```
[tox]
envlist = py37, py38, py39, py310
isolated_build = True
skip_missing_interpreters = True
```

Now we'll be testing Python versions from 3.7 though 3.10.

We also added the setting, skip_missing_interpreters = True. If skip_missing_interpreters is set to False, the default, tox will fail if your system is missing any of the versions of Python listed. With it set to True, tox will run the tests on any available Python version, but skip versions it can't find without failing.

The output is similar. This is an abbreviated output:

```
$ tox -c tox_multiple_pythons.ini
...
py37 run-test: commands[0] | pytest
...
py38 run-test: commands[0] | pytest
...
py39 run-test: commands[0] | pytest
...
py310 run-test: commands[0] | pytest
...
_____ summary _____
  py37: commands succeeded
  py38: commands succeeded
  py39: commands succeeded
  py310: commands succeeded
  congratulations :)
```

Note that the use of an alternate configuration than tox.ini is unusual. We just used tox -c tox_multiple_pythons.ini so that we can see different tox.ini settings with the same project.

Running tox Environments in Parallel

In the previous example, the different environments ran in a series. It's also possible to run them in parallel with the -p flag:

```
$ tox -c tox_multiple_pythons.ini -p
✓ OK py310 in 3.921 seconds
✓ OK py37 in 4.02 seconds
✓ OK py39 in 4.145 seconds
✓ OK py38 in 4.218 seconds
_____ summary _____
  py37: commands succeeded
  py38: commands succeeded
  py39: commands succeeded
  py310: commands succeeded
  congratulations :)
```

Note that the output is not abbreviated. This is actually all the output you see if everything passes.

Adding a Coverage Report to tox

With a couple of changes to the tox.ini file, tox can add coverage reports to its test runs. To do so, we need to add pytest-cov to the deps setting so that the pytest-cov plugin will be installed in the tox test environments. Pulling in pytest-cov will also include all of its dependencies, like coverage. We then extend the commands call to pytest to be pytest --cov=cards:

ch11/cards_proj/tox_coverage.ini
```
[testenv]
deps =
  pytest
  faker
  pytest-cov
commands = pytest --cov=cards
```

When using coverage with tox, it's also nice to set up a .coveragerc file to let coverage know which source paths should be considered identical:

ch11/cards_proj/.coveragerc
```
[paths]
source =
   src
   .tox/*/site-packages
```

This looks a little cryptic at first. tox creates virtual environments in the .tox directory (for example, in .tox/py310). The Cards source is in the src/cards directory before we run. But when tox installs our package into the environment, it will live in a site-packages/cards directory somewhere buried in .tox. For example, for Python 3.10, it shows up in .tox/py310/lib/python3.10/site-packages/cards.

The coverage source setting to the list including src and .tox/*/site-packages is shorthand to make the earlier code work such that the following output is possible:

```
$ tox -c tox_coverage.ini -e py310
...
py310 run-test: commands[0] | pytest --cov=cards
...
---------- coverage: platform darwin, python 3.x.y -----------
Name                    Stmts   Miss  Cover
--------------------------------------------
src/cards/__init__.py       3      0   100%
src/cards/api.py           72      0   100%
src/cards/cli.py           86      0   100%
src/cards/db.py            23      0   100%
--------------------------------------------
TOTAL                     184      0   100%

========================= 51 passed in 0.44s =========================
_____ summary _____
  py310: commands succeeded
  congratulations :)
```

In this example, note that we also used the -e py310 flag to choose a specific environment.

Specifying a Minimum Coverage Level

When running coverage from tox, it's also nice to set a baseline coverage percent to flag any slips in coverage. This is done with the --cov-fail-under flag:

ch11/cards_proj/tox_coverage_min.ini
```
[testenv]
deps =
  pytest
  faker
  pytest-cov
commands = pytest --cov=cards --cov=tests --cov-fail-under=100
```

This will add an extra line to the output:

```
$ tox -c tox_coverage_min.ini -e py310
...
Name                    Stmts   Miss  Cover
--------------------------------------------
src/cards/__init__.py       3      0   100%
src/cards/api.py           72      0   100%
```

```
src/cards/cli.py                    86      0    100%
...
tests/cli/test_version.py            3      0    100%
tests/conftest.py                   22      0    100%
-----------------------------------------------------
TOTAL                              439      0    100%
```

➤ Required test coverage of 100% reached. Total coverage: 100.00%

```
========================= 51 passed in 0.43s =========================
_____ summary _____
  py310: commands succeeded
  congratulations :)
```

We used a couple of other flags as well. In tox.ini, we added --cov=tests to the pytest call to make sure all of our tests are run. In the tox command line, we used -e py310. The -e flag allows us to run one specific tox environment.

Passing pytest Parameters Through tox

In the previous section we saw how using -e py310 enables us to zoom in on one environment to run. We could also zoom in on an individual test if we make one more modification to allow parameters to get to pytest.

The changes are as simple as adding {posargs} to our pytest command:

ch11/cards_proj/tox_posargs.ini
```
[testenv]
deps =
  pytest
  faker
  pytest-cov
commands =
  pytest --cov=cards --cov=tests --cov-fail-under=100 {posargs}
```

Then to pass arguments to pytest, add a -- between the tox arguments and the pytest arguments. In this case, we'll select test_version tests using keyword flag -k. We'll also use --no-cov to turn off coverage (no point in measuring coverage when we're only running a couple of tests):

```
$ tox -c tox_posargs.ini -e py310 -- -k test_version --no-cov
...
py310 run-test: commands[0] | pytest --cov=cards --cov=tests
  --cov-fail-under=100 -k test_version --no-cov
========================= test session starts =========================
collected 51 items / 49 deselected / 2 selected

tests/api/test_version.py .                                    [ 50%]
tests/cli/test_version.py .                                    [100%]

==================== 2 passed, 49 deselected in 0.10s ====================
```

```
_____ summary _____
  py310: commands succeeded
  congratulations :)
```

tox is capable of doing many other cool things. Check the tox documentation[2] for specific needs not covered here.

tox is not only awesome for automating testing processes locally, but also it helps with cloud-based CI. Let's move on to running pytest and tox using GitHub Actions.

Running tox with GitHub Actions

Even if you are careful to run tox all the time before committing or merging your code, it's really nice to have a CI system set up to *always* run tox on all changes. Even though GitHub Actions has only been available since 2019, it's already very popular for Python projects.

GitHub Actions[3] is a cloud-based CI system provided by GitHub. If you are using GitHub to store your project, Actions are a natural CI option.

CI Alternatives

 GitHub Actions is just one example of a continuous integration tool. There are many other great tools available, such as GitLab CI, Bitbucket Pipelines, CircleCI, and Jenkins.

To add Actions to a repository, all you have to do is add a workflow .yml file to .github/workflows/ at the top level of your project.

Let's look at main.yml for Cards:

ch11/cards_proj/.github/workflows/main.yml
```
name: CI

on: [push, pull_request]

jobs:
  build:

    runs-on: ubuntu-latest
    strategy:
      matrix:
        python: ["3.7", "3.8", "3.9", "3.10"]

    steps:
      - uses: actions/checkout@v2
      - name: Setup Python
```

---

2. https://tox.wiki/
3. https://github.com/features/actions

```
    uses: actions/setup-python@v2
    with:
      python-version: ${{ matrix.python }}
  - name: Install Tox and any other packages
    run: pip install tox
  - name: Run Tox
    run: tox -e py
```

Now let's walk through what this file is specifying:

- name can be anything. It shows up in the GitHub Actions user interface that we'll see in a bit.

- on: [push, pull_request] tells Actions to run our tests every time we either push code to the repository or a pull request is created. If we push code changes, our tests will run. If anyone creates a pull request, the tests will run. On pull requests, the result of the test run can be seen in the pull request interface. All action run results can be seen in the Actions tab on the GitHub interface. We'll see that shortly.

- runs-on: ubuntu-latest specifies which operating system to run the tests on. Here we're just running on Linux, but other OSs are available.

- matrix: python: ["3.7", "3.8", "3.9", "3.10"] specifies which Python version to run.

- steps is a list of steps. The name of each step can be anything and is optional.

- uses: actions/checkout@v2 is a GitHub Actions tool that checks out our repository so the rest of the workflow can access it.

- uses: actions/setup-python@v2 is a GitHub Actions tool that gets Python configured and installed in a build environment.

- with: python-version: ${{ matrix.python }} says to create an environment for each of the Python versions listed in matrix: python.

- run: pip install tox installs tox.

- run: tox -e py runs tox. The -e py is a bit surprising because we don't have a py environment specified. However, this works to select the correct version of Python specified in our tox.ini.

The Actions syntax can seem mysterious at first. Luckily it's documented well. A good starting point in the GitHub Actions documentation is the Building and Testing Python[4] page. The documentation also shows you how

---

4. https://docs.github.com/en/actions/guides/building-and-testing-python

to run pytest directly without tox and how to extend the matrix to multiple operating systems.

Once you've set up your workflow .yml file and pushed it to your GitHub repository, it will be run automatically.

Select the Actions tab to see previous runs, as shown in the following screenshot:

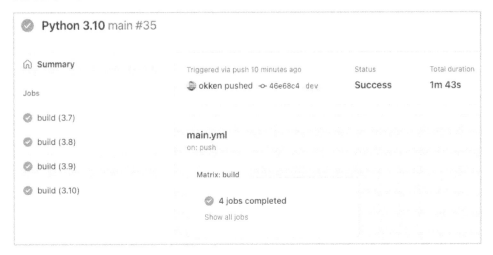

The different Python environments are listed on the left. Selecting one shows you the results for that environment, as shown in this screenshot:

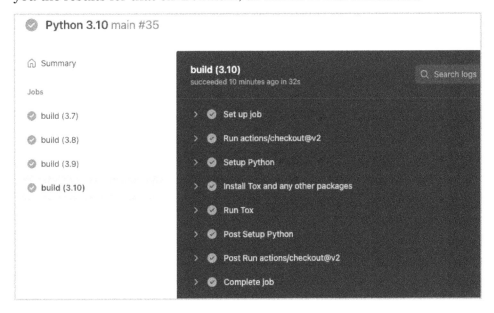

Notice how our top-level name setting, "Python package," shows up at the top, and the names for each step are shown as well.

Running Other Tools from tox and CI

 We used tox and GitHub Actions to run pytest. However, these tools can do so much more. Many projects use these tools to run other tools for static analysis, type checking, code format checks, and so on. Please visit the documentation for both tox and GitHub Actions to find out more.

Review

In this chapter, we set up both tox and GitHub Actions to run pytest on multiple Python versions. You also saw how to

- run tox environments in parallel,
- test with coverage,
- set a minimum coverage percentage,
- run specific environments,
- pass parameters from the tox command line to pytest, and
- run tox on GitHub Actions.

Exercises

Working with tox is even more fun than reading about it. Running through these exercises will help you realize how simple it is to work with tox. A small starter project with a starter tox.ini set to run tests using Python 3.10 is in the /path/to/code/exercises/ch11 folder. Use that project to complete the following exercises.

1. Go to /path/to/code/exercises/ch11. Install tox.

2. Run tox with the current settings.

3. Change envlist to also run Python 3.9.

4. Change commands to add coverage report, including making sure there is 100% coverage. Don't forget to add pytest-cov to deps.

5. Add {posargs} to the end of the pytest command. Run tox -e py310 -- -v to see the test names.

6. (*Bonus*) Set up GitHub Actions to run tox for this project, or some other Python project repository.

What's Next

We've been testing the Cards application for most of this book. Cards is a Python pip-installable package. However, lots of Python projects are not installed with pip, such as simple single-file scripts and larger applications that are deployed in ways other than pip.

When testing non-pip-installable Python code, there are some gotchas. For example, in order for a test file to import another module, the module needs to be in the Python search path. And, without pip install, we need some other way to get the application code into the search path. The next chapter addresses these issues and walks through some solutions.

## CHAPTER 12

Testing Scripts and Applications

The sample Cards application is an installable Python package that is installed with pip install. Once it is installed, the test code can simply import cards to access the application's capabilities, and test away. However, not all Python code is installable with pip, but still needs to be tested.

In this chapter, we'll look at techniques for testing scripts and applications that cannot be installed with pip. To be clear on terms, the following definitions apply in this chapter:

- A *script* is a single file containing Python code that is intended to be run directly from Python, such as python my_script.py.

- An *importable script* is a script in which no code is executed when it is imported. Code is executed only when it is run directly.

- An *application* refers to a package or script that has external dependencies defined in a requirements.txt file. The Cards project is also an application, but it is installed with pip. External dependencies for Cards are defined in its pyproject.toml file and pulled in during pip install. In this chapter, we'll specifically look at applications that cannot or choose to not use pip.

We'll start with testing a script. We'll then modify the script so that we can import it for testing. We'll then add an external dependency and look at testing applications.

When testing scripts and applications, a few questions often come up:

- How do I run a script from a test?

- How do I capture the output from a script?

- I want to import my source modules or packages into my tests. How do I make that work if the tests and code are in different directories?

- How do I use tox if there's no package to build?

- How do I get tox to pull in external dependencies from a requirements.txt file?

These are the questions this chapter will answer.

Don't Forget to Use a Virtual Environment

 The virtual environment you've been using in the previous part of the book can be used for the discussion in this chapter, or you can create a new one. Here's a refresher on how to do that:

```
$ cd /path/to/code/ch12
$ python3 -m venv venv
$ source venv/bin/activate
(venv) $ pip install -U pip
(venv) $ pip install pytest
(venv) $ pip install tox
```

Testing a Simple Python Script

Let's start with the canonical coding example, *Hello World!*:

ch12/script/hello.py
```
print("Hello, World!")
```

The run output shouldn't be surprising:

```
$ cd /path/to/code/ch12/script
$ python hello.py
Hello, World!
```

Like any other bit of software, scripts are tested by running them and checking the output and/or side effects.

For the hello.py script, our challenge is to (1) figure out how to run it from a test, and (2) how to capture the output. The subprocess module, which is part of the Python standard library,[1] has a run() method that will solve both problems just fine:

ch12/script/test_hello.py
```
from subprocess import run

def test_hello():
    result = run(["python", "hello.py"], capture_output=True, text=True)
    output = result.stdout
    assert output == "Hello, World!\n"
```

---

1. https://docs.python.org/3/library/subprocess.html#subprocess.run

The test launches a subprocess, captures the output, and compares it to "Hello, World!\n", including the newline print() automatically adds to the output. Let's try it out:

```
$ pytest -v test_hello.py
========================= test session starts =========================
collected 1 item

test_hello.py::test_hello PASSED                              [100%]

========================= 1 passed in 0.03s =========================
```

That's not too bad. Let's try it with tox.

If we set up a normal-ish tox.ini file, it won't really work. Let's try anyway:

ch12/script/tox_bad.ini
```
[tox]
envlist = py39, py310

[testenv]
deps = pytest
commands = pytest

[pytest]
```

Running this illustrates the problem:

```
$ tox -e py310 -c tox_bad.ini
ERROR: No pyproject.toml or setup.py file found. The expected locations are:
  /path/to/code/ch12/script/pyproject.toml or /path/to/code/ch12/script/setup.py
You can
  1. Create one:
     https://tox.readthedocs.io/en/latest/example/package.html
  2. Configure tox to avoid running sdist:
     https://tox.readthedocs.io/en/latest/example/general.html
  3. Configure tox to use an isolated_build
```

The problem is that tox is trying to build something as the first part of its process. We need to tell tox to not try to build anything, which we can do with skipsdist = true:

ch12/script/tox.ini
```
[tox]
envlist = py39, py310
skipsdist = true

[testenv]
deps = pytest
commands = pytest

[pytest]
```

Now it should run fine:

```
$ tox
...
py39 run-test: commands[0] | pytest
========================= test session starts =========================
collected 1 item

test_hello.py .                                                  [100%]

========================= 1 passed in 0.04s =========================
...
py310 run-test: commands[0] | pytest
========================= test session starts =========================
collected 1 item

test_hello.py .                                                  [100%]

========================= 1 passed in 0.04s =========================
_____ summary _____
  py39: commands succeeded
  py310: commands succeeded
  congratulations :)
$
```

Awesome. We tested our script with pytest and tox and used subprocess.run() to launch our script and capture the output.

Testing a small script with subprocess.run() works okay, but it does have drawbacks. We may want to test sections of larger scripts separately. That's not possible unless we split the functionality into functions. We also may want to separate test code and scripts into different directories. That's also not trivial with the code as is, because our call to subprocess.run() assumed hello.py was in the same directory. A few modifications to our code can clean up these issues.

Testing an Importable Python Script

We can change our script code a tiny bit to make it importable and allow tests and code to be in different directories. We'll start by making sure all of the logic in the script is inside a function. Let's move the workload of hello.py into a main() function:

ch12/script_importable/hello.py
```
def main():
    print("Hello, World!")

if __name__ == "__main__":
    main()
```

We call main() inside a if __name__ == '__main__' block. The main() code will be called when we call the script with python hello.py:

```
$ cd /path/to/code/ch12/script_importable
$ python hello.py
Hello, World!
```

The main() code won't be called with just an import. We have to call main() explicitly:

```
$ python
>>> import hello
>>> hello.main()
Hello, World!
```

Now we can test main() as if it were just any other function. In the modified test, we are using capsys (which was covered in Using capsys, on page 51):

ch12/script_importable/test_hello.py
```
import hello


def test_main(capsys):
    hello.main()
    output = capsys.readouterr().out
    assert output == "Hello, World!\n"
```

Not only can we test main(), but also as our script grows, we may break up code into separate functions. We can now test those functions separately. It's a bit silly to break up *Hello, World!*, but let's do it anyway, just for fun:

ch12/script_funcs/hello.py
```
def full_output():
    return "Hello, World!"


def main():
    print(full_output())


if __name__ == "__main__":
    main()
```

Here we've put the output contents into full_output() and the actual printing of it in main(). And now we can test those separately:

ch12/script_funcs/test_hello.py
```
import hello


def test_full_output():
    assert hello.full_output() == "Hello, World!"


def test_main(capsys):
    hello.main()
    output = capsys.readouterr().out
    assert output == "Hello, World!\n"
```

Splendid. Even a fairly large script can be reasonably tested in this manner. Now let's look into moving our tests and scripts into separate directories.

Separating Code into src and tests Directories

Suppose we have a bunch of scripts and a bunch of tests for those scripts, and our directory is getting a bit cluttered. So we decide to move the scripts into a src directory and the tests into a tests directory, like this:

```
script_src
├── src
│   └── hello.py
├── tests
│   └── test_hello.py
└── pytest.ini
```

Without any other changes, pytest will blow up:

```
$ cd /path/to/code/ch12/script_src
$ pytest --tb=short -c pytest_bad.ini
========================= test session starts =========================
collected 0 items / 1 error

=============================== ERRORS ================================
_____ ERROR collecting tests/test_hello.py _____
ImportError while importing test module
  '/path/to/code/ch12/script_src/tests/test_hello.py'.
...
tests/test_hello.py:1: in <module>
    import hello
E   ModuleNotFoundError: No module named 'hello'
======================= short test summary info =======================
ERROR tests/test_hello.py
!!!!!!!!!!!!!!!!! Interrupted: 1 error during collection !!!!!!!!!!!!!!!!!
========================== 1 error in 0.08s ===========================
```

Our tests—and pytest—don't know to look in src for hello. All import statements, either in our source code or in our test code, use the standard Python import process; therefore, they look in directories that are found in the Python module search path. Python keeps this search path list in the sys.path variable,[2] then pytest modifies this list a bit to add the directories of the tests it's going to run.

What we need to do is add the directories for the source code we want to import into sys.path. pytest has an option to help us with that, pythonpath. The option was introduced for pytest 7. If you need to use pytest 6.2, you can use the pytest-srcpaths plugin,[3] to add this option to pytest 6.2.x.

---

2. https://docs.python.org/3/library/sys.html#sys.path
3. https://pypi.org/project/pytest-srcpaths

First we need to modify our pytest.ini to set pythonpath to src:

ch12/script_src/pytest.ini
```
[pytest]
addopts = -ra
testpaths = tests
➤ pythonpath = src
```

Now pytest runs just fine:

```
$ pytest tests/test_hello.py
========================= test session starts =========================
collected 2 items

tests/test_hello.py ..                                           [100%]

========================= 2 passed in 0.01s =========================
```

That's great that it works. But when you first encounter sys.path, it can seem mysterious. Let's take a closer look.

Defining the Python Search Path

The Python search path is simply a list of directories Python stores in the sys.path variable. During any import statement, Python looks through the list for modules or packages matching the requested import. We can use a small test to see what sys.path looks like during a test run:

ch12/script_src/tests/test_sys_path.py
```python
import sys

def test_sys_path():
    print("sys.path: ")
    for p in sys.path:
        print(p)
```

When we run it, notice the search path:

```
$ pytest -s tests/test_sys_path.py
========================= test session starts =========================
collected 1 item

tests/test_sys_path.py sys.path:
/path/to/code/ch12/script_src/tests
/path/to/code/ch12/script_src/src
...
/path/to/code/ch12/venv/lib/python3.10/site-packages
.

========================= 1 passed in 0.00s =========================
```

The last path, site-packages, makes sense. That's where packages installed via pip go. The script_src/tests path is where our test is located. The tests directory is added by pytest so that pytest can import our test module. We can utilize this addition by placing any test helper modules in the same directory as the tests using it. The script_src/src path is the path added by the pythonpath=src setting. The path is relative to the directory that contains our pytest.ini file.

Testing requirements.txt-Based Applications

A script or application may have *dependencies*—other projects that need to be installed before the script or application can run. A packaged project like Cards has a list of dependencies defined in either a pyproject.toml, setup.py, or setup.cfg file. Cards uses pyproject.toml. However, many projects don't use packaging, and instead define dependencies in a requirements.txt file.

The dependency list in a requirements.txt file could be just a list of loose dependencies, like:

ch12/sample_requirements.txt
```
typer
requests
```

However, it's more common for applications to "pin" dependencies by defining specific versions that are known to work:

ch12/sample_pinned_requirements.txt
```
typer==0.3.2
requests==2.26.0
```

The requirements.txt files are used to recreate a running environment with pip install -r. The -r tells pip to read and install everything in the requirements.txt file.

A reasonable process would then be:

- Get the code somehow. For example, git clone <repository of project>.
- Create a virtual environment with python3 -m venv venv.
- Activate the virtual environment.
- Install the dependencies with pip install -r requirements.txt.
- Run the application.

For so many projects, packaging makes way more sense. However, this process is common for web frameworks like Django[4] and projects using higher-level packaging, such as Docker.[5] In those cases and others, requirements.txt files are common and work fine.

---

4.   https://www.djangoproject.com
5.   https://www.docker.com

Let's add a dependency to hello.py to see this situation in action. We'll use Typer[6] to help us add a command-line argument to say hello to a certain name. First we'll add typer to a requirements.txt file:

ch12/app/requirements.txt
```
typer==0.3.2
```

Notice that I also pinned the version to Typer 0.3.2. Now we can install our new dependency with either:

```
$ pip install typer==0.3.2
```

or

```
$ pip install -r requirements.txt
```

A code change is in order as well:

ch12/app/src/hello.py
```
import typer
from typing import Optional

def full_output(name: str):
    return f"Hello, {name}!"

app = typer.Typer()

@app.command()
def main(name: Optional[str] = typer.Argument("World")):
    print(full_output(name))

if __name__ == "__main__":
    app()
```

Typer uses type hints[7] to specify the type of options and arguments passed to a CLI application, including optional arguments. In the previous code we are telling Python and Typer that our application takes name as an argument, to treat it as a string, that it's optional, and to use "World" if no name is passed in.

Just for sanity's sake, let's try it out:

```
$ cd /path/to/code/ch12/app/src
$ python hello.py
Hello, World!
$ python hello.py Brian
Hello, Brian!
```

---

6. https://typer.tiangolo.com
7. https://docs.python.org/3/library/typing.html

Cool. Now we need to modify the tests to make sure hello.py works with and without a name:

ch12/app/tests/test_hello.py

```python
import hello
from typer.testing import CliRunner

def test_full_output():
    assert hello.full_output("Foo") == "Hello, Foo!"

runner = CliRunner()

def test_hello_app_no_name():
    result = runner.invoke(hello.app)
    assert result.stdout == "Hello, World!\n"

def test_hello_app_with_name():
    result = runner.invoke(hello.app, ["Brian"])
    assert result.stdout == "Hello, Brian!\n"
```

Instead of calling main() directly, we're using Typer's built in CliRunner() to test the app.

Let's run it first with pytest and then with tox:

```
$ cd /path/to/code/ch12/app
$ pytest -v
========================= test session starts =========================
collected 3 items

tests/test_hello.py::test_full_output PASSED                    [ 33%]
tests/test_hello.py::test_hello_app_no_name PASSED              [ 66%]
tests/test_hello.py::test_hello_app_with_name PASSED            [100%]

========================= 3 passed in 0.02s =========================
```

Great. Works with pytest. Now on to tox. Because we have dependencies, we need to make sure they are installed in the tox environments. We do that by adding -rrequirements.txt to the deps setting:

ch12/app/tox.ini

```ini
[tox]
envlist = py39, py310
skipsdist = true

[testenv]
deps = pytest
       pytest-srcpaths
       -rrequirements.txt
commands = pytest

[pytest]
addopts = -ra
```

```
testpaths = tests
pythonpath = src
```

That was easy. Let's try it out:

```
$ tox
py39 installed: ..., pytest==x.y,typer==x.y.z
...
========================= test session starts =========================
...
collected 3 items

tests/test_hello.py ...                                          [100%]

========================= 3 passed in 0.03s =========================
py310 ..., pytest==x.y,typer==x.y.z
...
========================= test session starts =========================
...
collected 3 items

tests/test_hello.py ...                                          [100%]

========================= 3 passed in 0.02s =========================
_____ summary _____
  py39: commands succeeded
  py310: commands succeeded
  congratulations :)
```

Yay! We have an application with an external dependency listed in a require-
ments.txt file. We are using pythonpath to specify the source code location. We
added -rrequirements.txt to tox.ini to get those dependencies installed in the tox
environments. And our tests run with pytest and with tox. Woohoo!

Review

In this chapter, we looked at how to use pytest and tox to test scripts and
applications. In the context of this chapter, *script* refers to a Python file that
is run directly, as in python my_script.py, and *application* refers to a Python script
or larger application that requires dependencies to be installed with require-
ments.txt.

In addition, you learned several techniques for testing scripts and applications:

- Using subprocess.run() and pipes to run a script and read the output
- Refactoring a script code into functions, including main()
- Calling main() from a if _name_ == "_main_" block
- Using capsys to capture output
- Using pythonpath to move tests into tests and source code into src
- Specifying requirements.txt in tox.ini for applications with dependencies

Exercises

Testing scripts can be quite fun. Running through the process on a second script will help you remember the techniques in this chapter.

The exercises start with an example script, sums.py, that adds up numbers in a separate file, data.txt.

Here's sums.py:

exercises/ch12/sums.py
```
# sums.py
# add the numbers in `data.txt`

sum = 0.0

with open("data.txt", "r") as file:
    for line in file:
        number = float(line)
        sum += number

print(f"{sum:.2f}")
```

And here's an example data file:

exercises/ch12/data.txt
```
123.45
 76.55
```

If we run it, we should get 200.00:

```
$ cd /path/to/code/exercises/ch12
$ python sums.py data.txt
200.00
```

Assuming valid numbers in data.txt, we need to test this script.

1. Write a test using subprocess.run() to test sums.py with data.txt.

2. Modify sums.py so it can be imported by a test module.

3. Write a new test that imports sums and tests it using capsys.

4. Set up tox to run your tests on at least one version of Python.

5. (*Bonus*) Move the tests and source into tests and src. Make necessary changes to get the tests to pass.

6. (*Bonus*) Modify the script to pass in a file name.

   - Run the code as python sums.py data.txt.
   - You should be able to use it on multiple files.
   - What different test cases would you add?

What's Next

A big part of writing and running tests that we haven't discussed much yet in this book is what to do when the tests fail. When one or more test fails, we need to figure out why. It's either a problem with the test, or a problem with the code we are testing. Either way, the process to figure it out is called *debugging*. In the next chapter, we'll look at the many flags and features that pytest has to help you with debugging.

## CHAPTER 13

Debugging Test Failures

Test failures happen. If they didn't, tests wouldn't be much use. What we do when tests fail is what counts. When tests fail, we need to figure out why. It might be the test or it might be the application. The process of determining where the problem lies and what to do about it is similar.

Integrated development environments (IDEs) and many text editors have graphical debuggers built right in. These tools are incredibly helpful for debugging, allowing us to add breakpoints, step through code, look at variable values, and much more. However, pytest also provides many tools that may help you solve the problem faster, without having to reach for a debugger. There are also times when IDEs may be difficult to use, such as while debugging code on a remote system or when debugging one tox environment. Python includes a builtin source code debugger called pdb, as well as several flags to make debugging with pdb quick and easy.

In this chapter, we're going to debug some failing code with the help of pytest flags and pdb. You may spot the bugs right away. Wonderful. We're just using the bug as an excuse to look at debugging flags and the pytest plus pdb integration.

We need a failing test to debug. For that, we'll go back to the Cards project—this time in developer mode—to add a feature and some tests.

Adding a New Feature to the Cards Project

Let's say we've been using Cards for a while and we now have some finished tasks:

```
$ cards list
```

```
 ID    state    owner    summary
 ─────────────────────────────────────────
 1     done              some task
 2     todo              another
 3     done              a third
```

We'd like to list all of the completed tasks at the end of the week. We can do this with cards list already, because it has some filter features:

```
$ cards list --help
Usage: cards list [OPTIONS]

  List cards in db.

Options:
  -o, --owner TEXT
  -s, --state TEXT
  --help              Show this message and exit.
```

```
$ cards list --state done
```

```
 ID    state    owner    summary
 ─────────────────────────────────────────
 1     done              some task
 3     done              a third
```

That works. But let's add a cards done command to do this filter for us. For that, we need a CLI command:

ch13/cards_proj/src/cards/cli.py

```python
@app.command("done")
def list_done_cards():
    """
    List 'done' cards in db.
    """
    with cards_db() as db:
        the_cards = db.list_done_cards()
        print_cards_list(the_cards)
```

This command calls an API method, list_done_cards(), and prints the results. The list_done_cards() API method really just needs to call list_cards() with a pre-filled state="done":

ch13/cards_proj/src/cards/api.py

```python
def list_done_cards(self):
    """Return the 'done' cards."""
    done_cards = self.list_cards(state="done")
```

Now let's add some tests for the API and CLI.

First, the API test:

ch13/cards_proj/tests/api/test_list_done.py

```python
import pytest

@pytest.mark.num_cards(10)
def test_list_done(cards_db):
    cards_db.finish(3)
    cards_db.finish(5)

    the_list = cards_db.list_done_cards()

    assert len(the_list) == 2
    for card in the_list:
        assert card.id in (3, 5)
        assert card.state == "done"
```

Here we set up a list of 10 cards and marked two as finished. The result of list_done_cards() should be a list of two cards with the correct index and with state set to "done". The @pytest.mark.num_cards(10) lets Faker generate the contents of the cards.

Now let's add the CLI test:

ch13/cards_proj/tests/cli/test_done.py

```python
import cards

expected = """\
  ID   state   owner   summary

   1   done            some task
   3   done            a third"""


def test_done(cards_db, cards_cli):
    cards_db.add_card(cards.Card("some task", state="done"))
    cards_db.add_card(cards.Card("another"))
    cards_db.add_card(cards.Card("a third", state="done"))
    output = cards_cli("done")
    assert output == expected
```

For the CLI test, we can't use the Faker data, as we have to know exactly what the outcome is going to be. Instead, we just fill in a few cards and set state to "done" for a couple of them.

If we try to run these tests in the same virtual environment in which we were testing Cards before, they won't work. We need to install the new version of Cards. Because we are editing the Cards source code, we'll need to install it in editable mode. We'll go ahead and install cards_proj in a new virtual environment.

Installing Cards in Editable Mode

When developing both source and test code, it's super handy to be able to modify the source code and immediately run the tests, without having to rebuild the package and reinstall it in our virtual environment. Installing the source code in editable mode is just the thing we need to accomplish this, and it's a feature built in to both pip and Flit.

Let's spin up a new virtual environment:

```
$ cd /path/to/code/ch13
$ python3 -m venv venv
$ source venv/bin/activate
(venv) $ pip install -U pip
...
Successfully installed pip-21.3.x
```

Now in our fresh virtual environment, we need to install the ./cards_proj directory as a local editable package. For this to work, we need pip version 21.3.1 or above, so be sure to upgrade pip if it's below 21.3.

Installing an editable package is as easy as pip install -e ./package_dir_name. If we run pip install -e ./cards_proj we will have cards installed in editable mode. However, we also want to install all the necessary development tools like pytest, tox, etc.

We can install cards in editable mode and install all of our test tools all at once using optional dependencies.

```
$ pip install -e "./cards_proj/[test]"
```

This works because all of these dependencies have been defined in pyproject.toml, in a optional-dependencies section:

ch13/cards_proj/pyproject.toml
```
[project.optional-dependencies]
test = [
    "pytest",
    "faker",
    "tox",
    "coverage",
    "pytest-cov",
]
```

Now let's run the tests. We are using --tb=no to turn off tracebacks:

```
$ cd /path/to/code/ch13/cards_proj
$ pytest --tb=no
```

```
========================= test session starts =========================
collected 55 items

tests/api/test_add.py .....                                    [  9%]
...
tests/api/test_list_done.py .F                                 [ 49%]
...
tests/cli/test_done.py .F                                      [ 80%]
...
tests/cli/test_version.py .                                    [100%]

======================= short test summary info =======================
FAILED tests/api/test_list_done.py::test_list_done - TypeError: objec...
FAILED tests/cli/test_done.py::test_done - AssertionError: assert '' ...
===================== 2 failed, 53 passed in 0.33s ====================
```

Awesome. There are a couple failures, which is just what we wanted. Now we can look at debugging.

Debugging with pytest Flags

pytest includes quite a few command-line flags that are useful for debugging. We will be using some of these to debug our test failures.

Flags for selecting which tests to run, in which order, and when to stop:

- *-lf / --last-failed*: Runs just the tests that failed last

- *-ff / --failed-first*: Runs all the tests, starting with the last failed

- *-x / --exitfirst*: Stops the tests session after the first failure

- *--maxfail=num*: Stops the tests after num failures

- *-nf / --new-first*: Runs all the tests, ordered by file modification time

- *--sw / --stepwise*: Stops the tests at the first failure. Starts the tests at the last failure next time

- *--sw-skip / --stepwise-skip*: Same as --sw, but skips the first failure

Flags to control pytest output:

- *-v / --verbose*: Displays all the test names, passing or failing
- *--tb=[auto/long/short/line/native/no]*: Controls the traceback style
- *-l / --showlocals*: Displays local variables alongside the stacktrace

Flags to start a command-line debugger:

- *--pdb*: Starts an interactive debugging session at the point of failure

- *--trace*: Starts the pdb source-code debugger immediately when running each test

- *--pdbcls*: Uses alternatives to pdb, such as IPython's debugger with --pdb-cls=IPython.terminal.debugger:TerminalPdb

For all of these descriptions, "failure" refers to a failed assertion or any other uncaught exception found in our source code or test code, including fixtures.

Re-Running Failed Tests

Let's start our debugging by making sure the tests fail when we run them again. We'll use --lf to re-run the failures only, and --tb=no to hide the traceback, because we're not ready for it yet:

```
$ pytest --lf --tb=no
========================= test session starts =========================
collected 27 items / 25 deselected / 2 selected
run-last-failure: re-run previous 2 failures (skipped 13 files)

tests/api/test_list_done.py F                                  [ 50%]
tests/cli/test_done.py F                                       [100%]

======================= short test summary info =======================
FAILED tests/api/test_list_done.py::test_list_done - TypeError: objec...
FAILED tests/cli/test_done.py::test_done - AssertionError: assert '' ...
=================== 2 failed, 25 deselected in 0.10s ===================
```

Great. We know we can reproduce the failure. We'll start with debugging the first failure.

Let's run just the first failing test, stop after the failure, and look at the traceback:

```
$ pytest --lf -x
========================= test session starts =========================
collected 27 items / 25 deselected / 2 selected
run-last-failure: re-run previous 2 failures (skipped 13 files)

tests/api/test_list_done.py F

============================== FAILURES ==============================
_____ test_list_done _____

cards_db = <cards.api.CardsDB object at 0x7fabab5288b0>

    @pytest.mark.num_cards(10)
    def test_list_done(cards_db):
        cards_db.finish(3)
        cards_db.finish(5)

        the_list = cards_db.list_done_cards()
```

```
>       assert len(the_list) == 2
E       TypeError: object of type 'NoneType' has no len()

tests/api/test_list_done.py:10: TypeError
======================= short test summary info ========================
FAILED tests/api/test_list_done.py::test_list_done - TypeError: objec...
!!!!!!!!!!!!!!!!!!!!!!!! stopping after 1 failures !!!!!!!!!!!!!!!!!!!!!!!!
==================== 1 failed, 25 deselected in 0.18s ====================
```

The error, TypeError: object of type 'NoneType' has no len() is telling us that the_list is None. That's not good. We expect it to be a list of Card objects. Even if there are no "done" cards, it should be an empty list and not None. Actually, that's probably a good test to add, checking that everything works properly with no "done" cards. Focusing on the problem at hand, let's get back to debugging.

Just to be sure we understand the problem, we can run the same test over again with -l/--showlocals. We don't need the full traceback again, so we can shorten it with --tb=short:

```
$ pytest --lf -x -l --tb=short
========================= test session starts =========================
collected 27 items / 25 deselected / 2 selected
run-last-failure: re-run previous 2 failures (skipped 13 files)

tests/api/test_list_done.py F

============================== FAILURES ===============================
_____ test_list_done _____
tests/api/test_list_done.py:10: in test_list_done
    assert len(the_list) == 2
E   TypeError: object of type 'NoneType' has no len()
        cards_db  = <cards.api.CardsDB object at 0x7f884a4e8850>
        the_list  = None
======================= short test summary info ========================
FAILED tests/api/test_list_done.py::test_list_done - TypeError: objec...
!!!!!!!!!!!!!!!!!!!!!!!! stopping after 1 failures !!!!!!!!!!!!!!!!!!!!!!!!
==================== 1 failed, 25 deselected in 0.18s ====================
```

Yep. the_list = None. The -l/--showlocals is often extremely helpful and sometimes good enough to debug a test failure completely. What's more, the existence of -l/--showlocals has trained me to use lots of intermediate variables in tests. They come in handy when a test fails.

Now we know that in this circumstance, list_done_cards() is returning None. But we don't know why. We'll use pdb to debug inside list_done_cards() during the test.

Debugging with pdb

pdb,[1] which stands for "Python debugger," is part of the Python standard library, so we don't need to install anything to use it. We'll get pdb up and running and then look at some of the most useful commands within pdb.

You can launch pdb from pytest in a few different ways:

- Add a breakpoint() call to either test code or application code. When a pytest run hits a breakpoint() function call, it will stop there and launch pdb.

- Use the --pdb flag. With --pdb, pytest will stop at the point of failure. In our case, that will be at the assert len(the_list) == 2 line.

- Use the --trace flag. With --trace, pytest will stop at the beginning of each test.

For our purposes, combining --lf and --trace will work perfectly. The combo will tell pytest to re-run the failed tests and stop at the beginning of test_list_done(), before the call to list_done_cards():

```
$ pytest --lf --trace
========================= test session starts =========================
collected 27 items / 25 deselected / 2 selected
run-last-failure: re-run previous 2 failures (skipped 13 files)

tests/api/test_list_done.py
>>>>>>>>>>>>>>>> PDB runcall (IO-capturing turned off) >>>>>>>>>>>>>>>>
> /path/to/code/ch13/cards_proj/tests/api/test_list_done.py(5)test_list_done()
-> cards_db.finish(3)
(Pdb)
```

Following are the common commands recognized by pdb. The full list is in the pdb documentation.[2]

Meta commands:

- *h(elp)*: Prints a list of commands
- *h(elp) command*: Prints help on a command
- *q(uit)*: Exits pdb

Seeing where you are:

- *l(ist)* : Lists 11 lines around the current line. Using it again lists the next 11 lines, and so on.

---

1.   https://docs.python.org/3/library/pdb.html
2.   https://docs.python.org/3/library/pdb.html#debugger-commands

- *l(ist) .*: The same as above, but with a dot. Lists 11 lines around the current line. Handy if you've use l(list) a few times and have lost your current position

- *l(ist) first, last*: Lists a specific set of lines

- *ll* : Lists all source code for the current function

- *w(here)*: Prints the stack trace

Looking at values:

- *p(rint) expr*: Evaluates expr and prints the value

- *pp expr*: Same as p(rint) expr but uses pretty-print from the pprint module. Great for structures

- *a(rgs)*: Prints the argument list of the current function

Execution commands:

- *s(tep)*: Executes the current line and steps to the next line in your source code even if it's inside a function

- *n(ext)*: Executes the current line and steps to the next line in the current function

- *r(eturn)*: Continues until the current function returns

- *c(ontinue)*: Continues until the next breakpoint. When used with --trace, continues until the start of the next test

- *unt(il) lineno*: Continues until the given line number

Continuing on with debugging our tests, we'll use ll to list the current function:

```
(Pdb) ll
  3      @pytest.mark.num_cards(10)
  4      def test_list_done(cards_db):
  5  ->      cards_db.finish(3)
  6          cards_db.finish(5)
  7
  8          the_list = cards_db.list_done_cards()
  9
 10          assert len(the_list) == 2
 11          for card in the_list:
 12              assert card.id in (3, 5)
 13              assert card.state == "done"
```

The -> shows us the current line, before it's been run.

We can use until 8 to break right before we call list_done_cards(), like this:

```
(Pdb) until 8
> /path/to/code/ch13/cards_proj/tests/api/test_list_done.py(8)test_list_done()
-> the_list = cards_db.list_done_cards()
```

And step to get us into the function:

```
(Pdb) step
--Call--
> /path/to/code/ch13/cards_proj/src/cards/api.py(82)list_done_cards()
-> def list_done_cards(self):
```

Let's use ll again to see the whole function:

```
(Pdb) ll
 82  ->      def list_done_cards(self):
 83                  """Return the 'done' cards."""
 84                  done_cards = self.list_cards(state='done')
```

Now let's continue until just before this function returns:

```
(Pdb) return
--Return--
> /path/to/code/ch13/cards_proj/src/cards/api.py(84)list_done_cards()->None
-> done_cards = self.list_cards(state='done')
(Pdb) ll
 82           def list_done_cards(self):
 83                  """Return the 'done' cards."""
 84  ->              done_cards = self.list_cards(state='done')
```

We can look at the value of done_cards with either p or pp:

```
(Pdb) pp done_cards
[Card(summary='Line for PM identify decade.',
      owner='Russell', state='done', id=3),
 Card(summary='Director season industry the describe.',
      owner='Cody', state='done', id=5)]
```

This looks fine, but I think I see the problem. If we continue out to the calling test and check the return value, we can make doubly sure:

```
(Pdb) step
> /path/to/code/ch13/cards_proj/tests/api/test_list_done.py(10)test_list_done()
-> assert len(the_list) == 2
(Pdb) ll
  3       @pytest.mark.num_cards(10)
  4       def test_list_done(cards_db):
  5           cards_db.finish(3)
  6           cards_db.finish(5)
  7
  8           the_list = cards_db.list_done_cards()
```

```
 9
10   ->      assert len(the_list) == 2
11           for card in the_list:
12               assert card.id in (3, 5)
13               assert card.state == "done"
(Pdb) pp the_list
None
```

Pretty clear now. We had the correct list in the done_cards variable within list_done_cards(). However, that value isn't returned. Because the default return value in Python is None if there isn't a return statement, that's the value that gets assigned to the_list in test_list_done().

If we stop the debugger, add a return done_cards to list_done_cards(), and re-run the failed test, we can see if that fixes it:

```
(Pdb) exit
!!!!!!!!!!!!!!! _pytest.outcomes.Exit: Quitting debugger !!!!!!!!!!!!!!!
=================== 25 deselected in 521.22s (0:08:41) ==================
$ pytest --lf -x -v --tb=no
========================= test session starts ==========================
collected 27 items / 25 deselected / 2 selected
run-last-failure: re-run previous 2 failures (skipped 13 files)

tests/api/test_list_done.py::test_list_done PASSED              [ 50%]
tests/cli/test_done.py::test_done FAILED                        [100%]

======================= short test summary info ========================
FAILED tests/cli/test_done.py::test_done - AssertionError: assert '  ...
!!!!!!!!!!!!!!!!!!!!!!!!! stopping after 1 failures !!!!!!!!!!!!!!!!!!!!!!!!!
=============== 1 failed, 1 passed, 25 deselected in 0.10s ==============
```

Wonderful. We fixed one bug. One more to go.

Combining pdb and tox

To debug the next test failure, we're going to combine tox and pdb. For this to work, we have to make sure we can pass arguments through tox to pytest. This is done with tox's {posargs} feature, which was discussed in Passing pytest Parameters Through tox, on page 158.

We've already got that set up in our tox.ini for Cards:

ch13/cards_proj/tox.ini
```
[tox]
envlist = py39, py310
isolated_build = True
skip_missing_interpreters = True

[testenv]
deps =
```

```
    pytest
    faker
    pytest-cov
➤ commands = pytest --cov=cards --cov=tests --cov-fail-under=100 {posargs}
```

We'd like to run the Python 3.10 environment, and start the debugger at the test failure. We could run it once with -e py310, then use -e py310 -- --lf --trace to stop at the entry point of the first failing test.

Instead, let's just run it once and stop at the failure point with -e py310 -- --pdb --no-cov. (--no-cov is used to turn off the coverage report.)

```
$ tox -e py310 -- --pdb --no-cov
...
py310 run-test: commands[0] | pytest --cov=cards --cov=tests
--cov-fail-under=100 --pdb --no-cov
========================= test session starts =========================
...
collected 53 items

tests/api/test_add.py .....                                    [  9%]
tests/api/test_config.py .                                     [ 11%]
...
tests/cli/test_delete.py .                                     [ 77%]
tests/cli/test_done.py F
>>>>>>>>>>>>>>>>>>>>>>>>>>>>>> traceback >>>>>>>>>>>>>>>>>>>>>>>>>>>>>>>

...
>          assert output == expected
...
tests/cli/test_done.py:15: AssertionError
>>>>>>>>>>>>>>>>>>>>>>>>>>>>>> entering PDB >>>>>>>>>>>>>>>>>>>>>>>>>>>>>

>>>>>>>>>>>>>>> PDB post_mortem (IO-capturing turned off) >>>>>>>>>>>>>>>
> /path/to/code/ch13/cards_proj/tests/cli/test_done.py(15)test_done()
-> assert output == expected
(Pdb) ll
 10     def test_done(cards_db, cards_cli):
 11         cards_db.add_card(cards.Card("some task", state="done"))
 12         cards_db.add_card(cards.Card("another"))
 13         cards_db.add_card(cards.Card("a third", state="done"))
 14         output = cards_cli("done")
 15  ->     assert output == expected
```

That drops us into pdb, right at the assertion that failed.

We can use pp to look at the output and expected variables:

```
(Pdb) pp output
➤ ('                                      \n'
   ' ID    state   owner   summary      \n'
   ' ──────────────────────────────────  \n'
   ' 1     done            some task  \n'
```

```
 '  3    done            a third')
(Pdb) pp expected
('\n'
 '  ID    state    owner    summary      \n'
 ' _____ \n'
 '  1    done             some task  \n'
 '  3    done             a third')
```

Now we can see the problem. The expected output starts with a line containing a single new line character, '\n'. The actual output contains a bunch of spaces before the new line. This problem would be difficult to spot with the traceback only, or even in an IDE. With pdb, it's not too hard to spot.

We can add those spaces to the test and re-run the tox environment with that one test failure:

```
$ tox -e py310 -- --lf --tb=no --no-cov -v
...
py310 run-test: commands[0] | pytest --cov=cards --cov=tests
  --cov-fail-under=100 --lf --tb=no --no-cov -v
========================= test session starts ==========================
...

tests/cli/test_done.py::test_done PASSED                        [100%]

==================== 1 passed, 41 deselected in 0.11s ====================
_____ summary _____
  py310: commands succeeded
  congratulations :)
```

And just for good measure, re-run the whole thing:

```
$ tox
...
Required test coverage of 100% reached. Total coverage: 100.00%

========================= 53 passed in 0.53s =========================
_____ summary _____
  py310: commands succeeded
  py310: commands succeeded
  congratulations :)
```

Woohoo! Defects fixed.

Review

We covered a lot of techniques for debugging Python packages with command-line flags, pdb, and tox:

- We installed an editable version of Cards with pip install -e ./cards_proj.

- We used many pytest flags for debugging. There's list of useful flags at Debugging with pytest Flags, on page 183.

- We used pdb to debug the tests. A subset of pdb commands is at Debugging with pdb, on page 186.

- We combined tox, pytest, and pdb to debug a failing test within a tox environment.

Exercises

The code files included in the code download for this chapter don't have the fixes. They just have the broken code. Even if you plan to do most of your debugging with an IDE, I encourage you to try the debugging techniques in this chapter to help you understand how to use the flags and pdb commands.

1. Create a new virtual environment and install Cards in editable mode.

2. Run pytest and make sure you see the same failures listed in the chapter.

3. Use --lf and --lf -x to see how they work.

4. Try --stepwise and --stepwise-skip. Run them both a few times. How are they different than --lf and --lf -x?

5. Use --pdb to open pdb at a test failure.

6. Use --lf --trace to open pdb at the start of the first failing test.

7. Fix both bugs and verify with a clean test run.

8. Add breakpoint() somewhere in the source code or test code and run pytest with neither --pdb or --trace.

9. (*Bonus*) Break something again and try IPython for debugging. (IPython[3] is part of the Jupyter[4] project. Please see their respective documentation for more information.)

   - Install IPython with pip install ipython.

   - You can run it with:

     – pytest --lf --trace --pdbcls=IPython.terminal.debugger:TerminalPdb
     – pytest --pdb --pdbcls=IPython.terminal.debugger:TerminalPdb
     – Put breakpoint() somewhere in the code and run pytest --pdbcls=IPython.terminal.debugger:TerminalPdb

---

3.   https://ipython.readthedocs.io/en/stable/index.html
4.   https://jupyter.org

What's Next

The next part of the book is intended to help you become more efficient with writing and running tests. Lots of common testing problems have been solved by someone else already and packaged as pytest plugins. We'll look at quite a few third-party plugins in the next chapter. After third-party plugins, we'll build our own plugin in Chapter 15, Building Plugins, on page 205. And then to finish up the book we'll revisit parametrization and look at some advanced techniques in Chapter 16, Advanced Parametrization, on page 221.

Part III

Booster Rockets

## CHAPTER 14

Third-Party Plugins

As powerful as pytest is right out of the box, it gets even better when we add plugins to the mix. The pytest code base is designed to allow customization and extensions, and there are hooks available to allow modifications and improvements through plugins.

It might surprise you to know that you've already written some plugins if you've worked through the previous chapters in this book. Any time you put fixtures and/or hook functions into a project's conftest.py file, you create a local plugin. It's just a little bit of extra work to convert these conftest.py files into installable plugins that you can share between projects, with other people, or with the world.

We'll start this chapter by looking at where to find third-party plugins. Quite a few plugins are available, so there's a decent chance someone has already written the change you want to make to pytest. We'll take a look at a handful of plugins that are broadly useful to many software projects. Finally, we'll explore the variety available by taking a quick tour of many types of plugins.

Finding Plugins

You can find third-party pytest plugins in several places.

https://docs.pytest.org/en/latest/reference/plugin_list.html
> The main pytest documentation site includes an alphabetized list of plugins pulled from pypi.org. It's a big list.

https://pypi.org
> The Python Package Index (PyPI) is a great place to get lots of Python packages, but it is also a great place to find pytest plugins. When looking for pytest plugins, it should work pretty well to search for pytest, pytest- or -pytest, as most pytest plugins either start with pytest- or end in -pytest. You

can also filter by classifier "Framework::Pytest", which will include packages that include a pytest plugin but aren't named pytest- or -pytest, such as Hypothesis and Faker.

https://github.com/pytest-dev

The pytest-dev group on GitHub is where the pytest source code is kept. It's also where you can find many popular pytest plugins. For plugins, the pytest-dev group is intended as a central location for popular pytest plugins and to share some of the maintenance responsibility. Refer to "Submitting Plugins to pytest-dev" on the docs.pytest.org website[1] for more information.

https://docs.pytest.org/en/latest/how-to/plugins.html

The main pytest documentation site has a page that talks about installing and using pytest plugins, and lists a few common plugins.

Let's look at the various ways you can install plugins with pip install.

Installing Plugins

pytest plugins are installed with pip, just like the other Python packages you've already installed in the earlier chapters in this book.

For example:

```
$ pip install pytest-cov
```

This installs the latest stable version from PyPI. However, pip is quite powerful and can install packages from other places like local directories and Git repositories. See Appendix 2, pip, on page 237 for more information.

Exploring the Diversity of pytest Plugins

The Plugin List from the main pytest documentation site[2] lists almost 1000 plugins last time I checked. That's a lot of plugins. Let's take a look at a small subset of plugins that are both useful to lots of people and show the diversity of what we can do with plugins.

All of the following plugins are available via PyPI.

---

1.   https://docs.pytest.org/en/latest/contributing.html#submitting-plugins-to-pytest-dev
2.   https://docs.pytest.org/en/latest/reference/plugin_list.html

Plugins That Change the Normal Test Run Flow

pytest, by default, runs our tests in a predictable flow. Given a single directory of test files, pytest will run each file in alphabetical order. Within each file, each test is run in the order it appears in the file.

Sometimes it's nice to change that order. The following plugins in some way change the normal test run flow:

- pytest-order—Allows us to specify the order using a marker
- pytest-randomly—Randomizes the order, first by file, then by class, then by test
- pytest-repeat—Makes it easy to repeat a single test, or multiple tests, a specific number of times
- pytest-rerunfailures—Re-runs failed tests. Helpful for flaky tests
- pytest-xdist—Runs tests in parallel, either using multiple CPUs on one machine, or multiple remote machines

Plugins That Alter or Enhance Output

The normal pytest output shows mostly dots for passing tests, and characters for other output. Then you'll see lists of test names with outcome if you pass in -v. However, there are plugins that change the output.

- pytest-instafail—Adds an --instafail flag that reports tracebacks and output from failed tests right after the failure. Normally, pytest reports tracebacks and output from failed tests after all tests have completed.
- pytest-sugar—Shows green checkmarks instead of dots for passing tests and has a nice progress bar. It also shows failures instantly, like pytest-instafail.
- pytest-html—Allows for html report generation. Reports can be extended with extra data and images, such as screenshots of failure cases.

Plugins for Web Development

pytest is used extensively for testing web projects, so it's no surprise there's a long list of plugins to help with web testing.

- pytest-selenium—Provides fixtures to allow for easy configuration of browser-based tests. Selenium is a popular tool for browser testing.

- pytest-splinter—Built on top of Selenium as a higher level interface, this allows Splinter to be used more easily from pytest.

- pytest-django and pytest-flask—Help make testing Django and Flask applications easier with pytest. Django and Flask are two of the most popular web frameworks for Python.

Plugins for Fake Data

We used Faker in Combining Markers with Fixtures, on page 88 to generate card summary and owner data. There are many cases in different domains where it's helpful to have generated fake data. Not surprisingly, there are several plugins to fill that need.

- Faker—Generates fake data for you. Provides faker fixture for use with pytest

- model-bakery—Generates Django model objects with fake data.

- pytest-factoryboy—Includes fixtures for Factory Boy, a database model data generator

- pytest-mimesis—Generates fake data similar to Faker, but Mimesis is quite a bit faster

Plugins That Extend pytest Functionality

All plugins extend pytest functionality, but I was running out of good category names. This is a grab bag of various cool plugins.

- pytest-cov—Runs coverage while testing

- pytest-benchmark—Runs benchmark timing on code within tests

- pytest-timeout—Doesn't let tests run too long

- pytest-asyncio—Tests async functions

- pytest-bdd—Writes behavior-driven development (BDD)–style tests with pytest

- pytest-freezegun—Freezes time so that any code that reads the time will get the same value during a test. You can also set a particular date or time.

- pytest-mock—A thin-wrapper around the unittest.mock patching API

While many may find the plugins listed in this section helpful, two plugins in particular find near universal approval in helping to speed up testing and finding accidental dependencies between tests: pytest-xdist and pytest-randomly. Let's take a closer look at those next.

Running Tests in Parallel

Usually all tests run sequentially. And that's just what you want if your tests hit a resource that can only be accessed by one client at a time. However, if your tests do not need to access a shared resource, you could speed up test sessions by running multiple tests in parallel. The pytest-xdist plugin allows you to do that. You can specify multiple processors and run many tests in parallel. You can even push off tests onto other machines and use more than one computer.

For example, let's look at the following simple test:

ch14/test_parallel.py
```
import time


def test_something():
    time.sleep(1)
```

Running it takes about one second:

```
$ cd /path/to/code/ch14
$ pytest test_parallel.py
========================= test session starts =========================
collected 1 item

test_parallel.py .                                            [100%]

========================= 1 passed in 1.01s =========================
```

If we use pytest-repeat to run it 10 times with --count=10, it should take about 10 seconds:

```
$ pip install pytest-repeat
$ pytest --count=10 test_parallel.py
========================= test session starts =========================
collected 10 items

test_parallel.py ..........                                   [100%]

========================= 10 passed in 10.05s =========================
```

Now we can speed things up by running those tests in parallel on four CPUs with -n=4:

```
$ pip install pytest-xdist
$ pytest --count=10 -n=4 test_parallel.py
========================= test session starts =========================
gw0 [10] / gw1 [10] / gw2 [10] / gw3 [10]
..........                                                    [100%]
========================= 10 passed in 3.49s =========================
```

We can use -n=auto to run on as many CPU cores as possible:

```
$ pytest --count=10 -n=auto test_parallel.py
========================= test session starts =========================
gw0 I / gw1 I / gw2 I ...
..........                                                      [100%]
========================= 10 passed in 2.16s =========================
```

This was running on a six-core processor. So it seems like maybe we should be able to run it six times on six cores and get it down to about one second again:

```
$ pytest --count=6 -n=6 test_parallel.py
========================= test session starts =========================
gw0 [6] / gw1 [6] / gw2 [6] / gw3 [6] / gw4 [6] / gw5 [6]
......                                                          [100%]
========================= 6 passed in 1.63s =========================
```

Not quite. 1.63 seconds. There is some overhead involved with spawning parallel processes and combining results in the end. However, the overhead is fairly constant, so for large jobs, it's worth it.

Here's the same -n=6 for 60 tests:

```
$ pytest --count=60 -n=6 test_parallel.py
========================= test session starts =========================
gw0 [60] / gw1 [60] / gw2 [60] / gw3 [60] / gw4 [60] / gw5 [60]
........................................................   [100%]
========================= 60 passed in 10.71s =========================
```

The overhead just grew a little with 10 times the tests, from 0.63 seconds to 0.71 seconds.

I've noted in these examples -n=6. However, it is a better practice to run on -n=auto to get the best speedup. I honestly don't know how this works as well as it does, but even though I have six cores, -n=auto is faster than -n=6:

```
$ pytest --count=60 -n=auto test_parallel.py
========================= test session starts =========================
gw0 I / gw1 I / gw2 I ...
........................................................   [100%]
========================= 60 passed in 6.14s =========================
```

That's a little over six seconds for 60 seconds of test work.

The pytest-xdist plugin has another nice feature bundled with it: the --looponfail flag. The --looponfail flag enables you to run tests repeatedly in a subprocess. After each run, pytest waits until a file in your project changes and then re-runs the previously failing tests. This is repeated until all tests pass after which again a full run is performed. This feature is pretty cool for debugging a bunch of test failures.

Randomizing Test Order

Generally we'd like each of our tests to be able to run independently of all other tests. Having independent tests allows for easy debugging if something ever fails. If test order inadvertently depends on the state of the system being tested, that independence is broken. One common way to test for order independence is to randomize the test run order.

The pytest-randomly plugin is excellent randomizing test order. It also randomizes the seed value for other random tools like Faker and Factory Boy. Let's try it out on a couple simple test files:

ch14/random/test_a.py
```
def test_one():
    pass


def test_two():
    pass
```

ch14/random/test_b.py
```
def test_three():
    pass


def test_four():
    pass
```

If we run these normally, we get tests one through four:

```
$ cd path/to/code/ch14/random
$ pytest -v
========================= test session starts =========================
collected 4 items

test_a.py::test_one PASSED                                      [ 25%]
test_a.py::test_two PASSED                                      [ 50%]
test_b.py::test_three PASSED                                    [ 75%]
test_b.py::test_four PASSED                                     [100%]

========================== 4 passed in 0.01s ==========================
```

test_a.py runs before test_b.py due to alphabetical order. Then the tests within the files run in the order they appear in the file.

To randomize the order, install pytest-randomly:

```
$ pip install pytest-randomly
$ pytest -v
========================= test session starts =========================
collected 4 items

test_b.py::test_four PASSED                                     [ 25%]
test_b.py::test_three PASSED                                    [ 50%]
```

```
test_a.py::test_two PASSED                                    [ 75%]
test_a.py::test_one PASSED                                    [100%]

========================= 4 passed in 0.01s ==========================
```

Making sure your tests run fine in random order may seem like a weird thing to care about. However, tests that aren't properly isolated have caused many a late-night debugging session. Randomizing your tests on a regular basis can help you avoid these problems.

Review

In this chapter, we looked at where to find plugins:

- https://pypi.org (search for pytest-)
- https://github.com/pytest-dev
- https://docs.pytest.org/en/latest/how-to/plugins.html
- https://docs.pytest.org/en/latest/reference/plugin_list.html

We quickly looked at the variety of plugins available, and specifically tried out using pytest-randomly, pytest-repeat, and pytest-xdist.

Exercises

pytest is incredibly powerful by itself. However, it's important to understand the range and power achievable with the additions of plugins. Taking a moment to explore the resources available and trying a few plugins really will help you to remember where to look when you actually need help on a real testing project.

1. Head over to pypy.python.org with your favorite browser. Search for pytest-.

   - How many projects are listed?

2. Activate the virtual environment you were using in Chapter 13.

   - Run the full test suite.
   - How long does it take?

3. Install pytest-xdist.

   - Re-run the tests with --n=auto.
   - What was the time for the test suite?

What's Next

One of the reasons there are so many pytest plugins available is that it's rather simple to create a plugin and share it with the world. In the next chapter, we'll walk through developing, testing, and sharing a plugin of your own.

## CHAPTER 15

Building Plugins

In the last chapter, we talked about the wealth of plugins available. As you progress with using pytest, you will undoubtedly create fixtures and new command-line flags and all sorts of new cool things that you will want to use on more than one project. You may even want to share the modifications with others and publish your changes. This chapter is exactly about how to share pytest modifications by building your own plugins.

Starting with a Cool Idea

Maybe "cool idea" is too strong a phrase. An idea doesn't have to be really that cool to deserve being made into a plugin. It just needs to be helpful. You may have a fixture or command-line flag that's useful on one project, and you want to use on other projects. That's good enough for plugin-hood.

As an example, we'll grab an idea from the pytest documentation about slow tests. The pytest documentation[1] includes an examples page with a description of how to skip tests that are marked with @pytest.mark.slow automatically.

Here's the idea (the documentation actually uses --runslow, but we'll use --slow because it's shorter and seems like a better flag to me):

- Mark tests with @pytest.mark.slow that are so slow you don't want to always run them.

- When pytest collects tests to run, intercept that process by adding an extra mark—@pytest.mark.skip(reason="need --runslow option to run")—on all tests marked with @pytest.mark.slow. That way, these tests will be skipped by default.

---

1. https://docs.pytest.org/en/7.0.x/example/simple.html#control-skipping-of-tests-according-to-command-line-option

- Add the --slow flag so that users can override this behavior and actually run the slow tests. Under normal circumstances, whenever you run pytest, the tests marked slow will be skipped. However, the --slow flag will run all the tests, including the slow tests.

- To run just the slow tests, you can still select the marker with -m slow, but you have to combine it with --slow, so -m slow --slow will run only the slow tests.

This actually seems like a very useful idea. We'll develop this idea into a full plugin in this chapter. Along the way, you'll learn how to test plugins, how to package them, and how to publish them on PyPI. You'll also learn about hook functions, as we'll use them to implement this plugin.

We can already use markers to select or exclude specific tests. With --slow, we're just trying to change the default to exclude tests marked with "slow":

Behavior	Without plugin	With plugin
Exclude slow	pytest -m "not slow"	pytest
Include slow	pytest	pytest --slow
Only slow	pytest -m slow	pytest -m slow --slow

I set up a short test file and configuration file as a playground for the original behavior.

The test file looks like this:

ch15/just_markers/test_slow.py
```
import pytest


def test_normal():
    pass


@pytest.mark.slow
def test_slow():
    pass
```

And here's the configuration file to declare "slow":

ch15/just_markers/pytest.ini
```
[pytest]
markers = slow: mark test as slow to run
```

The behavior we're trying to make easier, avoiding slow tests, looks like this:

```
$ cd path/to/code/ch15/just_markers
$ pytest -v -m "not slow"
```

```
========================= test session starts ==========================
collected 2 items / 1 deselected / 1 selected

test_slow.py::test_normal PASSED                                  [100%]

==================== 1 passed, 1 deselected in 0.01s ====================
```

Great. Now that we know what we're shooting for, let's begin.

Building a Local conftest Plugin

We'll start by making changes in a conftest.py file and testing our changes locally before moving the code to a plugin.

To modify how pytest works, we need to utilize pytest hook functions. *Hook functions*[2] are function entry points that pytest provides to allow plugin developers to intercept pytest behavior at certain points and make changes. The pytest documentation lists a lot of hook functions.[3] We'll use three in this chapter:

- pytest_configure()—Allows plugins and conftest files to perform initial configuration. We'll use this hook function to pre-declare the slow marker so users don't have to add slow to their config files.

- pytest_addoption()—Used to register options and settings. We'll add the --slow flag with this hook.

- pytest_collection_modifyitems()—Called after test collection has been performed and can be used to filter or re-order the test items. We need this to find the slow tests, so we can mark them for skipping.

Let's start with pytest_configure() and declare the slow marker:

ch15/local/conftest.py
```
import pytest


def pytest_configure(config):
    config.addinivalue_line("markers", "slow: mark test as slow to run")
```

Now we need to use pytest_addoption() to add the --slow flag:

ch15/local/conftest.py
```
def pytest_addoption(parser):
    parser.addoption(
        "--slow", action="store_true", help="include tests marked slow"
    )
```

---

2. https://docs.pytest.org/en/6.2.x/writing_plugins.html#writinghooks
3. https://docs.pytest.org/en/latest/reference/reference.html#hook-reference

The call to parser.addoption() creates the flag and the configuration setting. The action="store_true" parameter tells pytest to store a true in the slow configuration setting when the --slow flag is passed in, and false otherwise. The help="include tests marked slow" creates a line in the help output to describe the flag:

```
$ cd path/to/code/ch15/local
$ pytest --help
...
custom options:
  --slow                 include tests marked slow
...
```

Now for the fun part—actually modifying the tests that get run:

ch15/local/conftest.py
```python
def pytest_collection_modifyitems(config, items):
    if not config.getoption("--slow"):
        skip_slow = pytest.mark.skip(reason="need --slow option to run")
        for item in items:
            if item.get_closest_marker("slow"):
                item.add_marker(skip_slow)
```

This code uses the suggestion in the pytest documentation to add a skip marker to any test that already includes the slow marker. We use config.getoption("--slow") to get the slow setting. We can also use config.getoption("slow"). Both work the same. But I find that including the dashes is more readable.

The items value passed to pytest_collection_modifyitems() will be the list of tests pytest intends to run. Specifically, it's a list of Node objects. Now we're really getting into the guts of pytest implementation.

The Node interface[4] includes two methods we care about: get_closest_marker() and add_marker(). get_closest_marker("slow") will return a marker object if there is a "slow" marker on the test. If there is no "slow" marker on the test, the get_closest_marker("slow") will return None. Here we're using the return value as a boolean True or False to see if "slow" is a marker on the test. If it is, we add the skip marker. If the method returns an object, it will act like a True value in an if clause. A None value evaluates to False in an if clause. Let's try it out:

```
$ pytest -v
========================= test session starts =========================
collected 2 items

test_slow.py::test_normal PASSED                              [ 50%]
test_slow.py::test_slow SKIPPED (need --slow option to run)   [100%]

===================== 1 passed, 1 skipped in 0.01s =====================
```

---

4.   https://docs.pytest.org/en/latest/reference/reference.html#node

By default, we avoid our slow test by skipping it. It's not quite the same as deselecting it. However, it is nice that the reason is listed in the verbose output.

We can also include the test with --slow:

```
$ pytest -v --slow
========================= test session starts =========================
collected 2 items

test_slow.py::test_normal PASSED                                  [ 50%]
test_slow.py::test_slow PASSED                                    [100%]

========================= 2 passed in 0.01s =========================
```

And to run just the slow tests, use -m slow --slow:

```
$ pytest -v -m slow --slow
========================= test session starts =========================
collected 2 items / 1 deselected / 1 selected

test_slow.py::test_slow PASSED                                    [100%]

==================== 1 passed, 1 deselected in 0.01s ====================
```

We have now created a local conftest plugin. Because it's entirely contained in a conftest.py file, we can use it as is. However, packaging it as an installable plugin will make it easier to share with other projects.

Creating an Installable Plugin

In this section, we'll walk through the process of going from local conftest plugin to installable plugin. Even if you never put your own plugins up on PyPI, it's good to walk through the process at least once. The experience will help you when reading code from open source plugins, and you'll be better equipped to judge if the plugins can help you or not.

First, we need to create a new directory for our plugin code. The name of the top-level directory doesn't really matter. We'll call it pytest_skip_slow:

```
pytest_skip_slow
├── examples
│   └── test_slow.py
└── pytest_skip_slow.py
```

Here test_slow.py was moved into an examples directory. We'll use it as-is later when automating tests for the plugin. Our conftest.py file is copied directly to pytest_skip_slow.py. The name pytest_skip_slow.py also is up to you. However, use a descriptive name, as the file will end up in our virtual environments site-packages directory when we pip install it later.

Now we need to create some Python packaging-specific files for the project. Specifically, we need to fill in a pyproject.toml file, a LICENSE file, and a README.md. We'll use Flit to help us with the pyproject.toml file and LICENSE. We'll have to modify pyproject.toml, but Flit will give us a good start on it. Then we'll have to write our own README.md. We're choosing Flit because it's easy, and the Cards project also uses it.

We start by installing Flit and running flit init inside a virtual environment and in the new directory:

```
$ cd path/to/code/ch15/pytest_skip_slow
$ pip install flit
$ flit init
Module name [pytest_skip_slow]:
Author: Your Name
Author email: your.name@example.com
Home page: https://github.com/okken/pytest-skip-slow
Choose a license (see https://choosealicense.com/ for more info)
1. MIT - simple and permissive
2. Apache - explicitly grants patent rights
3. GPL - ensures that code based on this is shared with the same terms
4. Skip - choose a license later
Enter 1-4: 1

Written pyproject.toml; edit that file to add optional extra info.
```

flit init asks you a handful of questions. Answer the best you can. For example, "Home page" is required for flit init, but I often don't know what to put there. For projects that I have no intent on publishing to GitHub or PyPI, I fill this field in with my company URL, my blog site, or whatever.

Let's now look at what pyproject.toml looks like right after flit init:

```
[build-system]
requires = ["flit_core >=3.2,<4"]
build-backend = "flit_core.buildapi"

[project]
name = "pytest_skip_slow"
authors = [{name = "Your Name", email = "your.name@example.com"}]
classifiers = ["License :: OSI Approved :: MIT License"]
dynamic = ["version", "description"]

[project.urls]
Home = "https://github.com/okken/pytest-skip-slow"
```

This isn't correct yet. The defaults are a good start, but we need to modify it for pytest plugins.

Here's the final pyproject.toml:

```
ch15/pytest_skip_slow_final/pyproject.toml
[build-system]
requires = ["flit_core >=3.2,<4"]
build-backend = "flit_core.buildapi"

[project]
name = "pytest-skip-slow"
authors = [{name = "Your Name", email = "your.name@example.com"}]
readme = "README.md"
classifiers = [
    "License :: OSI Approved :: MIT License",
    "Framework :: Pytest"
]
dynamic = ["version", "description"]
dependencies = ["pytest>=6.2.0"]
requires-python = ">=3.7"

[project.urls]
Home = "https://github.com/okken/pytest-skip-slow"

[project.entry-points.pytest11]
skip_slow = "pytest_skip_slow"

[project.optional-dependencies]
test = ["tox"]

[tool.flit.module]
name = "pytest_skip_slow"
```

What changed:

- name is changed to "pytest-skip-slow". Flit assumes the module name and package name will be the same. That's not true of pytest plugins. pytest plugins usually start with pytest- and Python doesn't like module names with dashes.

- The actual name of the module is set in the [tool.flit.module] section with name = "pytest_skip_slow". This module name will also show up in the entry-points section.

- The section [project.entry-points.pytest11] is added, with one entry pytest_skip_slow = "pytest_skip_slow.py". This section name is always the same for pytest plugins. It's defined by pytest.[5] The section needs one entry, name_of_plugin = "plugin_module". In our case, this is skip_slow = "pytest_skip_slow".

- The classifiers section has been extended to include "Framework :: Pytest", a special classifier specifically for pytest plugins.

---

5. https://docs.pytest.org/en/latest/how-to/writing_plugins.html#making-your-plugin-installable-by-others

- readme points to our README.md file, which we haven't written yet. It's optional, but weird to not have one.

- dependencies lists dependencies. Because pytest plugins require pytest, we list pytest. We've specified it with a requirement that pytest must be version 6.2.0 or above. Pinning the pytest version is optional, but I like to specify the versions I specifically test against. Start with the pytest version you are using. Then expand to older versions if you've tested against them and they work.

- requires-python is optional. However, I only intend to test against Python versions 3.7 and above.

- Section [project.optional-dependencies], test = ["tox"] is also optional. When we test our plugin, we're going to want pytest and tox. pytest is already part of the dependencies, but tox is not. Setting test = ["tox"] tells Flit to install tox when we install our project in editable mode.

Check out the Flit documentation for a good write-up of all you can put in pyproject.toml.[6]

We're almost ready to build our package. However, there are still a few things missing. We still need to:

1. Add a docstring describing the plugin to the top of pytest_skip_slow.py.
2. Add a _version_ string to pytest_skip_slow.py.
3. Create a README.md file. (It doesn't have to be fancy; we can add to it later.)

Luckily, at this point, if we try to run flit build without some of these items, Flit will tell us what's missing.

Here's a docstring and version in pytest_skip_slow.py:

ch15/pytest_skip_slow_final/pytest_skip_slow.py

```
"""
A pytest plugin to skip `@pytest.mark.slow` tests by default.
Include the slow tests with `--slow`.
"""

import pytest

__version__ = "0.0.1"

# ... the rest of our plugin code ...
```

And a simple starter README.md:

---

6.   https://flit.readthedocs.io/en/latest/pyproject_toml.html

```
ch15/pytest_skip_slow_final/README.md
# pytest-skip-slow

A pytest plugin to skip `@pytest.mark.slow` tests by default.
Include the slow tests with `--slow`.
```

Now we can use flit build to build an installable package:

```
$ flit build
Built sdist: dist/pytest-skip-slow-0.0.1.tar.gz              I-flit_core.sdist
Copying package file(s) from .../pytest_skip_slow.py         I-flit_core.wheel
Writing metadata files                                       I-flit_core.wheel
Writing the record of files                                  I-flit_core.wheel
Built wheel: dist/pytest_skip_slow-0.0.1-py3-none-any.whl    I-flit_core.wheel
```

Woohoo! We have an installable wheel. Now we can do whatever we want with
it. We can email the .whl file to someone to try out. We can install the wheel
directly to try it out ourselves:

```
$ pip install dist/pytest_skip_slow-0.0.1-py3-none-any.whl
Processing ./dist/pytest_skip_slow-0.0.1-py3-none-any.whl
...
Installing collected packages: pytest-skip-slow
Successfully installed pytest-skip-slow-0.0.1
$ pytest examples/test_slow.py
========================= test session starts =========================
collected 2 items

examples/test_slow.py .s                                        [100%]

===================== 1 passed, 1 skipped in 0.01s =====================
$ pytest --slow examples/test_slow.py
========================= test session starts =========================
collected 2 items

examples/test_slow.py ..                                        [100%]

========================= 2 passed in 0.00s ===========================
```

Sweet. It works.

If we want to stop here, there are a few more steps you should remember to do:

- Make sure _pycache_ and dist are ignored by your version control system.
  For Git, add these to .gitignore.

- Commit   LICENSE,   README.md,   pyproject.toml,   examples/test_slow.py,   and
  pytest_skip_slow.py.

However, we're not going to stop here. In the next sections we're going to add
tests and walk through publishing the plugin.

Testing Plugins with pytester

Plugins are code that needs to be tested just like any other code. However, testing a change to a testing tool is a little tricky. When we tested the plugin manually with test_slow.py, we

- ran with -v to make sure the slow marked test was skipped,
- ran with -v --slow to make sure both tests ran, and
- ran with -v -m slow --slow to make sure just the slow test ran.

We're going to automate those tests with the help of a plugin called pytester. pytester ships with pytest but is disabled by default. The first thing we need to do then, is to enable it in conftest.py:

ch15/pytest_skip_slow_final/tests/conftest.py
```
pytest_plugins = ["pytester"]
```

Now we can use pytester to write our test cases. pytester creates a temporary directory for each test that uses the pytester fixture. The pytester documentation[7] lists a bunch of functions to help populate this directory:

- makefile() creates a file of any kind.
- makepyfile() creates a python file. This is commonly used to create test files.
- makeconftest() creates conftest.py.
- makeini() creates a tox.ini.
- makepyprojecttoml() creates pyproject.toml.
- maketxtfile() ... you get the picture.
- mkdir() and mkpydir() create test subdirectories with or without __init__.py.
- copy_example() copies files from the project's directory to the temporary directory. This is my favorite and what we'll be using for testing our plugin.

After we have our temporary directory populated, we can runpytest(), which returns a RunResult object.[8] With the result, we can check the outcome of the test run and examine the output.

Let's look at an example:

ch15/pytest_skip_slow_final/tests/test_plugin.py
```
import pytest

@pytest.fixture()
def examples(pytester):
    pytester.copy_example("examples/test_slow.py")
```

```
def test_skip_slow(pytester, examples):
    result = pytester.runpytest("-v")
    result.stdout.fnmatch_lines(
        [
            "*test_normal PASSED*",
            "*test_slow SKIPPED (need --slow option to run)*",
        ]
    )
    result.assert_outcomes(passed=1, skipped=1)
```

copy_example() copies our example test_slow.py into the temporary directory we're using for testing. I've put the copy_example() call into the examples fixture so it can be reused in all of the tests. This is just to keep the tests a bit cleaner by moving common setup out of the individual tests. The examples directory is in our project directory, which is what copy_example() uses as its top directory. That can be changed by setting pytester_example_dir in our project settings file. However, I like the explicitness of leaving the relative path in the copy_example() call.

test_skip_slow() calls runpytest("-v") to run pytest with -v. runpytest() returns a result, which allows us to examine stdout and assert_outcomes(). There are a bunch of ways to look at stdout, but I find fnmatch_lines() the handiest. The name comes from the fact that it's based on fnmatch from the standard library.[9] We provide fnmatch_lines() with a list of lines that we want matched, in relative order. The * is a wildcard and is rather important to get any reasonable results from it.

The outcomes can be checked with assert_outcomes(), which has you pass in the expected outcomes and does the assert for you, or parseoutcomes(). parseoutcomes() returns a dictionary of outcomes. We can then assert ourselves against that. We'll use parseoutcomes() in one of our tests, to see how that works.

Let's look at the next test:

ch15/pytest_skip_slow_final/tests/test_plugin.py
```
def test_run_slow(pytester, examples):
    result = pytester.runpytest("--slow")
    result.assert_outcomes(passed=2)
```

Well, dang, that's simple. We're reusing the examples fixture to copy test_slow.py. So we just need to run pytest with --slow and assert that both tests pass. Why don't we need to look at the output with fnmatch_lines()? We could do that. However, there are only two tests, so if two pass, there's not much else to test. I used fnmatch_lines in the first test to make sure the expected test was passing and the expected test was skipped.

---

9. https://docs.python.org/3/library/fnmatch.html#fnmatch.fnmatch

Let's use parseoutcomes() in the next test (mostly so that there's something new to learn):

ch15/pytest_skip_slow_final/tests/test_plugin.py
```python
def test_run_only_slow(pytester, examples):
    result = pytester.runpytest("-v", "-m", "slow", "--slow")
    result.stdout.fnmatch_lines(["*test_slow PASSED*"])
    outcomes = result.parseoutcomes()
    assert outcomes["passed"] == 1
    assert outcomes["deselected"] == 1
```

For test_run_only_slow(), I've added back in the -v so we can look at the output. We have two tests and we only want to run one, the slow one. fnmatch_lines() is being used to make sure it's the correct test.

The parseoutcomes() call returns a dictionary that we can assert against. In this case, we want one 'passed' test and one 'deselected'.

Now just for fun, let's make sure our help text shows up with --help:

ch15/pytest_skip_slow_final/tests/test_plugin.py
```python
def test_help(pytester):
    result = pytester.runpytest("--help")
    result.stdout.fnmatch_lines(
        ["*--slow * include tests marked slow*"]
    )
```

That's pretty good behavior coverage for our plugin.

Before we run this, let's test against the editable code:

```
$ cd /path/to/code/ch15/pytest_skip_slow_final
$ pip uninstall pytest-skip-slow
$ pip install -e .
```

The dot (.) in pip install -e . means the current directory. Remember that pip needs to be version 21.3 or later for this to work.

Now we know we're testing the same code we're looking at.

```
$ pytest -v
========================= test session starts =========================
collected 4 items

tests/test_plugin.py::test_skip_slow PASSED                    [ 25%]
tests/test_plugin.py::test_run_slow PASSED                     [ 50%]
tests/test_plugin.py::test_run_only_slow PASSED                [ 75%]
tests/test_plugin.py::test_help PASSED                         [100%]

========================= 4 passed in 0.20s =========================
```

Cool. Looking good. Next, let's use tox to test our plugin against a few Python versions.

Testing Multiple Python and pytest Versions with tox

In Chapter 11, tox and Continuous Integration, on page 151, we used tox to test Cards against multiple versions of Python. We're going to do the same thing with our plugin, but also test against a couple versions of pytest.

Here's our tox.ini for our plugin:

```
ch15/pytest_skip_slow_final/tox.ini
[pytest]
testpaths = tests

[tox]
envlist = py{37, 38, 39, 310}-pytest{62,70}
isolated_build = True

[testenv]
deps =
    pytest62: pytest==6.2.5
    pytest70: pytest==7.0.0

commands = pytest {posargs:tests}
description = Run pytest
```

We are using a couple of new tricks for tox:

• envlist = py{37, 38, 39, 310}-pytest{62,70}. The curly brackets and dashes are creating a test environment matrix. This is a shorthand that tells tox to create environments for all combinations of the four listed versions of Python and the two listed versions of pytest. See tox docs[10] for more information.

• The deps section has two rows, pytest62: pytest==6.2.5 and pytest70: pytest==7.0.0. This tells tox that for every environment that ends with -pytest62, it should install pytest 6.2.5. Likewise, for -pytest70 environments, install pytest 7.0.0.

And now we just run it:

```
$ tox -q --parallel
...
_____ summary _____
  py37-pytest62: commands succeeded
  py37-pytest70: commands succeeded
  py38-pytest62: commands succeeded
```

---

10. https://tox.wiki/en/latest/example/basic.html#compressing-dependency-matrix

```
py38-pytest70: commands succeeded
py39-pytest62: commands succeeded
py39-pytest70: commands succeeded
py310-pytest62: commands succeeded
py310-pytest70: commands succeeded
congratulations :)
```

The -q reduces the output of tox, and --parallel tells tox to run the environments in parallel. Since the 4x2 matrix creates eight test environments, running them in parallel saves a bit of time.

Now let's move on to publishing.

Publishing Plugins

Now that we have a plugin built and tested, we'd like to share it with other projects, our company, or even the world. Bwahahahaha!

To publish your plugin, you can:

- Push your plugin code to a Git repository and install from there.

    - For example: pip install git+https://github.com/okken/pytest-skip-slow
    - Note that you can list multiple git+https://... repositories in a requirements.txt file and as dependencies in tox.ini.

- Copy the wheel, pytest_skip_slow-0.0.1-py3-none-any.whl, to a shared directory somewhere and install from there.

    - cp dist/*.whl path/to/my_packages/
    - pip install pytest-skip-slow --no-index --find-links=path/to/my_packages/

- Publish to PyPI.

    - Check out the Uploading the distribution archives[11] section in Python's documentation on packaging.

    - Also see the Controlling package uploads[12] section of the Flit documentation.

Review

Wow. In this chapter, we created a plugin and left it inches away from being able to push it to PyPI. We looked at how to move from hook functions in a conftest.py file to an installable and distributable packaged pytest plugin.

---

11. https://packaging.python.org/tutorials/packaging-projects/#uploading-the-distribution-archives
12. https://flit.readthedocs.io/en/latest/upload.html#controlling-package-uploads

In addition, we

- used a conftest.py and simple test code to manually develop hook functions for our plugin;

- moved conftest.py code into a new directory and pytest_skip_slow.py;

- moved test code into an examples directory;

- used flit init to create a pyproject.toml file, then modified the file for the special needs of pytest plugins;

- tried building with flit build and manually testing with built wheel;

- developed test code that utilized pytester and an example test file; and

- looked at different ways to distribute a package.

Exercises

Walking through the steps to go from pytest-skip-slow to pytest-skip-slow-full will help you learn how to build and test a plugin.

The supplied source code includes the following:

- local (the local conftest plugin)
- pytest-skip-slow (just the copy from local into new names)
- pytest-skip-slow-full (a possible final layout for the completed plugin)

1. Try out -v, --slow, and -v -m slow --slow in the local directory.

2. Go to the pytest-skip-slow directory.

3. pip install flit and run flit init. Use your own information.

4. Modify the pyproject.toml file as described in the chapter.

5. Run flit build and try out the generated wheel.

6. Add tests and a tox.ini file to run tests with either pytest or tox.

7. (*Bonus*) Create a plugin with a fixture, instead of hook functions. Especially within teams or a large project, using common fixtures can really speed up test development. The fixture could be something that returns interesting data, or fake data, or a connection to a temporary database, filled or empty. This really could be anything. Try to make it useful for something you are interested in or useful for a project you are working on.

What's Next

The final chapter is a flashback to parametrization. We've parametrized tests with a single parameter and simple values, like strings. In the next chapter, we'll use multiple values, objects for values, and even generate parameter values in custom functions. We'll also look at custom identifiers to help keep our test node names expressive to what we are trying to test.

## CHAPTER 16

Advanced Parametrization

We're going to wrap up this book by swinging back to parametrization and look at some advanced techniques. In Chapter 5, Parametrization, on page 61, we looked at parametrizing tests and fixtures, and you learned how to implement parametrized testing with the hook function, pytest_generate_tests(). However, we left the chapter with some pretty simple parametrizations of a test using one parameter with string values. We're going to do so much more in this chapter.

In this chapter we'll look at:

- Using data structures or objects as values. That complicates the test case identifier slightly, but we'll use custom identifiers to make the test node IDs readable.

- Using dynamic values. We'll use a function to dynamically generate the values at runtime.

- Using multiple parameters. We'll use multiple parameters per test case, and then stack parametrize decorators to generate a matrix of values.

- Intercepting values with a fixture using a technique called "indirect parametrization."

Using Complex Values

Sometimes you might want to parametrize using data structures or objects as values. Let's start with a string value parametrization from Chapter 5, Parametrization, on page 61, and modify it to use Cards objects.

Here's the function parametrization we used earlier in Chapter 5:

ch16/test_ids.py
```
@pytest.mark.parametrize("start_state", ["done", "in prog", "todo"])
def test_finish(cards_db, start_state):
    c = Card("write a book", state=start_state)
    index = cards_db.add_card(c)
    cards_db.finish(index)
    card = cards_db.get_card(index)
    assert card.state == "done"
```

This code includes one parameter, start_state, with string values statically listed in the parametrize() decorator.

This results in test node names that are easy to read:

```
$ cd /path/to/code/ch16
$ pytest -v test_ids.py::test_finish
========================= test session starts =========================
collected 3 items

test_ids.py::test_finish[todo] PASSED                            [ 33%]
test_ids.py::test_finish[in prog] PASSED                         [ 66%]
test_ids.py::test_finish[done] PASSED                            [100%]

========================= 3 passed in 0.01s =========================
```

Make Sure Cards and pytest Are Installed

 We're back to using an installed version of the Cards project. You can use a virtual environment from an early chapter, or create a new one. Install Cards and pytest with cd /path/to/code; pip install ./cards_proj; pip install pytest.

Let's make one small change to this test. Instead of passing in an initial card state, which is used to create a starting card, let's actually pass in the starting card:

ch16/test_ids.py
```
@pytest.mark.parametrize(
    "starting_card",
    [
        Card("foo", state="todo"),
        Card("foo", state="in prog"),
        Card("foo", state="done"),
    ],
)
def test_card(cards_db, starting_card):
    index = cards_db.add_card(starting_card)
    cards_db.finish(index)
    card = cards_db.get_card(index)
    assert card.state == "done"
```

Here we moved the construction of the Card() objects to inside the parametrized list of values.

When you do that, you are no longer using string values but object values, and pytest doesn't really know what to use for identifiers:

```
$ pytest -v test_ids.py::test_card
========================= test session starts =========================
collected 3 items

test_ids.py::test_card[starting_card0] PASSED                    [ 33%]
test_ids.py::test_card[starting_card2] PASSED                    [ 66%]
test_ids.py::test_card[starting_card1] PASSED                    [100%]

========================= 3 passed in 0.07s =========================
```

Therefore, for objects that don't have an obvious string value, pytest numbers them: "starting_card0," "starting_card1,"and so on. Numbered identifiers work to distinguish the node IDs, but they are not meaningful to us. We can remedy these confusing identifiers by using one of several available methods to create custom identifiers.

Creating Custom Identifiers

You can define a function to generate identifiers by using the ids parameter. Often the builtin str or repr functions work fine.

Let's try using str as an ID function:

```
ch16/test_ids.py
card_list = [
    Card("foo", state="todo"),
    Card("foo", state="in prog"),
    Card("foo", state="done"),
]

➤ @pytest.mark.parametrize("starting_card", card_list, ids=str)
def test_id_str(cards_db, starting_card):
    ...
```

Here we added ids=str. We also moved the list of cards to a named variable to allow shorter code samples in the rest of this section.

Here's what our node IDs look like now:

```
$ pytest -v test_ids.py::test_id_str
========================= test session starts =========================
collected 3 items

test_ids.py::test_id_str[Card(summary='foo', owner=None,
                     state='todo', id=None)]              PASSED [ 33%]
```

```
test_ids.py::test_id_str[Card(summary='foo', owner=None,
                        state='in prog', id=None)]          PASSED [ 66%]
test_ids.py::test_id_str[Card(summary='foo',
                        owner=None, state='done', id=None)] PASSED [100%]

========================= 3 passed in 0.01s =========================
```

That's a bit hard to read for Card objects. For smaller structures, like small tuples and lists, str or repr might work fine as an ID function. For classes, even small ones like the Card class, using str or repr is a bit too verbose and hides the important details. The important detail is that the state is different. But that information is buried in a lot of other noise. We can fix that by writing our own function.

Writing Custom ID Functions

Let's define our own ID function. It needs to take a Card object and return a string. And we'll set ids to our new function:

ch16/test_ids.py
```python
def card_state(card):
    return card.state


➤ @pytest.mark.parametrize("starting_card", card_list, ids=card_state)
def test_id_func(cards_db, starting_card):
    ...
```

That works so much better at highlighting the state difference in the test cases:

```
$ pytest -v test_ids.py::test_id_func
========================= test session starts =========================
collected 3 items

test_ids.py::test_id_func[todo] PASSED                          [ 33%]
test_ids.py::test_id_func[in prog] PASSED                       [ 66%]
test_ids.py::test_id_func[done] PASSED                          [100%]

========================= 3 passed in 0.02s =========================
```

Many ID functions will be short. If it's a one-line function, a lambda function works great:

ch16/test_ids.py
```python
➤ @pytest.mark.parametrize(
➤     "starting_card", card_list, ids=lambda c: c.state
➤ )
def test_id_lambda(cards_db, starting_card):
    ...
```

The output will look just the same:

```
$ pytest -v test_ids.py::test_id_lambda
========================= test session starts =========================
collected 3 items

test_ids.py::test_id_lambda[todo] PASSED                        [ 33%]
test_ids.py::test_id_lambda[in prog] PASSED                     [ 66%]
test_ids.py::test_id_lambda[done] PASSED                        [100%]

========================= 3 passed in 0.02s =========================
```

The ids feature is available with parametrized fixtures and pytest_generate_tests as well. There are two more methods to create custom identifiers: pytest.param and id lists.

Adding an ID to pytest.param

In Marking Files, Classes, and Parameters, on page 82, we used pytest.param to add markers to parametrization values. pytest.param can also be used to add IDs. In the following example, we'll add a "special" ID to one parameter:

```
ch16/test_ids.py
c_list = [
    Card("foo", state="todo"),
➤   pytest.param(Card("foo", state="in prog"), id="special"),
    Card("foo", state="done"),
]

@pytest.mark.parametrize("starting_card", c_list, ids=card_state)
def test_id_param(cards_db, starting_card):
    ...
```

This method is especially useful in combination with others. In this example, we've specified the one "special" ID with pytest.param, and let ids=cards_state() generate the rest of the IDs.

The resulting test run looks like this:

```
$ pytest -v test_ids.py::test_id_param
========================= test session starts =========================
collected 3 items

test_ids.py::test_id_param[todo] PASSED                         [ 33%]
test_ids.py::test_id_param[special] PASSED                      [ 66%]
test_ids.py::test_id_param[done] PASSED                         [100%]

========================= 3 passed in 0.02s =========================
```

Using pytest.param for an ID is great if you just have one or two that need special treatment. If you want to hand write all of the IDs, pytest.param can be cumbersome. If you want to write custom IDs for all values, using a list might be more maintainable.

Using an ID List

You can supply a list to ids, instead of a function, like this:

```
ch16/test_ids.py
id_list = ["todo", "in prog", "done"]

@pytest.mark.parametrize("starting_card", card_list, ids=id_list)
def test_id_list(cards_db, starting_card):
    ...
```

You have to be extra careful to keep the lists synchronized. Otherwise, the IDs are wrong. One way to keep the IDs and values together is to use the ID as a key to a dictionary. Then you can use .keys() as the list of IDs and .values() as the list of parameters. Using a dictionary in this manner is especially useful when the IDs are not easily generated with a function:

```
ch16/test_ids.py
text_variants = {
    "Short": "x",
    "With Spaces": "x y z",
    "End In Spaces": "x    ",
    "Mixed Case": "SuMmArY wItH MiXeD cAsE",
    "Unicode": "i¢£¤¥¦§¨©ª«¬®¯°±²³´µ¶·¸¹º»¼½¾",
    "Newlines": "a\nb\nc",
    "Tabs": "a\tb\tc",
}

@pytest.mark.parametrize(
    "variant", text_variants.values(), ids=text_variants.keys()
)
def test_summary_variants(cards_db, variant):
    i = cards_db.add_card(Card(summary=variant))
    c = cards_db.get_card(i)
    assert c.summary == variant
```

One nice feature of the dictionary technique is that the ID is at the front of the line of code instead of at the end, as in pytest.param.

Using dictionaries like this can be surprising to people who have been conditioned to never trust the order of dictionaries. However, keys() and values() return view objects into the dictionary.[1] As long as no changes are made to the dictionary between calls, Python guarantees that the elements of keys() and values() will be lined up one to one.

We've looked at several methods to create custom identifiers. Next, let's explore dynamic values.

---

1. https://docs.python.org/3/library/stdtypes.html#dictionary-view-objects

Parametrizing with Dynamic Values

In the previous example using dictionaries, the parameter values came from a function, text_variants.values(). We can write our own functions to generate parameter values.

Let's move the generation of text variants into a function, text_variants(), which we'll define shortly. We can then call that function for our parameter values:

```
ch16/test_param_gen.py
@pytest.mark.parametrize("variant", text_variants())
def test_summary(cards_db, variant):
    i = cards_db.add_card(Card(summary=variant))
    c = cards_db.get_card(i)
    assert c.summary == variant
```

Now we need to define our text_variants() function. It can really be anything, but let's use a dictionary like before, and use it to generate pytest.param objects, complete with parameter value and ID set:

```
ch16/test_param_gen.py
def text_variants():
    variants = {
        "Short": "x",
        "With Spaces": "x y z",
        "End in Spaces": "x     ",
        "Mixed Case": "SuMmArY wItH MiXeD cAsE",
        "Unicode": "¡¢£¤¥¦§¨©ª«¬®¯°±²³´µ¶·¸¹º»¼½¾",
        "Newlines": "a\nb\nc",
        "Tabs": "a\tb\tc",
    }
    for key, value in variants.items():
        yield pytest.param(value, id=key)
```

The text_variants() function still has fixed data in the code, but it doesn't have to. It could easily be reading the data from a file or a database or an API endpoint. The sky's the limit. Or rather, computer memory is the limit. The entire list will be loaded before the test starts during pytest's test collection phase.

Using Multiple Parameters

So far we've looked at tests with one parameter variation per test or fixture. However, you can use more than one. Let's say you have a list of summaries, owners, and states and we want to test the cards_db.add_card() method against all combinations of summary, owner, state:

```
ch16/test_multiple.py
summaries = ["short", "a bit longer"]
owners = ["First", "First M. Last"]
states = ["todo", "in prog", "done"]
```

You can use multiple parameters and pass in a tuple or list of values to line up with these parameters. In the example that follows, we're using a comma-separated list of parameter names: "summary, owner, state". You can also use a list of strings, or ["summary", "owner", "state"]. The former involves a little less typing:

```
ch16/test_multiple.py
@pytest.mark.parametrize(
    "summary, owner, state",
    [
        ("short", "First", "todo"),
        ("short", "First", "in prog"),
        # ...
    ],
)
def test_add_lots(cards_db, summary, owner, state):
    """Make sure adding to db doesn't change values."""
    i = cards_db.add_card(Card(summary, owner=owner, state=state))
    card = cards_db.get_card(i)

    expected = Card(summary, owner=owner, state=state)
    assert card == expected
```

This works okay if you have a small number of combinations:

```
$ pytest test_multiple.py::test_add_lots -v
========================= test session starts =========================
collected 2 items

test_multiple.py::test_add_lots[short-First-todo] PASSED     [ 50%]
test_multiple.py::test_add_lots[short-First-in prog] PASSED  [100%]

========================= 2 passed in 0.01s =========================
```

However, if you really want to test all combinations, stacking parameters is the way to go:

```
ch16/test_multiple.py
@pytest.mark.parametrize("state", states)
@pytest.mark.parametrize("owner", owners)
@pytest.mark.parametrize("summary", summaries)
def test_stacking(cards_db, summary, owner, state):
    """Make sure adding to db doesn't change values."""
    ...
```

This will act rather like cascading for loops, looping on the parameters from the bottom decorator to the top:

```
$ pytest test_multiple.py::test_stacking -v
============================ test session starts ==============================
collected 12 items

test_multiple.py::test_stacking[short-First-todo] PASSED                 [  8%]
test_multiple.py::test_stacking[short-First-in prog] PASSED              [ 16%]
test_multiple.py::test_stacking[short-First-done] PASSED                 [ 25%]
...
test_multiple.py::test_stacking[a bit longer-First M. Last-done] PASSED [100%]

============================ 12 passed in 0.03s ==============================
```

Because we have two summaries, two owners, and three states, we get 2 x 2 x 3 = 12 test cases.

Using Indirect Parametrization

The final parametrization technique we're going to look at is indirect parametrization. An *indirect parameter* is one that gets passed to a fixture before it gets sent to the test function. Indirect parametrization allows us to perform work based on the parameter value.

The way it works is to set indirect to a list of parameter names you want to be indirect, like indirect=["param1", "param2"]. You can also set indirect=True if you want all parameters to be indirect. Then you need a fixture with the same name as the parameter.

As an example, let's say we have expanded Cards to have different access rights for different user roles. We can parametrize a test with a user parameter:

ch16/test_indirect.py
```
@pytest.mark.parametrize(
    "user", ["admin", "team_member", "visitor"], indirect=["user"]
)
def test_access_rights(user):
    print(f"Test access rights for {user}")
```

Here we've set user to be indirect with indirect=["user"]. We could have also used indirect=True since user is the only parameter. We also need a user fixture:

ch16/test_indirect.py
```
@pytest.fixture()
def user(request):
    role = request.param
    print(f"\nLog in as {role}")
    yield role
    print(f"\nLog out {role}")
```

The fixture is able to retrieve the value through request.param, just like it can with parametrized fixtures.

Now with each value of user, the user fixture will be called by pytest:

```
$ pytest -s -v test_indirect.py
=========================== test session starts ===========================
collected 3 items

test_indirect.py::test_access_rights[admin]
Log in as admin
Test access rights for admin
PASSED
Log out admin

test_indirect.py::test_access_rights[team_member]
Log in as team_member
Test access rights for team_member
PASSED
Log out team_member

test_indirect.py::test_access_rights[visitor]
Log in as visitor
Test access rights for visitor
PASSED
Log out visitor

=========================== 3 passed in 0.01s ===========================
```

Indirect parameters can also be used to select a subset of values from a parametrized fixture.

Selecting a Subset of Fixture Parameters

Let's say we have parametrized our user fixture:

ch16/test_subset.py
```
@pytest.fixture(params=["admin", "team_member", "visitor"])
def user(request):
    ...
```

We can use it as normal for tests that use all user roles:

ch16/test_subset.py
```
def test_everyone(user):
    ...
```

We can also use it for tests that just need one or a subset of the fixture parameters:

ch16/test_subset.py
```
@pytest.mark.parametrize("user", ["admin"], indirect=["user"])
def test_just_admin(user):
    ...
```

When we run both of these tests, we'll see test_everyone() testing against all user roles, and test_just_admin() only running against the admin role:

```
$ pytest -v test_subset.py
========================= test session starts =========================
collected 5 items

test_subset.py::test_everyone[admin] PASSED                     [ 20%]
test_subset.py::test_everyone[author] PASSED                    [ 40%]
test_subset.py::test_everyone[editor] PASSED                    [ 60%]
test_subset.py::test_everyone[visitor] PASSED                   [ 80%]
test_subset.py::test_just_admin[admin] PASSED                   [100%]

========================= 5 passed in 0.01s =========================
```

Indirect parameters essentially let us parametrize a fixture, while keeping the parameter values with the test function, instead of with the fixture function. This allows different tests to use the same fixture with different parameter values.

Creating an Optional Indirect Fixture

One last fun aspect of indirect parameters to play with is the use of an optional indirect fixture. This technique allows us to use the same fixture that expects a value with both parametrized and non-parametrized tests.

To use this technique, we need a fixture that checks if the test is parametrized and uses a default value if not:

```
ch16/test_optional.py
@pytest.fixture()
def user(request):
    role = getattr(request, "param", "visitor")
    print(f"\nLog in as {role}")
    return role
```

In this example, we used getattr(request, "param", "visitor") to check if there is a parameter value. If a test is parametrized, pytest will set request.param to the value, and getattr() will find it. Otherwise, the default of "visitor" will be used.

The user fixture can be used by non-parametrized tests:

```
ch16/test_optional.py
def test_unspecified_user(user):
    ...
```

And by parametrized tests that specify user as indirect:

```
ch16/test_optional.py
@pytest.mark.parametrize(
    "user", ["admin", "team_member"], indirect=["user"]
)
def test_admin_and_team_member(user):
    ...
```

Now both parametrized and non-parametrized tests can use the same fixture:

```
$ pytest -v -s test_optional.py
========================= test session starts =========================
collected 3 items

test_optional.py::test_unspecified_user
Log in as visitor
PASSED
test_optional.py::test_admin_and_team_member[admin]
Log in as admin
PASSED
test_optional.py::test_admin_and_team_member[team_member]
Log in as team_member
PASSED

========================= 3 passed in 0.01s =========================
```

The indirect feature is also available with pytest_generate_tests.

Review

There's a lot of parametrization fun in this chapter! We covered

- using data structures and objects as parameter values and how that results in numbered test IDs;

- creating custom identifiers using ids and ID functions, including repr, str, custom functions, and lambdas;

- using the id setting of pytest.param for identifiers;

- using a list for IDs and using dictionaries to keep track of test cases and identifiers;

- using functions for parameter values, which allow us to dynamically create values at test collection time;

- using multiple parameters and even stacking parametrize decorators to create a test matrix, and

- moving parameter values from fixture to test function using indirect parametrization.

Exercises

We went through quite a few techniques in this chapter at a fairly quick pace. Going through the techniques yourself will help you remember these features when you really need them.

1. Start at the beginning of the chapter and read and understand the code examples for each technique.

2. Run pytest for each example.

3. Be sure to understand all of the custom identifier techniques. They all become useful eventually.

4. When we stacked parameters in Using Multiple Parameters, on page 227, "summary" was in the bottom, and "state" was on the top. Try reversing them. What effect does that have on the test node IDs?

What's Next

You're definitely ready to go out and try pytest with your own projects. If you've kept up with most of the book, good job. There is a lot of material here. If you also went through the code examples yourself and did the exercises, I dare say that you are well above average in pytest knowledge. Pat yourself on the back. Unless that hurts, then don't do that; have someone else pat you on the back gently.

pytest is not a static tool. It's a dynamic project with lots of amazing people volunteering to keep it great and add features. I recommend keeping in touch. I will continue to write about pytest and software development, testing, and related topics on my blog, pythontest.com,[2] and talk about it on my podcasts, Test & Code[3] and PythonBytes.[4]

And you will continue to learn and possibly want to share what you've learned. Feel free to reach out to me through the blog, podcast, or Twitter at @brianokken.[5] I'm always interested in great stories and cool techniques!

---

2. https://pythontest.com
3. https://testandcode.com
4. https://pythonbytes.fm
5. https://twitter.com/brianokken

Virtual Environments

Python virtual environments enable you to set up a Python sandbox with its own set of packages separate from the system site-packages in which to work. There are many reasons to use virtual environments, such as if you have multiple services running with the same Python installation, but with different packages and package version requirements. In addition, you might find it handy to keep the dependent package requirements separate for every Python project you work on. Virtual environments let you do that.

As of Python 3.3, the venv virtual environment module is included as part of the standard library. However, some problems with venv have been reported on some versions of Linux. If you have any trouble with venv, use virtualenv instead. Just remember to pip install virtualenv first.

The basic workflow for using venv:

- Create

  - python -m venv env_dir_name [--prompt my_proj]

- Activate

  - source env_dir_name/bin/activate to activate on macOS and Linux.
  - env_dir_name\Scripts\activate.bat to activate on Windows.
  - env_dir_name\Scripts\Activate.ps1 to activate on Windows with PowerShell.

- Deactivate

  - deactivate when done

You can choose whatever directory name you want. However, it's a fairly common convention to use either venv or .venv as the directory name. The --prompt parameter is optional. If you don't supply one, the prompt will match the directory name. As of Python 3.9, providing --prompt . (using just a dot as the prompt name), will tell venv to use the parent directory as the prompt.

For example, here's how to set up a virtual environment in macOS and Linux:

```
$ mkdir proj_name
$ cd proj_name
$ python3 -m venv venv --prompt .
$ source venv/bin/activate
(proj_name) $ which python
/path/to/proj_name/venv/bin/python
... do your work ...
(proj_name) $ deactivate
```

In Windows, there's a change to the activate line. Here's an example for cmd.exe:

```
C:/> mkdir proj_name
C:/> cd proj_name
C:/> python3 -m venv venv --prompt .
➤ C:/> venv\Scripts\activate.bat
(proj_name) C:/>
... do your work ...
(proj_name) C:/> deactivate
```

And for PowerShell:

```
PS C:/> mkdir proj_name
PS C:/> cd proj_name
PS C:/> python3 -m venv venv --prompt .
➤ PS C:/> venv\Scripts\Activate.ps1
(proj_name) PS C:/>
... do your work ...
(proj_name) PS C:/> deactivate
```

When you're done with a virtual environment, you can delete the directory.

venv is a flexible tool with many options. Here we just looked at basics and common use case of venv. Be sure to check out python -m venv --help. Also, the Python docs on venv[1] are worth reading. Also, if you have any issues with creating a virtual environment, the venv docs may help. There is a note about PowerShell execution policies, for example.

---

1.   https://docs.python.org/3/library/venv.html

pip

pip is the tool used to install Python packages, and it is installed as part of your Python installation. pip supposedly is a recursive acronym that stands for *Pip Installs Python* or *Pip Installs Packages.* If you have more than one version of Python installed on your system, each version has its own pip package manager.

By default, when you run pip install something, pip will:

1. Connect to the PyPI repository at https://pypi.org/pypi.

2. Look for a package called something.

3. Download the appropriate version of something for your version of Python and your system.

4. Install something into the site-packages directory of your Python installation that was used to call pip.

This is a gross understatement of what pip does—it also does cool stuff like setting up scripts defined by the package, wheel caching, and more.

As mentioned, each installation of Python has its own version of pip tied to it. If you're using virtual environments, pip and python are automatically linked to whichever Python version you specified when creating the virtual environment. If you aren't using virtual environments, and you have multiple Python versions installed, such as python3.9 and python3.10, use python3.9 -m pip or python3.10 -m pip instead of pip directly. It works just the same.

To check the version of pip and which version of Python it's tied to, use pip --version:

```
(venv) $ pip --version
pip 21.2.4 from /path/to/code/venv/lib/python3.10/site-packages/pip
    (python 3.10)
```

To list the packages you have currently installed with pip, use pip list. If there's something there you don't want anymore, you can uninstall it with pip uninstall something.

For example:

```
(venv) $ pip list
Package    Version
---------- -------
pip        21.2.4
setuptools 57.4.0a
(venv) $ pip install pytest
...
Installing collected packages: pyparsing, toml, py, pluggy, packaging,
    iniconfig, attrs, pytest
Successfully installed ...
...
(venv) $ pip list
Package    Version
---------- -------
attrs      21.2.0
iniconfig  1.1.1
packaging  21.0
pip        21.2.4
pluggy     1.0.0
py         1.10.0
pyparsing  2.4.7
pytest     6.2.5
setuptools 57.4.0
toml       0.10.2
```

As shown here, pip installs the package we want and also any dependencies that aren't already installed.

pip is pretty flexible. It can install things from other places, such as GitHub, our own servers, a shared directory, or a local package we're developing.

You can also use pip to install packages with version numbers from pypi.org if it's a release version PyPI knows about:

```
$ pip install pytest==6.2.5
```

You can use pip to install packages directly from a Git repository. For example, from GitHub:

```
$ pip install git+https://github.com/pytest-dev/pytest-cov
```

You can also specify a version tag:

```
$ pip install git+https://github.com/pytest-dev/pytest-cov@v2.12.1
```

Or you can specify a branch:

```
$ pip install git+https://github.com/pytest-dev/pytest-cov@master
```

Installing from a Git repository is especially useful if you're storing your own work within Git, or if the plugin or plugin version you want isn't on PyPI.

You can use pip to install a local package:

```
$ pip install /path/to/package
```

Use ./package_name if in the same directory as the package:

```
$ cd /path/just/above/package
$ pip install my_package # pip is looking in PyPI for "my_package"
$ pip install ./my_package # now pip looks locally
```

You can use pip to install packages that have been downloaded as zip files or wheels without unpacking them.

You can also use pip to install a lot of packages at once using a requirements.txt file:

```
(venv) $ cat requirements.txt
pytest==6.2.5
pytest-xdist==2.4.0

(venv) $ pip install -r requirements.txt
...
Successfully installed ... pytest-6.2.5 pytest-xdist-4.2.0
```

You can use pip to download a bunch of various versions into a local cache of packages, and then point pip there instead of PyPI to install them into virtual environments later, even when offline.

The following downloads pytest and all dependencies:

```
(venv) $ mkdir ~/.pipcache
(venv) $ pip download -d ~/pipcache pytest
Collecting pytest
...
Successfully downloaded pytest attrs pluggy py iniconfig packaging pyparsing toml
```

Later, even if you're offline, you can install from the cache:

```
(venv) $ pip install --no-index --find-links=~/pipcache pytest
Looking in links: /Users/okken/pipcache
...
Successfully installed attrs-21.2.0 iniconfig-1.1.1 packaging-21.0 pluggy-1.0.0
    py-1.10.0 pyparsing-2.4.7 pytest-6.2.5 toml-0.10.2
```

This is great for situations like running tox or continuous integration test suites without needing to grab packages from PyPI. I also use this method to grab a bunch of packages before taking a trip so that I can code on the plane.

The Python Packaging Authority documentation[1] is a great resource for more information on pip.

---

1.   https://pip.pypa.io

Index

Thank you!

How did you enjoy this book? Please let us know. Take a moment and email us at support@pragprog.com with your feedback. Tell us your story and you could win free ebooks. Please use the subject line "Book Feedback."

Ready for your next great Pragmatic Bookshelf book? Come on over to https://pragprog.com and use the coupon code BUYANOTHER2022 to save 30% on your next ebook.

Void where prohibited, restricted, or otherwise unwelcome. Do not use ebooks near water. If rash persists, see a doctor. Doesn't apply to *The Pragmatic Programmer* ebook because it's older than the Pragmatic Bookshelf itself. Side effects may include increased knowledge and skill, increased marketability, and deep satisfaction. Increase dosage regularly.

And thank you for your continued support.

The Pragmatic Bookshelf

Pragmatic Bookshelf

SAVE 30%!
Use coupon code
BUYANOTHER2022

Python Brain Teasers

We geeks love puzzles and solving them. The Python programming language is a simple one, but like all other languages it has quirks. This book uses those quirks as teaching opportunities via 30 simple Python programs that challenge your understanding of Python. The teasers will help you avoid mistakes, see gaps in your knowledge, and become better at what you do. Use these teasers to impress your co-workers or just to pass the time in those boring meetings. Teasers are fun!

Miki Tebeka
(116 pages) ISBN: 9781680509007. $18.95
https://pragprog.com/book/d-pybrain

Pandas Brain Teasers

This book contains 25 short programs that will challenge your understanding of Pandas. Like any big project, the Pandas developers had to make some design decisions that at times seem surprising. This book uses those quirks as a teaching opportunity. By understanding the gaps in your knowledge, you'll become better at what you do. Some of the teasers are from the author's experience shipping bugs to production, and some from others doing the same. Teasers and puzzles are fun, and learning how to solve them can teach you to avoid programming mistakes and maybe even impress your colleagues and future employers.

Miki Tebeka
(110 pages) ISBN: 9781680509014. $18.95
https://pragprog.com/book/d-pandas

Complex Network Analysis in Python

Construct, analyze, and visualize networks with networkx, a Python language module. Network analysis is a powerful tool you can apply to a multitude of datasets and situations. Discover how to work with all kinds of networks, including social, product, temporal, spatial, and semantic networks. Convert almost any real-world data into a complex network—such as recommendations on co-using cosmetic products, muddy hedge fund connections, and online friendships. Analyze and visualize the network, and make business decisions based on your analysis. If you're a curious Python programmer, a data scientist, or a CNA specialist interested in mechanizing mundane tasks, you'll increase your productivity exponentially.

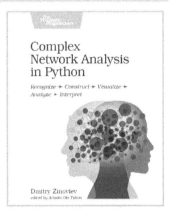

Dmitry Zinoviev
(260 pages) ISBN: 9781680502695. $35.95
https://pragprog.com/book/dzcnapy

Data Science Essentials in Python

Go from messy, unstructured artifacts stored in SQL and NoSQL databases to a neat, well-organized dataset with this quick reference for the busy data scientist. Understand text mining, machine learning, and network analysis; process numeric data with the NumPy and Pandas modules; describe and analyze data using statistical and network-theoretical methods; and see actual examples of data analysis at work. This one-stop solution covers the essential data science you need in Python.

Dmitry Zinoviev
(224 pages) ISBN: 9781680501841. $29
https://pragprog.com/book/dzpyds

Portable Python Projects

Discover easy ways to control your home with the powerful new Raspberry Pi hardware. Program short Python scripts that will detect changes in your home and react with the instructions you code. Use new add-on accessories to monitor a variety of measurements, from light intensity and temperature to motion detection and water leakage. Expand the base projects with your own custom additions to perfectly match your own home setup. Most projects in the book can be completed in under an hour, giving you more time to enjoy and tweak your autonomous creations. No breadboard or electronics knowledge required!

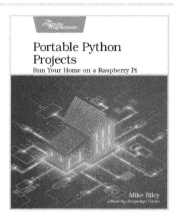

Mike Riley
(180 pages) ISBN: 9781680508598. $45.95
https://pragprog.com/book/mrpython

Pythonic Programming

Make your good Python code even better by following proven and effective pythonic programming tips. Avoid logical errors that usually go undetected by Python linters and code formatters, such as frequent data look-ups in long lists, improper use of local and global variables, and mishandled user input. Discover rare language features, like rational numbers, set comprehensions, counters, and pickling, that may boost your productivity. Discover how to apply general programming patterns, including caching, in your Python code. Become a better-than-average Python programmer, and develop self-documented, maintainable, easy-to-understand programs that are fast to run and hard to break.

Dmitry Zinoviev
(150 pages) ISBN: 9781680508611. $26.95
https://pragprog.com/book/dzpythonic

Intuitive Python

Developers power their projects with Python because it emphasizes readability, ease of use, and access to a meticulously maintained set of packages and tools. The language itself continues to improve with every release: writing in Python is full of possibility. But to maintain a successful Python project, you need to know more than just the language. You need tooling and instincts to help you make the most out of what's available to you. Use this book as your guide to help you hone your skills and sculpt a Python project that can stand the test of time.

David Muller
(140 pages) ISBN: 9781680508239. $26.95
https://pragprog.com/book/dmpython

Practical Programming, Third Edition

Classroom-tested by tens of thousands of students, this new edition of the best-selling intro to programming book is for anyone who wants to understand computer science. Learn about design, algorithms, testing, and debugging. Discover the fundamentals of programming with Python 3.6—a language that's used in millions of devices. Write programs to solve real-world problems, and come away with everything you need to produce quality code. This edition has been updated to use the new language features in Python 3.6.

Paul Gries, Jennifer Campbell, Jason Montojo
(410 pages) ISBN: 9781680502688. $49.95
https://pragprog.com/book/gwpy3

The Pragmatic Bookshelf

The Pragmatic Bookshelf features books written by professional developers for professional developers. The titles continue the well-known Pragmatic Programmer style and continue to garner awards and rave reviews. As development gets more and more difficult, the Pragmatic Programmers will be there with more titles and products to help you stay on top of your game.

Visit Us Online

This Book's Home Page
https://pragprog.com/book/bopytest2
Source code from this book, errata, and other resources. Come give us feedback, too!

Keep Up to Date
https://pragprog.com
Join our announcement mailing list (low volume) or follow us on twitter @pragprog for new titles, sales, coupons, hot tips, and more.

New and Noteworthy
https://pragprog.com/news
Check out the latest pragmatic developments, new titles and other offerings.

Save on the ebook

Save on the ebook versions of this title. Owning the paper version of this book entitles you to purchase the electronic versions at a terrific discount.

PDFs are great for carrying around on your laptop—they are hyperlinked, have color, and are fully searchable. Most titles are also available for the iPhone and iPod touch, Amazon Kindle, and other popular e-book readers.

Send a copy of your receipt to support@pragprog.com and we'll provide you with a discount coupon.

Contact Us

Online Orders: *https://pragprog.com/catalog*
Customer Service: *support@pragprog.com*
International Rights: *translations@pragprog.com*
Academic Use: *academic@pragprog.com*
Write for Us: *http://write-for-us.pragprog.com*
Or Call: +1 800-699-7764

Milton Keynes UK
Ingram Content Group UK Ltd.
UKHW050712311023
431598UK00003B/7